THE PIERRE
HOTEL AFFAIR

THE PIERRE
HOTEL AFFAIR

How Eight Gentleman Thieves Orchestrated
the Largest Jewel Heist in History

DANIEL SIMONE

WITH NICK SACCO

PEGASUS CRIME

NEW YORK LONDON

Note: The Pierre Hotel is a trademark of the Taj Hotels Resorts
and Palaces which has neither authorized nor endorsed this book.

THE PIERRE HOTEL AFFAIR

Pegasus Books Ltd.
148 W 37th Street, 13th Floor
New York, NY 10018

First Pegasus Books cloth edition May 2017

Interior design by Maria Fernandez

Library of Congress Cataloging-in-Publication Data is available.

ISBN: 978-1-68177-402-2

10 9 8 7 6 5 4 3 2 1

Printed in the United States of America
Distributed by W. W. Norton & Company

This is dedicated in part to Frank and Antoinette, who have been in my heart throughout the arduous effort of producing this book. You know who you are. My soulmate, BJ, also deserves a dedication for her unconditional support, as does my dearest son.

—Daniel Simone

To my mother, stepfather, and grandmother:
I only pass this way one time, and if I am to be remembered, I must leave my mark upon this earth.

—Nick Sacco

CAST OF CHARACTERS

BOBBY COMFORT. He was charming, well-spoken, and polite, and had the appearance and demeanor of a white-collar professional; perhaps an accountant, or a lawyer, or a doctor, or a Wall Street type. And as a jewel thief, when the need arose he'd comfortably assume those roles. He was fair-minded, even-handed, intelligent, and sensible, though he had been a juvenile delinquent and a burglar since his preadolescent years. Bobby Comfort was crafty, and irrespective of the dangers or difficulties he faced, his temperament and coolness seldom faltered, and never resorted to violence. He strived to gain financial security for his dear wife and children, and above all that was his priority.

MILLIE COMFORT. She was Bobby's unconditionally devoted wife, though her husband's unconventional ways to earn a living caused her stress and despair. Millie was the ideal loving wife, mother, and homemaker. But how could she continue to live with the constant fear that the authorities might one day knock down her door and arrest Bobby for a burglary, or who knew what? This wasn't fair to her and their child. To what extent should she suffer while mired in her steadfast loyalty to him?

NICK "THE CAT" SACCO. He is the co-author of this book. In his childhood, his father abandoned the family, leaving a cold void in the household. And seeing his mom grovel to keep a roof over their heads and food on the table, little Nick felt a compunction to lighten her burdens. That prompted him to delve into thieveries at the age of nine, and in no time he became proficient at it, though, like Bobby Comfort, he was dedicated to averting violence. Dodging the authorities, he stole here and robbed there until he accumulated enough cash to relocate his mother to a respectable home. Sacco grew into adulthood, and because of his wit and physical limberness was known as "the Cat." But what also grew was his penchant for a fast-track life of womanizing and luxuries. And gambling.

SAMMY "THE ARAB" NALO. Nalo's trademarks were his long bushy sideburns, and the dense curly wigs he wore during a robbery—and when he would court women, who were mainly topless dancers and part-time prostitutes. He was a genius at planning armed robberies and applied his meticulousness to carry out those bold ventures. His wardrobe was fashionable and of high quality. Nalo was always bedecked in jewelry and exotic watches, as though a formal soiree awaited him. But he was apathetic and antisocial, save for his lady friends. Perhaps his mind was too preoccupied by his insurmountable gambling debts.

CHRISTIE "THE TICK" FURNARI. He held the distinction as the Lucchese Family consigliere, a coveted rank in the Mafia organization. Typically, this position was reserved for astute, steady-tempered members who were not prone to reacting on impulse and reaching premature unmeasured decisions. And Furnari fit that mold in an exemplary fashion. He also had a keen intuition to foresee undetectable developments with potential liabilities for him and the family. A true statesman.

AL VISCONTI. He, too, held a distinction, though not as prestigious as Furnari's. Al Visconti was known to be gay, the reason the Lucchese bosses did not elevate him to "a made man," despite his ingenious means as an "earner." He had an uncanny resemblance to Rocky Marciano. And coincidentally, Visconti had a brief stint as a professional heavyweight boxer. His bid as a ranked contender, though, was lackluster, and he wisely retired his boxing gloves, thus resuming his criminal career.

BOBBIE GERMAINE. He was a cordial, smooth-talking burglar and veteran stickup artist who treated his victims with the utmost care and civility. But another form of art was Germaine's foremost desire: his ambition to become a crime writer, preferably an author who would chronicle his own litany of felonies.

AL GREEN. This chap, an African American, was a numbers runner who operated in the Harlem section of New York City. Green would roam about, flanked by a bevy of "sistahs," dabbling as a pimp. Characteristic of "big time" black bookies, as a diversion he owned a raunchy bar, the Black Pussycat, where streetwalkers, lowly drug dealers, social welfare fraudsters, drunkards, and numbers runners lounged, frittering away time after a day of hard work.

ALI-BEN. He was a native of Turkey ingrained with the archaic close-minded mentality of a desert nomad. Ali-Ben tended toward viciousness and bore no respect for human life. The well-being of a goat or a camel meant more to him than that of a person. But when he partook in heists sanctioned by Christie Furnari and his gunmen, he knew that weapons were just for show, and violence was off-limits.

DONALD "THE GREEK" FRANKOS. His primary occupation was defined as freelance contract killing. Frankos was associated with "Mad Dog" Sullivan, the head of the Westies, a murderous gang founded by Irish immigrants. The Greek also killed for Genovese underboss "Fat Tony" Salerno. However, on the few occasions when he collaborated with Nick Sacco in performing jewel heists, Frankos left his cold-blooded contract killer hat behind and switched to a nonaggressive posture.

JOANNE RINALDI. The woman's beauty and promiscuity were the qualities with which she bartered for anything that fancied her. Adventure and men of power, who tap danced in mine fields, inebriated and electrified her. Unlike Millie Comfort, Joanne would not have been content to be a homemaker; she loved men, the masculine types, and would rather have fun than to have a baby. Indeed, the Manhattan nightlife inspired her, and she lived for it.

DETECTIVE GEORGE BERMUDEZ. He personified the NYPD's police officers of the '60s and '70s when corruption within the New York City Police Department was as corrosive as acid. Detective Bermudez was always in search for a "score," an illegal path to riches, and he found it—thanks to one of the Pierre Hotel robbers. But because of that sudden boon Bermudez learned that one's most priceless assets were honor and integrity, and not material wealth.

FBI AGENT MATT HAMMER. Weighing in on the opposite end of the scale from George Bermudez's deceitful and dishonorable inclinations, Agent Hammer was a law enforcer who subscribed to the highest standards of morals, and adhered to the FBI's strictest rules and regulations. But at times, someone who is too honest, too ethical, and too conservative sacrifices productivity and results.

ASSISTANT DISTRICT ATTORNEY DOUG POPE. Mr. Pope, an African American, was reared in a ghetto by a single mother. Against all odds, he repelled the temptation to emulate the dominant forces of his neighborhood. Driven by irrepressible motivations, he climbed above the 1950s stereotypical expectations of his race, and attained his goal: to be a prosecutor and invoke his people's civil rights and protect them from racial injustice. In the 1970s, though, to ADA Pope's dismay, combating racial injustice was no less a feat than fighting Goliath. And just when he felt totally defeated, he was given charge of the Pierre Hotel robbery investigation, a nationally famous case that, if. . .if he could only nab the perpetrators, it would surely propel him to stardom—or so he wished.

LAUREN BAKER. Since her adolescence, her dad had not bestowed to her love and affection, and she sought a father figure. For that reason, she married a much older man who happened to be of means. But Lauren came with a generous trust fund and didn't need anyone's financial support; though after her husband's passing, she being so young and vibrant, wealth alone could not allay her loneliness. And it is the desperate longing for companionship that often goads a man or a woman into an irreversible commitment to a mate who may not be suitable.

JUDGE ANDREW TYLER. The Honorable Judge Tyler, another African American component of this story, wasn't so honorable. He had been the focus of a succession of improprieties, which led to disciplinary consequences. The consensus of the investigators who reviewed his string of infractions was that he had no reservations in tapping into the authority of his judgeship for self-serving gains. Moreover, His Honor had tendencies to disregard the importance of his responsibilities on the bench. Judge Tyler's professional derelictions, it could be said, were a scar on the judicial system; on the other hand, his indiscretions might've been to the advantage of the defendants who appeared before him.

CHAPTER 1

NICK SACCO

I wasn't born a thief, but at thirteen years of age I was already a pro. I was running with the big dogs, stealing rolls of cables from the phone company and selling the copper to scrap yards. I had to; my father skipped town, and I was helping my mother make ends meet. I had a knack for getting in and out of tight spots as if I were double-jointed, even though I was quite tall for my age, eventually growing to six foot two. Because of my agility, my mother, may she rest in peace, nicknamed me "the Cat." And it kind of fit nicely with the rest of my name: Nick "the Cat" Sacco.

As I got older, I specialized in stealing jewels. I didn't get rich from this kind of work, but it was a living that let me afford to move my mother into a decent little house. In 1972, though, it all changed for me when I was pulled into the score of scores, the robbery that has never been topped. I was asked to work with the two slickest and smartest jewel thieves I've ever known, Bobby Comfort and Sammy "the Arab" Nalo.

But when these two guys first told me about the plan to break into the Pierre Hotel's safe deposit boxes, I thought they had lost their senses. I was afraid we'd all get arrested and wind up in a federal joint for thirty years.

The Pierre, on Fifth Avenue and 61st Street in Manhattan, is one of the ritziest hotels in the world. It has hosted presidents, kings, and queens, literally. Some of the permanent residents there are princesses, wealthy socialites, celebrities, and reclusive moguls.

Bobby Comfort and Sammy Nalo were so sure they'd figured out a way to break into the vault room, where hundreds of safe deposit boxes were encased in the walls. But I wasn't persuaded. They figured that on certain nights those damn boxes, all combined, might net us twenty to thirty million dollars in jewels, bearer bonds, and cash. (In today's value that would equate to a quarter of a billion dollars.) I'm now paying attention with an open mind. Soon, Comfort and Nalo's scheme made sense. It was well thought out, and it had to do with taking over the entire hotel at four in the morning for two and a half hours, holding hostage the night shift staff and anybody else who might've been awake. Two and a half hours! It sounded like something out of a movie. How can you take over a forty-story hotel with four hundred guests without a hint that a bunch of armed robbers were smashing into deposit boxes in the vault room?

Well, it wasn't easy or simple. Not to get caught, a thousand things had to go right, and just one had to go wrong to get pinched.

It's been forty-four years since Comfort, Nalo, five other thieves, and myself, all armed, barged into the Pierre hell-bent on cleaning out the deposit boxes. Of course, nothing goes as you wanted to. And although we had rehearsed every step, and thought we'd nailed it better than a stage dance, hair-raising incidents cropped left and right, and the unexpected took us by surprise. More unforgettably, many of the Pierre's guests, rich and influential, were eccentric, bizarre characters whose lives were as weird as a vegetarian wolf.

When it was over, whatever happened became history, and I buried those memories deep in my mind, never thinking about the Pierre. But today, a gray, snowy afternoon, I was walking through Central Park nearing 61st Street, and the peak of that famed hotel came into view high above the trees; and the daring adventure of 1972 re-lighted in my head as if it was going on at that very moment.

1971

Bobby Comfort and Sammy "the Arab" Nalo, a black brief case swinging at his side, were walking briskly on Canal Street in the Diamond District of lower Manhattan, weaving through the crowded sidewalk of inattentive pedestrians. The air was fouled with the exhaust of diesel fuel from the caravan of delivery trucks inching through the narrow streets. "Let's first give it a go with Hyman," Comfort said. "He's pretty quick at making up his mind."

Nalo side-glanced him and snickered. "Most of the times. Any way you look at it, he's a cheap old shyster."

Comfort nodded ahead. "We got another block to go. And there's his place. If we don't make a deal with Hyman, we'll go back to Delancey Street, and see if we can do business with Abe Saperstein."

Nalo sucked on his teeth and side-glanced Comfort. "Abe! Another swindler."

Comfort and Nalo strutted into H&M Jewelers, a long, narrow store, a glass showcase spreading the entire length of it. A dozen shoppers were hunched over the display cabinets intently gazing at the jewelry. Hyman Bloom, the proprietor, saw Comfort and Nalo and fast-stepped to the end of the showcase, where Nalo had placed his briefcase. Hyman, an Orthodox Jew, flashed a smile of brownish, crooked teeth. "Eet's nice to see you boyz." He put out his hand, fingers thin and bony, and Comfort shook it hardily, Hyman's curls, *the peyess*, bouncing on the sides of his head, resembling two slinkies. "So how's business?" he asked in his Yiddish accent.

Nalo swept his hand across the store. "*Your* business looks pretty damn good. Maybe you'll loosen up with your money."

Hyman petted his pewter-gray beard, the elderly man's cloudy eyes dimming. "Eh! You should know. Nothing is the way it looks." He bent over the counter and whispered, "Aha! The overhead. It's a killer. A killer!" But he quickly perked up. "So tell me, what do you have for me today?"

Nalo unclasped the briefcase and turned it to face Hyman. The scrawny gent, short and stoop-shouldered, peered through his thick bifocals, eyes twinkling and fleeting furtively. Twenty feet down behind the glass counter, three or four salesmen with yarmulkes and unruly black beards, oily curls of hair, the *peyess* winding below the ears, were busy tending to the shoppers.

Hyman nodded toward them. "Eh, let's move down a little, know what I mean?" Hand trembling, he took the loupe that hung on his chest and wedged it under his right eyebrow. Hyman began inspecting the valued stones inside the briefcase one by one. The goods were a range of loose diamonds, rubies, opals, and emeralds. Fifteen minutes into his examination, the jeweler let the loupe drop to his chest, and looked upward at the taller Comfort. "Tell me, how much you boys want for all this?"

Nalo, edgy and wiry, shifted from one foot to the other. And beating his partner to the answer, he said with firmness, "Six hundred and fifty grand."

Hyman grunted. "Follow me to my office. I have to take a closer look at what you have here. I don't know how many of these stones are numbered. As you boys know, whenever you shave off the numbers you lose a half to a karat."

"It don't matter, Hyman. Six hundred and fifty gives you plenty of wiggling room," Comfort countered. "First of all, most of the diamonds, as you see, are at least eight carats and up. And look at the brilliance. We're talking about *FVVS2* clarity rating. Also, notice the shapes, Marquise, Princess, Emerald. And they're perfect cuts. These are top quality. You know that."

The jeweler sing-sang: "Clarity clackity, shapes apes, cuts buts already; it all means nothing unless a customer steps up to the plate and shows the color of his money. And now, the way the economy is, everybody squeezes the nickel until the bull shits."

"I'll tell you right up front, we ain't takin' less than six hundred," Nalo snipped.

Comfort raised an open palm at his partner. "Take it easy, Sammy. We can work things out with our friend Hyman."

Comfort, Nalo, and Hyman huddled in his office, a tiny space hardly spacious for three men. A small jeweler's scale, a primitive brass contraption mounted on a wooden case, stood amid a cluttered desk. Hyman, slowly and deliberately, one by one weighed the stones, jotting on a scrap pad the weight of each one. Twenty more minutes of Hyman's assessment of the gems and another fifteen of *hondling* with the sellers funneled down to an agreed price of $567,000.

The jeweler, bald and frail, dabbed his forehead with a napkin, saliva bubbling in the corners of his dry lips. "I need a couple of hours to get you boys the gelt. Okay?" (*Gelt*, a Yiddish term for money, is pronounced *ghelt*.)

"As long as the gelt is in US dollars," Nalo quipped smirking, his deep, black eyes that told of dark deeds skipping from Comfort to Hyman.

"My gelt is nothing but US dollars. What do you think I'm gonna pay you with kosher chickens?"

The transaction was consummated, and Comfort and Nalo took a deep breath. They had just liquidated the majority of the gems plucked when they had forayed into Sophia Loren's suite at the Hampshire House hotel on Central Park South in New York City. Six months ago, in October of 1970, Comfort and two gunmen had taken over the hotel lobby. Nalo, posing as a service technician, encroached into Ms. Loren's apartment, held the Italian actress at gunpoint, and stripped the distressed woman of her jewelry. He then cut the phone lines and ran off without harming Ms. Loren and her two-year-old son. Nalo fled by means of the stairway rather than the elevator, vanishing in seconds.

Hyman well understood the stones were swag. Fifty percent of the jewelers in the Diamond District buy and sell hot products. This is an unknown commonality, but not to FBI Agent Matt Hammer, who was the lead investigator of the Loren case, *and* had been fast creeping at Comfort and Nalo's heels.

CHAPTER 2

NOVEMBER 1971

Bobby Comfort, in his late forties and looking tailored in a taupe, three-quarter length Burberry trench coat, was frittering away time in the exquisitely decorated lounge of a midtown Manhattan hotel. The lounge itself, Café Pierre, was sunken three feet lower than the lobby level, and the elaborate wrought iron scrolling of the three-step brass hand railings were inspired by the rococo style. Two etched glass doors lent the café privacy and quietude. The twelve round tables there, topped with black granite, each accommodated four green leather upholstered club chairs.

Comfort's brown eyes, roaming and inquisitive, were obscured by dark sunglasses, his face hidden behind a copy of the *New York Times*. The headlines read: NIXON PLANS TRIP TO NEW YORK FIRST WEEK OF NEW YEAR. On prior travels to Manhattan, President Richard Nixon had lodged at the Pierre, and presumably he'd do the same on his next visit. This might pose a dilemma and interfere with Comfort's plot.

On this evening at 11:40, the café's twenty-six-foot bar, tastefully veneered with golden-colored brushed stainless steel, was sparse of people. At twenty-minute intervals, Comfort had been ambling nonchalantly into the black-and-white-checkered-floor lobby, his gray tweed Totes hat pulled snugly over his forehead. He had followed this practice on numerous nights, occasionally parking himself at the Café Pierre's softly lit bar, drinking Dewars and soda.

"Care for another?" asked the bartender, timely striking a match to light the cigarette Comfort had stuck between his lips.

"Yes, but this time I'll have a shot of Baileys." He leaned in closer to the bartender for him to light his Pall Mall. "Thanks." Comfort drew on the cigarette and exhaled a puff, his eyelids squinting from the smoke. It was a rarity to see him not smoking. "By the way, what's your name?"

"Dean. And yours?"

"I'm George St. John. Pleased to meet you, Dean." Comfort's diction was polished and deliberate, and he chose his words to connote an educated background.

Dean turned his back to fetch the Baileys from the liquor rack, and Comfort said, "Not many people here tonight" To the casual listener this might've been idle talk, confabulation. Not at all, Comfort was collecting intelligence. He tasted the Baileys' dense sweetness and surveyed the surroundings, sumptuousness everywhere.

Dean, an engaging smile on his face, and always apt with a witty phrase, pulled on his own cigarette. "This is not unusual. After eleven o'clock it quiets down. Sometimes I can fall asleep." He winked and added, "By the way, this late, when everything is nice and quiet, the right fish might walk in. Know what I mean?"

Comfort returned the wink and downed his drink. "I sure do know what you mean." He bid Dean good night, and perused the ground floor of the sleepy lobby. He was waiting to see at what time of night the hotel's bookkeeper shut the cast iron door to the vault, where the guests' safe deposit boxes were. At 12:05, the vault's door was still open. But rather than mill about at this late hour, possibly looking suspicious, he thought it best to leave, and adjourn his stakeout until the next evening.

The following afternoon, a bone-chilling, rainy weather, Comfort, his long sideburns trimmed, face clean-shaven, tinting his complexion in a greenish shadow, paid another visit to the same hotel. In a black double-breasted suit, he walked with a purposeful gait to the registration desk, a black-marbled ebony counter. A six-foot, predominantly powder-blue painting hung behind it, flanked by two beige marble columns.

Comfort, his Burberry raincoat draped over the left arm as he lugged along a Louis Vuitton garment bag, accosted the reception clerk. "Good day. I'd like a room for the night," he said, sternness and formality in his voice.

The clerk's garnet uniform was custom fitted, a beige handkerchief folded in the breast pocket, and he had the faintness of a British accent. "Good afternoon, sir. Welcome. Will it be just one night?"

"Yes. My name is Dr. George St. John," Comfort said. His black hair combed to the side in a neat part, fingernails manicured, certainly befitting the image and comportment of a physician. Earlier that day, at Nalo's apartment in the Hell's Kitchen quarter of Manhattan, Comfort had applied heavy makeup to lessen two revolting scars on his face: one over the left eyebrow, and the other to the right of his mouth.

The clerk assigned Room 2169, and Comfort gave him a credit card, an American Express. The card holder's name read: Dr. George St. John. A bogus account. The clerk consulted the weekly bulletin of invalid and stolen credit cards, and indeed, Dr. St. John's account was in good standing. The clerk laid the Amex onto the credit card hand printer, swiped it with the roller and placed the receipt on the desktop for the customer to sign. "It's been a pleasure to be of service to you, Doctor. Please put your John Hancock here." Then almost forgetting, he said, "Oh, Doctor, here's the key to your room."

Comfort smiled politely and wandered to the elevators in the main hallway of the hotel. Before the advent of computers, credit card merchants received from banks a weekly bulletin of lost and fraudulent account numbers. The time that lapsed between the reporting of a card theft and the storekeepers' receipt of the advisory was twenty-one days. Inside that window, fraudsters could axe out a costly spending spree.

The lift operator, a black man in a black uniform and a crop of white hair under his hat, sprung into a stance of attention. "What floor, sir?"

"Twenty-first floor, please."

The elevator thrust into a heart fluttering ascent. When it slowed to a bumpy halt, Comfort disembarked and went to his suite.

Comfort's purpose to lodge at this hotel was to track the daily practices of the management and the staff, and of greater importance, to pinpoint the hour of night the bookkeeper locked the vault.

Bobby Comfort settled into the room—the walls veneered with peach-sand satin wallpaper—and undressed to shower and shampoo his wavy, jet-black hair. Although a few hours earlier he had showered at Nalo's apartment, the stressful ordeal of assuming an alter ego, Dr. St. John, and passing a stolen American Express, a film of clamminess was seeping in his underarms. Tired, Comfort lumbered into the shower stall, and lay under the hot, foggy water for twenty minutes. He dried off and napped until the early evening. Rested and perfumed, he dressed and centered the gray Totes hat on his head, casting an aura of erudition.

Comfort strode down to the lounge, and a different bartender welcomed him. Dean was off that evening. A woman, her legs crossed, had been sitting on one of the barstools nursing a cocktail, rattling the ice in her tumbler. The bartender asked Comfort, "Can I get you something, sir?"

Comfort scanned the bottles behind the bar. "Let's see . . . uh, how about a Remy cognac?"

"Certainly, sir."

"That's a good choice. Cognac warms my insides on a cold, lonely night," intruded the lady on the barstool to his right, her voice low and smoky as if she'd just wakened.

Comfort stole a glance at her partly uncovered legs. "Yes, a dry cognac warms me all over as well." He put out his arm for a handshake. "I'm Professor T. Phillip Pickens. Madame?"

The brunette, appealing and sprightly, tilted her head as though she were in awe, and placed her hand in his. "I'm Glenda. Glenda Atkins. Pleased to meet you Professor Pickens."

"Oh, please call me Phillip. *And* will you join me for a drink?"

To Comfort's fluster, she held on to his hand. "Sure, I'll have a Remy, too." And she moved over onto the stool beside his.

He ordered for Glenda, and with an inquisitive look in her black, olive-size eyes, she asked, "What do you teach, Phillip?"

"I'm an archeologist."

"An archeologist! What are you doing in New York? I wouldn't have thought you'd find dinosaur bones in Manhattan."

Comfort raised his index finger as if he were about to give a lesson. "Actually, after extensive research my colleagues and I have formed a consensus and . . ."

"What's a consensus?"

Comfort knew that word would stump Glenda, who was from Queens. "*Consensus* means an accord . . . an agreement among a group." He rubbed his chin and cleared his throat. "Anyway, we have reasons to believe that fossils of behemoth prehistoric animals may lie beneath the 42nd Street subway station." He was having fun.

Glenda didn't know the word *behemoth* either, but not to further lay bare her ignorance of the language, she tuned to a different frequency. "Interesting stuff! And you, too, Phillip, you're an interesting man." She brushed her hand on the lapel of his jacket. "Uh, I love your gray tweed blazer. And your yellow V-neck wool vest matches so well." She stared at him as if something had struck her nosiness, a smile opening to fairly nice rows of teeth. "Do you always wear sunglasses in the dark?"

He touched and jiggled the frame of his glasses. "I'm sensitive to light." Comfort chortled to move the conversation along. "Are you here regularly?"

"You can say that, Phillip. I work in the hotel, and after I'm done I come into the lounge and have a drink . . . or two."

She works here! Perfect, Comfort thought. "What do you do here, Glenda?"

She patted Comfort's wrist and pursed her succulent lips as if in a moment of confusion. "Oh, you mean what kind of work I do?" Glenda recrossed her legs, revealing meaty thighs. "Well, I'm the assistant to the bookkeeper who keeps track of the inventories inside the guests' safe deposit boxes."

Comfort gulped. *This is getting better by the minute.* What a wonderful coincidence.

NICK SACCO

Whenever Bobby Comfort was on a mission, he was as smooth as silk. He could hoodwink a cop, an FBI agent, a judge, or a lady. He was loyal to his marriage and loved his wife. And if he got involved with another woman, it was strictly business and nothing personal.

Comfort was one of the smartest jewel thieves in the country, and most of all, he wouldn't cheat you out of a penny. Except for smoking, he was free of vices. The man was ultracautious, and always on the alert. That's how he survived.

CHAPTER 3

A taxi cab slowed in front of 280 Broadway, the NYC Building Department, and Sammy "the Arab" Nalo, bald, five-foot-three, of Turkish descent, paid the fare. A cup of hot tea in hand, in the jerky strides of a short man he ran inside there, hurrying to stop the closing doors of the elevator. He made it in time, and walked out on the eighth floor, where the land records were warehoused. These premises were smoke-polluted and had the drabness of an ancient municipal facility. There, for the past month, pretending to be an architect, Nalo had been poring over certain architectural floor plans. He drew the attention of the records custodian, a plump, graying woman of retirement age whose straw hair could've been a bird's nest. Sourly, she asked, "Same file, young man?"

"Uh, yeah. Same file. Two East 61st Street."

"How many times do I gotta tell you? You have to give me the Section, Block, and Lot numbers, otherwise I gotta go through the whole drawer in the cabinet to look it up."

Nalo patted his dense, curly wig as if he had to ensure it was still in place, and put on a red baseball cap. When he didn't wear it, you could see that his dome-like bald scalp was as white as milk. "All right, all right."

"You better, 'cause this is the last time I'm doin' this for you."

Under his breath, he muttered, "Do everybody a favor and get yourself a four-hundred-volt dildo. That'll keep you in a nicer mood."

"And the next time, you should bring me a box of chocolate for my troubles."

Yeah, I'll bring you chocolate, all right. Chocolate with razor blades, Nalo was tempted to say.

The woman, her two chins sloshing loosely, had found the file and slapped it onto his chest. "Here, and remember: next time, no Section, Block, and Lot numbers, no shirtie."

The pudgy, forty-six-year-old Nalo carried the manila folder under his arm, looked about the room, and settled the paperwork onto an empty table, a scratched, splintering antique from the turn of the century. A dozen or so other researchers had been inconvenienced by the bantering between him and the spunky attendant. He shot the nosey-bodies a sinister glare and all heads lowered. Nalo emptied the folder on the table and unfolded a set of blueprints of the targeted hotel.

Looking sneakily as if in the midst of a subterfuge act—a fake beard on his cheeks and the red baseball cap overshadowing the eyes—he was copying into his notebook notations from the legend of a specific architectural drawing, the ground floor of the chosen hotel. Skimming over those plans, Nalo noted the locations of the elevator shafts, the stairwells, the distance from the side entrance to the vault room, and the square footage inside there. Also crucial for him to trace were the height of the ceiling in the vault and the thickness of the cement separating the first from the second floor. He then flipped to the electrical page of the blueprints and pinpointed the light switches in the various areas of the hotel lobby and stairwells.

At 3:45, the nagging clerk clapped her hands and announced for all to hear: "All right, everybody turn in your files. This office is closing in fourteen minutes. Let's go."

Nalo tidied the official documents, restuffed them into the folder, and rested it on her desk. A cab drove him to one of his pads, "the safe house," on 51st and Tenth Avenue. He paid the driver and fast-stepped around the corner to his apartment building, a brick structure where panhandlers and loiterers congregated. Suddenly stricken with paranoia, Nalo believed, as always, that someone might've been tailing him, possibly an FBI informant. He quickened his stride, ankles wobbling due to the two-inch lifts in his shoes.

He was looking forward to a quiet evening at home. One of Nalo's mistresses, Lupe, a twenty-three-year-old illegal immigrant from Ecuador, had been dwelling in his apartment. Lupe, an aspiring ballerina, freelanced as a topless pole dancer. Nalo unlocked the door, and as he opened it a raspy voice said, "Welcome home, Sammy."

Nalo strained to peer into the darkish apartment. As his eyes adjusted to the dimness, he saw Lupe, her hands tied behind her back. More alarming, an oversize, obese man, a stiletto knife in one hand, was clutching the girl's arm, and lightly gouging her throat. The trespasser was a collector for the bookmaker to whom Nalo owed $17,000.

CHAPTER 4

Comfort looked at his diamond pavé Piaget, a watch he only wore on special occasions. Ten-forty P.M., and Café Pierre was teeming with drinkers, a cloud of smoke hovering above the bar. Piano music sifting through hidden speakers was playing a medley of Bach opuses, and Comfort and Glenda were on the fourth cocktail. He was upbeat about her job in the vault room, and she was of interest to him. The liquor was dissolving the formalities, and tempted by Glenda's long lashes and what he visualized as her apple-shaped breasts, he said, "I'm staying the night here, and this evening the Rangers' hockey game is televised on closed circuit TV. I'm a die-hard fan and never miss a game. So I'm ready to go to my suite and tune in. Would you . . ." He paused as if he thought it too bold to ask. "Eh . . . would you care to join me? It's a very exciting sport to watch."

"I never watched a hockey game," she said, slurring. "My husband is closed-minded. He's into football and nothing else." Glenda swilled her cocktail and added bitterly, "His whole life is football, football, and football. I could be gone for days, and he won't even know it."

"Sounds like he lacks social vitality. Well, let me to introduce you to hockey," Comfort chanced, sort of tugging at her arm but with gentleness.

"I . . . I don't know, Phillip . . . I mean, my husband works nights, and he don't get home until seven in the morning and all that, but . . ."

"Oh, for God's sake. The game will be over in less than an hour." In actuality, the Rangers vs. Montreal game had already ended, and Comfort knew that. He glanced at his watch. "It's only a quarter to eleven. You live in Queens, so at the latest you'll be home by one."

Glenda slung her head back. "Oh, what the hell. But let's get another cognac and take it to the room with us."

Drink in hand, she kicked off the red, six-inch pumps and crammed them into her purse. They frolicked across the lobby, and the concierge, who saw his co-worker, noticed the tipsy couple. The new lovers blended into the main corridor leading to the elevators. Freshly polished oak panels and brass sconces were the signature of the Pierre's masterfully built elevators.

He unlocked the door of his suite, a soothing scent in the air. In the main room was a king-size bed attached to a beige padded headboard, and a rusty-tan tufted blanket lent it richness, an inviting warmth on this windy November night. A leather settee upholstered in a garnet damask fabric lay across the foot of the bed. Glenda, though an employee of the Pierre, had never been in any of the rooms and, astonished by this splendor, forgot about the hockey game, relieving Comfort from inventing a reason why in truth it wasn't on television.

Rather than sipping her cognac, she downed it in one swallow, and he knew it was time to charm her. He suggested, jokingly, it might be more comfortable if she slipped off her white, low neckline mini-dress and drape herself in one of the fluffy terry cloth robes supplied by the hotel.

To Comfort's surprise *and* delight, she said, "I've been up and running since eight this morning, and I can use a bit of unwinding."

He helped her disrobe, and pulled down the long zipper of the dress, sliding his palms along her neck and shoulders, whiffing Glenda's Chanel No. 5. Her back was silky and flat until it reached the buttocks, a pair of round buns that Comfort could've buttered and eaten right there and then. She leaned her head back in ecstasy, her breathing accelerating. "You got soft hands, Phillip."

Indeed he had, because moments later, standing behind the fast-heating Glenda, he was sensually pinching her nipples. "I love the feel of your pomegranate-size papayas."

Her panting slowed, and she asked in a labored voice, "What's a pomegranate?"

"Uh . . . it's a cross between a grapefruit and a tomato." An outright lie.

"Oh, Phillip, you're so educated." And her breathing hissed again.

Comfort untied Glenda's robe, nudged her onto the bed, setting ablaze flashes of surging lust. At 5:30 the next morning, as the autumn-violet daylight sneaked in through the pleated sheer panels she did not resemble her painted face of the night before. He woke the hung-over woman, and half-carried her into the bathroom. The shower stall, commodious and marbled, was enclosed with a glass door that had a chrome towel rack affixed to it, fluffy white towels hanging from it. He rushed her along so she'd be home before her husband. He wished for Glenda to avert a beating by her husband.

Comfort, tactfully, didn't broach the subject of the vault room; he'd save that for another day. Discretion was one of Bobby Comfort's qualities. Glenda slipped into the white dress, powdered her cheeks, and accentuated the eyelids with eyeliner. They embraced, and Comfort touched her chin. "Why don't we see each other tonight? Same time, but not the same place."

On his first visit to the hotel lounge, Comfort had told Dean, the bartender, that his name was George St. John. But last night Dean wasn't on duty, and he, Comfort, had presented himself to Glenda and the second bartender as Professor Phillip T. Pickens. And should Dean be working this evening, not to hazard his multiple identities colliding, he said to her, "When you're done with your shift, come straight to my room. I'll have champagne on ice waiting. What do you say?"

She upped on her toes to reach his mouth and smacked a wet kiss there. "See you later, handsome."

"And leave your wedding band home. Okay?"

Comfort offered to escort Glenda to her car, but she didn't want her co-workers to surmise she'd spent the night in one of the hotel guests' rooms. They kissed and she was gone.

Sammy Nalo did not have as delightful a night. From sundown to sunup, the nasty bookmaker's collector had been pressing him. An hour into this, he said, "If you ain't got my money, borrow it. I don't give a fuck how you do it. Just give me my fuckin' money. Understand?"

Nalo had blown his stake of the Sophia Loren score on gambling. Worse yet, Agent Hammer was advancing in solving the case, aligning Nalo in the FBI's crosshairs. And the collector, Gus, was torturing the South American Lupe, carving Nalo's name on her neck. Her screaming was unbearable, and Nalo couldn't bear it. "Look, Gus. Leave the girl alone. Give . . . give me twenty-four hours. I'll raise the cash." It was hot in the apartment, and beads of sweat streamed out from under Sammy Nalo's toupee. His brashness and tough-guy disposition had recoiled into meekness, a sheen of humidity glistening above his curved, narrow mouth, bringing to mind the perfectly painted lips of a doll.

Gus said, "I'll tell you what. I'm stayin' here with this broad and wait for you to come back with the dough." He pointed the knife at Nalo. "If you ain't back in twelve hours, I'll cut her tits off, and when I get to you I'll stuff them down your throat. Now get your ass in gear before I ream it with a Roto-Rooter."

NICK SACCO

Sammy was his own worst enemy. He was a degenerate gambler, but that was none of my business. I mean, I did a lot of gambling of my own, and went through millions of dollars. But Sammy had a worse habit. He couldn't be trusted; he'd screw his own partners. He was always in need of money and an inch away from getting killed. If you gamble, usually you lose borrowed money, and not the kind that comes from banks. It's cash you got from loansharks at five percent a week, and with such an outrageous vig you can never pay down the principal. Now you have shylocks breathing down your neck, and the first time you miss a vig payment they'll put you in a hospital. The second time, you'll be in the hospital longer. The third time, they won't bother paying a couple of goons to break your bones; they'll just kill you. It's cheaper. Me, I never gambled with borrowed money; fortunately I always had plenty of it.

That's why gambling makes a thief out of someone who's addicted to it, and Sammy was exactly that. If he had a chance to grab money that didn't belong to him, he'd beat his own mother out of it. And now, once again Sammy was scrambling to stay alive.

CHAPTER 5

The 19th Hole was a nightclub/restaurant in Bensonhurst, Brooklyn, covertly owned by Lucchese crime family consigliere Christie "the Tick" Furnari. The club, fiery with scantily dressed waitresses, music of the big band era in the background, was a front and nerve center for Furnari's illegal operations. There his underlings and fellow Mafia gangsters flocked and hashed out the scheme of the day. One of Furnari's affiliates was the Bypass Gang, a band of thieves who mapped out burglaries. Nick "the Cat" Sacco, a component of the gang, was Furnari's most entrusted.

On November 26, 1971, Christmas in the air, holiday decorations and pine-scented garlands festooned the walls and windows of the 19th Hole, softening the hard saloon atmosphere. Sacco was perched on a barstool, a vodka glass in hand, daydreaming about a cocktail waitress he had met last evening at 21 Club on West 52nd Street in Manhattan. To him, the Nordic-looking young lady resembled the actress Brigitte Nielsen.

Two colleagues strolled into the 19th Hole and meandered toward the bar. One was Donald "the Greek" Frankos, who affectionately slapped Sacco on his back, jolting him from his reverie. "How yah doin', Nick?"

"All right . . . all right, Greek. What's up?"

Frankos bent over close to Sacco's ear. "Nick, I gotta talk to you about a hell of a score."

Sacco put down his vodka. "Why don't you guys have a drink?"

The second friend, Al Visconti, a two-hundred-pound, five-foot-ten bruiser, also a burglar of Furnari's Bypass Gang, welcomed the offer. "Sounds like a good idea. Make mine Canadian Club on the rocks."

"I'll have the same," Frankos the Greek said.

Sacco hailed the bartender, Julie, a bouncy redhead whose lips seemed to be permanently puckered. "Julie, bring these guys two CC's on ice, will you?" He then said to Frankos, "So what's this score all about, Greek?"

Grinning, the Greek, square-jawed and lanky, cocked his head to the side and shook it in a way that said *Wait 'til you hear this*.

Julie served the cocktails and Visconti raised his glass. "Hey, cheers." He was strong and had a trunk-like neck, and you could see the contours of his biceps and shoulders under his shirt.

Sacco and Frankos answered in a chorus, "Cheers." And in restrained excitement, Frankos told Sacco that he had been asked to take part in a theft of mammoth proportions.

"Greek, can you give me a hint of what it's about?" Sacco's hazel eyes crinkled with curiosity.

Frankos looped his arm around the broad-shouldered, six-foot-two Sacco, and darted his head to the left and to the right as if someone might've been eavesdropping. "Look Pal, this is too big a job. A lot of money can be taken. I mean *a lot* of money, and I don't wanna say too much right here and now. All I can tell you is that Bobby Comfort and that miserable Turk, Sammy Nalo, are the ones putting together this score."

"I understan'. I understan'," Sacco said as Visconti listened in.

Frankos petted his black mustache, his jaw muscles flexing from edginess. "Nick, I want you to get Christie Furnari to sit down with us." He waved his forefinger in circles, implying a bond between them. "We're all gonna be in on it. You, Al, me, all of us. And if Christie comes through with what Comfort and Nalo need to pull it off, guess what?" The Greek raised his palms. "We'll be set for good. I mean, I'm talkin' about twenty-five to thirty million bucks."

Frankos' details were sketchy, and Sacco was skeptical and didn't commit to anything. The Greek sensed Sacco's reluctance and underscored, "Nick, like I said, we're lookin' at twenty-five to thirty million dollars, man."

It sank in, and Sacco nodded enthusiastically. "Christie doesn't come here a lot, even though it's his joint. But he's supposed to be here tomorrow, and I'll ask him if he'll jump on this ride."

The three jewel thieves called for another round of drinks and salivated at the prospect of a potential super score.

NICK SACCO

I had been friends with Greek for years, and we trusted each other more than if we'd been brothers. We'd done a lot of jobs together and never had an argument. He didn't talk much and at times acted as if he had the charm of a hippopotamus. But that was Greek's way to throw you off balance. On the other hand, if he put his mind to it he could con the devil out of his balls. He was a contract killer primarily for the Genovese family underboss, Fat Tony Salerno. Greek was all business and had no time for games or bullshit. And if he didn't want to go into details about a score he'd bring to me, I understood his reasoning. For one thing, he didn't want to talk about it in a public place where anybody might've been snooping. If another thief happens to overhear you talking about a burglary, he could pull it off before you do, or if he's an informant he could rat you out. And when you go to do the job, you find yourself in a hornet's nest, and get arrested without ever knowing what the hell hit you.

CHAPTER 6

The promise of a windfall from the undertaking Frankos had put forth kept Nick Sacco awake the whole night. The next morning, the Cat was having breakfast with Christie Furnari, who, too, was drooling for a slice of so humongous a theft. And before finishing a saucer of espresso spiked with anisette, the Lucchese consigliere, a busy person, said he was willing to hear about Frankos and his partners' idea over lunch. Furnari poured himself and Sacco a second round of the aromatic Italian coffee and raised his cup in toast. "*Salut!* Look Cat, let's not waste time. Set up a meeting with the Greek and his boys, and we'll see what can be done."

Sacco inhaled a drag of nicotine, and before sipping his coffee said, "*Salut* to you Christie. I'll call the Greek as soon as I leave here."

The luncheon at the 19th Hole with Furnari was set for 12:30. Nick Sacco and the respected Lucchese consigliere had been at the bar chit-chatting while waiting to hear about Comfort and Nalo's supposed mega-robbery. But annoyingly, frequent interruptions by runners, who delivered greetings and messages to Furnari, disrupted the conversation. The lunch customers were beginning to drift in, and the cooking flavors from the kitchen rustled Sacco's hunger, the song "My Way" sounding from the ceiling speakers.

The forty-seven-year-old Furnari nodded at *his* table. "Nick, let's go sit down over there." He raised his hand, and courteously called out to the bartender, "Freshen up our espressos, please." Plowing through the restaurant's patrons and tightly spaced tables, Sacco and Furnari walked to the corner table, a reserved spot exclusively for the Lucchese consigliere. He sat, his back to the wall, a Mafia precautionary tradition to avoid a bullet from behind. Furnari looked at his watch and sighed, impatience in his eyes. "It's a quarter to one. They're late, and already I don't like it." He was as punctual as the changing of the lunar faces and didn't tolerate lateness. And one of the reasons why he appreciated Nick Sacco was for his timeliness. But Sacco had other characteristics that singled him out. The Cat was of his word, a man whose eyes affirmed what he said.

"They're comin' from Hell's Kitchen and probably got caught in traffic," Sacco said apologetically.

Furnari's nose was slightly bent to the right, as if his face had been quartered and reassembled off-center. His mouth also lay askew, particularly when he'd get mad or upset, which he was at this moment. He waved a hand in disagreement. "Ah, that's no excuse. If a man is late for an appointment, he'll be late paying what he owes you. Remember that."

At last, Frankos strolled into the 19th Hole, Bobby Comfort and Sammy "the Arab" Nalo in tow. "Greek, over here," Sacco hollered, his arm up high waving him over.

The newly arrived sat opposite Furnari and Sacco. Amid the clanging of dishes and glasses, and the loud chatter from the crowd, Frankos introduced Comfort and Nalo, cigarette smoke thickening the air. Everyone shook hands, and as they settled at the table Furnari said, "So, Greek, let's hear what your friends have to say."

Frankos, five-foot-ten, his sparse black hair parted to the side, held his chin. "Well, Christie, why don't I have Bobby here give you the whole rundown?"

Everyone seemed uneasy in Furnari's presence, especially Comfort and Nalo. After all, to be face-to-face with the renowned Lucchese consigliere could fray one's nerves, though it was a humbling experience for anybody who had the privilege of his company. But Comfort, articulate and collected, rose to the occasion. "Mr. Furnari, first of all, I want to . . ."

Furnari interrupted him. "Call me Christie."

"Uh, thanks." Comfort said, indicating Nalo. "Sammy and I want to thank you for taking the time. We know a lot about you, and by all accounts you're a man of reason."

"That he is, that he is," Sacco asserted, winking at Furnari.

A few of minutes of wide-ranging conversations passed, and Comfort sketched out the bare essence of "the master scheme," Nalo sporadically interjecting as he picked at his cuticles. Before coming to this summit, they had decided not to divulge details until Furnari confirmed his pledge to the project. But the consigliere, wise and a man of a few words, always insisted on *all* the particulars, and would not settle for Comfort and Nalo's hazy proposition. And in his sedate but authoritative tone, he said, "Look, Bobby . . . what's your partner's name again?"

"Sammy," Comfort answered.

Furnari pointed a fork at Comfort and Nalo. "Listen hotshots, as a practice I don't swim in murky waters. If I can't see the bottom of the pool, I stay out of it. I gotta know the whole story about this job. But all you're giving me is an empty glass and double talk. I think you're not for me. Now if you'll excuse me." Christie Furnari stood and was about to say goodbye.

CHAPTER 7

Furnari was on the verge of walking away. Comfort and Nalo swallowed hard, knowing the opportunity to gain the support and backing of a Mafia boss, a consigliere no less, was fading faster than a candle in a hurricane. Startled and embarrassed, Frankos, Comfort, and Nalo glanced at Sacco, who gently grasped Furnari's elbow and said to his guests, "Christie here wants to know the whole deal upfront so he knows exactly what he's gettin' into. Understand?" He raised his eyes up at Furnari. "Christie, I don't think Bobby and Sammy meant to hold back." The Cat pointed at the consigliere's seat. "Here, sit. We can hash this out."

"Yeah," Frankos chimed in, "they're not here to play games. Please . . . please sit Christie and let's start over." He plucked a pack of Pall Malls from his shirt pocket and offered a cigarette to Furnari and to everybody else at the table. The consigliere declined, but Sacco accepted, sliding one out and sticking it in his lips. Frankos lighted it, as he did one for himself, shaking the match to snuff it out.

Taking the lead, and grateful for the second chance, Bobby Comfort signaled to Nalo not to do the talking. He leaned into the table and began a more thorough narration of his plot. The tension was easing, and the strategy seemed doable.

Sacco let out a stream of smoke and flicked his cigarette into an ashtray. "What's everybody's cut gonna be?"

Comfort opened his palms, a display of sincerity. "We'll do an even split among all of us."

Sacco looked to Furnari. "What about Christie? What does he get?"

Comfort cleared his throat as if he were afraid his answer might be rejected. "Uh . . . twenty percent."

Sacco and Furnari glanced at one another and chuckled. The consigliere said, "Thanks but no thanks."

"Well, I mean . . . eh that's negotiable," Comfort stammered, and Frankos fidgeted clumsily, Nalo still picking at his cuticles.

Furnari slurped his espresso and gazed slyly at Comfort over the rim of his cup. "You haven't yet said what you want from me."

"Christie, we need things like a late model limo, two untraceable trail cars, weapons, and other odds and ends. And should something go wrong, we need your political contacts."

"That's what I figured." Furnari folded his arms across the chest, leaned back in the chair, and allowed his thoughts to linger. Everyone else stopped breathing. "For me to consider all this, I gotta get thirty-five percent of the take." This resounded as if it were a bolt of thunder.

"That's what he usually gets," Frankos stressed to Comfort and Nalo, who were not accustomed to partnering with a high-ranking Mafia associate the likes of Furnari.

Sacco nodded. "That's what it is."

Comfort and Nalo didn't reply, and Furnari said, "I learned in life not to ask for anything that's unreasonable. So what's it gonna be, boys?" He called them boys to make Comfort and Nalo ill at ease. He waved at a waiter and asked for more coffee. "By the way, does anybody want anything to eat? Now's the time to order." But anxieties to reconcile this meeting with Furnari on board had stifled the appetites.

All eyes were on Comfort and Nalo, who were musing in silence, considering Furnari's most invaluable contributions—his connections to the judges, high level law enforcement agents, and key politicians. And putting matters into perspective, should they get collared or fall under suspicion, armed robbery is a Class A violent felony, packing a mandatory twenty-year sentence. And Furnari's coveted acquaintances could quash such a dire prospect. Comfort gave Nalo a final glance and said to Furnari, "Okay, Christie, thirty-five percent will be your end."

"I don't know why it took so long for you to come to your senses," Furnari said.

Sacco said, "Good, good!"

Furnari, icing his stone-faced stare, said to his off-balance audience, "I'll sleep on it."

Disappointed to end the luncheon inconclusively, the table disbanded and Sacco turned away from Furnari and winked at the others. "I'll be in touch with you guys."

CHAPTER 8

Two days had passed since the unproductive encounter at the 19th Hole. In the absence of a reply from Nick Sacco, Frankos, Comfort, and Nalo were growing discouraged, and contemplated soliciting the backing of a Colombo family made man, Vinnie Aloi. The drawback, though, was Aloi's insatiable greed. And more disconcerting, Vinnie was brutally vicious. But who else could they go to? Comfort and Nalo's stratagem to steal so large a prize was foolproof—at least on paper—and they were not about to scrap it. In so far as Aloi's hair-trigger ruthlessness, well, they'd have to play fair and pray for smooth sailing.

In the past, Frankos had collected loansharked debts on behalf of Aloi, and Vinnie had praise for him. Comfort and Nalo had never met Aloi, and it fell on Frankos to open the lines of communication with the Colombo wiseguy. "Hello, Vinnie, it's the Greek."

"Hey, Greek. How're you doin'?" asked the grossly overweight Aloi.

"Good, good, man. But listen, a couple of buddies of mine and me wanna hook up with you. Got somethin' to talk to you about, Vinnie."

"Sure, sure, Greek. Come down to my place. Say tomorrow afternoon at two-thirty."

"We'll be there, Vinnie."

Entering Aloi's basement makeshift office, a stench of cat urine overpowered the visitors' nostrils. At the first impression of him, Comfort and Nalo were revolted, if not frightened by his grotesqueness, and became more unwilling to align themselves with him. Frankos handled the introductions, and less any pleasantries, Aloi asked what the purpose of this call was. Comfort openly steered him through the preliminaries. Aloi, seeing the huge possibilities of this mouthwatering, high-stakes score, hinted he was interested. At that moment his phone rang. Resembling the bouncing of an oversized beach ball, he hobbled to his desk, flab around his belly sloshing beneath the soiled polo shirt, and lifted the phone receiver, his hand bloated like rising dough. "Hello," he said. His voice sounded as if he were gurgling. Moments later, he yelled into the phone, "What! I'll be right there." And Aloi flung the handset. In a fret, he said to his guests, "Somethin's come up. I gotta go. Come back tomorrow at the same time, and we'll wrap up this deal."

Again disillusioned, Comfort, Nalo, and the Greek walked up Aloi's basement steps, the wooden stairway creaking, and thought that, perhaps, this aborted meeting might've been an omen of sorts. Even so, they looked forward to returning tomorrow, hoping to finalize an understanding with Vinnie Aloi. But a concern was chewing on Frankos's mind, one he hadn't shared with his partners. Aloi only settled for a seventy-percent stake, a rather disproportionate cut. But what could you expect from a coldhearted loanshark? Certainly not fairness.

The next afternoon, just as the trio of super *bandoleros* were about to exit Nalo's Manhattan safe house for the trip to Aloi's office in Maspeth, Queens, the phone rang. Nalo answered it. "Hello."

"Hello, it's Nick Sacco. Is this Sammy?" He had recognized Nalo's high-octave voice.

"Yeah, it's Sammy. Got good news, Nick?" Nalo pointed at the receiver, and mouthed to Frankos and Comfort, "It's Sacco."

"That deal we talked about the other day; you-know-who says it's a go," Sacco was pleased to announce.

A smile came on Nalo's thin lips. As Frankos and Comfort were looking on eagerly, Nalo made a ring by curling his thumb and forefinger, the international sign that means all is well. "All right! And are you in, Nick?"

"Sure, I'm in," Sacco said.

Comfort was glad they didn't have to deal with the gluttonous Aloi and called for a minor celebration, though he told Frankos to place a courtesy phone call to the Colombo mobster and cancel their appointment. But hesitance was on the Greek's face, and Comfort asked, "What's the matter?"

Frankos scratched his chin and glanced from Nalo to Comfort. Frankos was stalling, and Nalo asked, "Greek, what's the problem? Any reason you don't wanna phone Aloi?"

Frankos lit a cigarette, puffed on it, and let out a swirling loop of smoke. "See, I know this guy like a book. And he's not gonna like us backin' out. We already told him it's gonna be a big, big score, and he's probably hot for it. Now he's gonna wanna know why we're not taking him in on it. And he'll be even more pissed when he finds out we're going with Furnari."

Comfort flopped onto a frayed velour couch. "So what if this fat fuck of a slob will be pissed. So what! We just got word that Furnari is behind us. And one of the reasons we went to Furnari in the first place is for protection; protection not only from the cops, but also from scumbags like Aloi. Right?"

"That's right!" Nalo said. "Let's go to the 19th Hole and see what Sacco says."

They walked two blocks east in the Hell's Kitchen district of New York City to where Frankos had parked his green Ford Thunderbird, and drove south to the 19th Hole.

Nick Sacco was in a large room furnished and dedicated to private affairs. He and Al Visconti were playing gin rummy. A waitress came in and informed the Cat that three individuals were at the bar asking for him. Sacco put his hand of cards down, and always on the alert, asked her, "Do they look like cops?"

"I doubt it. Their clothes are too tasteful and expensive."

Sacco pushed himself away from the card table, upped and went into the bar area of the restaurant. On seeing Frankos and his new partners, he said, "Here I am. What's up?"

Comfort asked, "Nick, can we talk somewhere more privately?"

"Sure." Sacco led them to the private room and told the waitress to ask everyone what they wanted to drink. She did and walked back to the bar. The Cat asked, "What's on your minds, guys?"

Quite candidly, Comfort told Sacco what had occurred in respect to Vinnie Aloi. And Frankos laid out the predicament at hand: the likelihood that Aloi would feel betrayed and threatened in some way.

Sacco listened and understood the pickle they had gotten themselves into. "But why didn't you guys wait before you jumped the gun and went to that fat bastard?"

"That's water under the bridge," Nalo said, draining a snifter of scotch. "The question is, what do we do now?"

Sacco shrugged. "I don't know. We're gona have to talk to Christie Furnari, and see how he wants to handle Aloi."

Vinnie Aloi eventually learned that Frankos, Comfort, and Nalo had canceled on him, and as anticipated this snubbing infuriated the Colombo captain. He was hell-bent on revenge.

CHAPTER 9

As delicately as he could, Sacco told Furnari about the Aloi flammable situation. The Lucchese consigliere's reaction was a seething one. In an attempt to soothe him, Sacco said, "Christie, Comfort and Nalo hadn't heard from us, and they figured you weren't interested. That's why they reached out to Aloi." Sacco poured more coffee for Furnari. "Not that I'm defending these guys, but they're pressed for time. They did say the job has to go down the day after the first of the year. I mean, we're already into the middle of November, and they got a lot of things to put in place."

Furnari tore open a bag of Sweet'N Low and dumped it in his espresso, stirring the muddy coffee. As an afterthought, he added a half ounce of Frangelico. "I don't wanna lose this score to Aloi." He took a swill of his espresso concoction and savored it, smacking his tongue. A few seconds passed, and Furnari aimed his spoon at Sacco. "I'm gonna call for a *sit down* with good ol' Vinnie, and I'll tune him up."

At the sit down, in the cellar of Don Peppe, an Italian restaurant on Lefferts Boulevard in Ozone Park, Queens, Aloi ranted and raved, complaining he'd been strung along by "three two-bit burglars" who used him as a wedge against the Lucchese family. And to add insult to injury, Aloi implied, Furnari was beating him out of a "big score just for spite."

But Aloi's grievances were unfounded; Comfort, and Nalo hadn't meant to mislead him. Their first choice of backing was Furnari, and perhaps it might've been in poor judgment to have prematurely contacted Aloi. In truth, if they were to be blamed for anything, it should've been for their impulsiveness. Nevertheless, this pair of non–Mafia members was on the verge of inciting a deadly confrontation between two clashing underworld figures.

Lucchese consigliere Furnari wielded far more power and clout than Vincent Aloi, who as a made man was lesser in rank and status. Aloi had ended his denunciation, and it was Furnari's turn to make his case. In his hardly audible voice, he began, "Does anybody here ever know me to go behind somebody's back and take somethin' that I wasn't entitled to?" Furnari glanced about the room, searching everyone's eyes, homing into Aloi's. No one answered, but in support some gave a faint shaking of the head. Furnari was the type of leader whose unblinking look affirmed his intentions, and those who knew him understood this.

Seven people were there, and five had cigarettes dangling from their mouths, the air smoky and thick, and as stale as the awful odor of a dirty ashtray. More discomforting, this humid, darkish subterranean level was noisy from the energetic footsteps of the waiters and customers in the restaurant above. Furnari, addressing Aloi, said, "Vinnie, you've been reading the wrong bible. You just made a lot of accusations against me in front of these folks, whom I'd like to think respect me *not* for who I am but for what *I do*." The consigliere swept his hand in an arc at the people seated. "I would never accuse you of anything unless I was a thousand percent sure. And yet, you made statements without first checking the facts."

"Like what?" Aloi yelped arrogantly.

Furnari ingested a deep breath and nodded at Comfort and Nalo. "Like what? These boys came to me about a week ago. And, I must admit, it's my fault that afterward they came to you. How is it my fault, you may ask? Here's why: I shouldn't have put off giving Mr. Comfort and Mr. Nalo my answer about what they had proposed to me. And not hearing from me after three days, they figured I wasn't on board. Understan', Vinnie?" Furnari paused and pointed at Comfort and Nalo. "Vinnie, these boys weren't trying to jerk you around. And I wasn't lookin' to take the score away from you. See, it wasn't yours in the first place."

Furnari had everybody's ears, and Aloi threw up his arms, interrupting with a provocative rudeness by challenging, "What're you mean it wasn't mine in the first place?"

The Lucchese consigliere, who never forfeited his dignity, didn't allow Aloi's contentious inciting to draw him into a heated argument. "Let me ask you this, Vinnie: when these guys came to you, did you give them an answer?"

"No, somethin' came up, and I told them I wanted to see them the next day."

Christie Furnari spread his palms at chest level. "Then you made the same mistake I made. I also had to take care of somethin' that came up. That's why I didn't get back to Mr. Comfort and Mr. Nalo as fast as I would've liked to."

A chorus of approvals rang out in the room. One of the listeners said, "That's right."

"Damn right," concurred another.

"Right on, Christie."

A Colombo family capo, Vic Orena was representing Aloi. Orena, short, his right eye lazy, had heard enough. "Christie, I'm with you on this." He then said to Aloi. "As for you, Vinnie, like Christie said, next time get it straight before you start talkin' out of your asshole." And Orena was compelled to dismiss Aloi's pretenses.

Everybody crowded the winner of the sit down, shaking hands and patting him on the back, and even kissing his cheeks. Frankos said to Comfort and Nalo, "See, Christie always comes through."

Sacco stood and rested his hands on Comfort and Nalo's shoulders. "That's for sure. Christie 'the Tick' is someone you can count on."

Nalo, his mistrusting tendency always switched on, asked Frankos to step away with him. When they were out of earshot, he whispered to the Greek, "How long have you known Furnari?"

"A few years. Why?" Frankos asked, curiosity in his coal-like eyes.

"I mean, can he be trusted?"

Frankos sighed and slung his head back. "Can Christie be trusted?! Lemme say this, Sammy, Christie Furnari is straighter than the pole your wife dances on. Does that make him straight enough?"

No one seemed to notice that Aloi had left, and on realizing this, Vic Orena nudged Furnari's arm and remarked, "In my book, you're all right. But that Vinnie is a sore loser. You gotta watch him. He's as unpredictable as a cornered rat. Know what I'm talkin' about, Christie?"

NICK SACCO

Everybody in our circles liked Christie Furnari because he was fair, even-handed, and sensible. Most of all, he never took what didn't belong to him. And he expected the same of those whom he dealt with; unlike Vinnie Aloi who was unreasonable, and he'd take your eyes out if he could. Furnari hadn't had much schooling, but he'd hold his own in any situation.

CHAPTER 10

On 257 West 29th Street, Port Said (pronounced *saheed*), a Middle Eastern nightclub featuring belly dancers, catered to a blend of regulars, scaling from Arabic extract to liberal, middle class New Yorkers who hosted a fondness for Middle Easterners. The management advertised "Exotic Belly Dancers from Turkey and Iran." The club was partly owned by Sammy Nalo. There, in his improvised office, he chartered "the robbery of the century" that the squadron of chosen gunmen would undertake. One of the robbers, Al Visconti, felt privileged to have been drafted into this elite squad. But at this moment, his mind was elsewhere. He couldn't wait to escape Nalo's confining, incense-filled office and enjoy cocktails in the dimly-lit cabaret setting of the club, where on the dance floor the belly dancers' bodies were sizzling, oozing shimmering droplets of perspiration. "Hey Sammy," Visconti asked, "the sign outside says your girls are fresh from the Middle East. But do they still smell like the camels they slept with?"

"I don't think that's funny, Al. Why don't you stop playin' around and pay attention to what we're talkin' about here?"

"Yeah, this ain't no time for jokes," added Bobby Germaine, a veteran stickup man who'd also been selected for this highly classified assignment.

"He's right, Al. You gotta take this serious, or else I'm out," Sacco said, snuffing his cigarette in an ashtray. "One small mistake, and we can wind up in the can for thirty years. So either get with it or bail out now." He glanced at the others for approval. "Right, guys?" Everyone nodded in agreement.

Comfort stood and yawned. "Excuse me," he said covering his mouth. "I didn't have much sleep last night. But you raised a good point, Nick. And I'll say that all of us gotta be into this with body, mind, and soul." He tapped Sacco's shoulder. "Nick's right. One small mistake, and we're all up shit's creek without a paddle." He then turned to Visconti. "Look, there'll be plenty of time for jokes."

Nalo cut in, "Let's break for tonight and meet here tomorrow at the same time." He, too, yawned, but wasn't as polite as Comfort, and didn't cover his mouth. "I'm kind o' tired myself."

"Good idea, Sammy," Frankos said, shuffling and reshuffling a deck of cards. "I gotta drive to Brooklyn and take care of some business tonight." Everybody here could've guessed Frankos's agenda this evening. Murder for hire. And most probably, at the behest of Anthony "Fat Tony" Salerno, a Genovese family titan. But any activities of violence had no business in the scheme of the planned robbery. And none of these bandits cared to know about Frankos's affairs; they trusted that his own dealings would not affect *or* infect theirs.

Comfort ran a hand through his hair and said in agreement, "Yeah, let's call it a night. Tomorrow, we'll go over what we talked about tonight, and then I'll walk you all through the rest of the details." He looked at his watch. "I gotta hook up with my contact at the Pierre. I'll see you guys tomorrow evening. Take it easy."

Before leaving, Comfort paused at the doorway, and glanced back at Ali-Ben and Al Green, the two last-minute recruits. "You two haven't asked a question the whole night. Either you understood everything or weren't paying attention. Which is it?"

Ali-Ben, an ill-tempered 190-pound Turk, who physically per-sonified an Arab from the dunes of the desert, had no more regard for a human life than he did for that of a fly. He answered in an indistinguishable accent, "Nah, nah." He flitted a finger from Al Green to himself. "Don't worry, Bobby. Al and me got it straight." He slapped Green on the back and chortled hoarsely. "Right, Al?"

"No doubt, man," Green said. He was tall and slender, and had a tawny complexion, and a quashed nose that looked as though it was sprawled all over his cheeks. "If any questions come up, we'll hash 'em out tomorrow."

Nalo dawdled behind, and everybody, save for Sacco and Vis-conti, went out the building through the rear delivery door. Sacco said to Nalo, "I think you and Bobby put together a good plan. Congratulations." The Cat paying a compliment was a rarity; he was a socially detached and secretive.

Nalo drew a swig from a pint bottle of ouzo and smacked his lips, relishing the bluish Greek beverage. "Thanks, and don't be late tomorrow night. Okay?" Nalo said in his bossy manner, jabbing a hand at the air.

Sacco didn't appreciate that order and walked out coldly, no goodbyes or cordialities. He and Visconti didn't leave. Instead, they walked into Port Said's lounge, mainly because Middle Eastern nightclubs were a novelty—at least on Sacco and Visconti. Neither one had been there before. But common knowledge had it that the club was not profitable, and the true purpose for Nalo to retain ownership of it was to attract and lure females into dating him.

Near the entrance, a hostess of Egyptian origin—the length of her black hair brushing the hips—was outfitted in a sparkly, red ankle-length gown. She led Sacco and Visconti to a table that had a square view of the stage. A three-piece band of musicians playing Turkish G clarinets was strumming what sounded to Sacco as repeti-tive twangs of Middle Eastern music. The main attraction, though, was a belly dancer in a purple and yellow glittery bra, her hips and legs veiled in a violet sheer, who barefoot and like a nymph in heat jutted her hips to the rhythm of the lulling melody. Fluidly flapping her sleekly outstretched arms, she flexed her belly, an inviting midsection that looked as supple as velvet. The curvy performer's makeup sparkled under the spotlights as if gleaming stars dappled her face. The dancer's wrists were adorned with jingling bracelets, her perspiring skin glistening as though it were wrapped in a film of cellophane.

Sacco and Visconti, watching the tireless performer—who was casting flirting glances at the gawkers closer to the stage—sat and adjusted themselves in the black velour club chairs. The Cat, still chafing from Nalo's rude order, said in a sulking mood, "You know, Al, I only know this fuckin' Sammy a week, and already can't stomach him. He thinks who the fuck he is, and if he keeps it up, I'll show him who *I* am."

"Yeah, I kinda got the same feelin'," Visconti answered, though distracted, his attention wholeheartedly on the steamy dancer.

"He must've been conceived by anal sex, 'cause he's a real ass-hole." Sacco gazed at Visconti for his reaction, and they erupted into a hearty laugh.

A waitress appeared from the dimness of the dining salon. She, in a blue dress, baring rounded shoulders and part of her gelatin-like mammary glands, asked, "Will you be dining, or are you just having drinks?" She flaunted a wide smile, her aquiline nose longish and thin.

"Just drinks," Sacco said. "I'll have bourbon on the rocks."

The waitress bent over to place napkins on the table, breasts dangling dangerously. And Visconti gaped unconsciously at the intoxicating sight, sweet perfume wafting from her deep cleavage. Pretending to rearrange the candle holder on the tabletop, she let him enjoy her luscious pom-poms for a few seconds. Then she asked sweetly, "And what will it be for you?"

That stirred Visconti. "Uh . . . same as my friend here."

On the stage, the tempo of the music sped as the hands of the percussionist, in blurring movements, frantically slapped a pair of bongos. The dancer's steps seemingly floated and raced nimbly in sync with the tune. She twirled gracefully, bending at the waist forward and backward, arms high above the head, the customary cymbals clacking in her hands.

The following evening, Comfort and Nalo navigated the Pierre Brigade through the minutest details, reviewing for the final time every action and movement they'd carry out in the spawning morning hours of January 2, 1972.

CHAPTER 11

THE PREDAWN HOURS OF JANUARY 2, 1972

Nalo's apartment in Hell's Kitchen was on the third floor of a graf-fiti-defaced, ramshackle building, one that even rats had vacated. The rusting wrought iron fire escapes hung precariously, and many of the windows were cracked or covered with brown paper. On entering the ground level hallway, the wooden door squeaking and caked with coats and coats of sloppily applied paint, a stench of overcooked cabbage gassed Sacco's nostrils. Nalo's apartment, Middle Eastern music droning on, was musty from years of sealed windows, and tonight had taken on the male scent of the occupants who were there in preparation for the imminent heist. Months of accumulated dust had lightened the maroon Persian rug that lay in the center of the room to a dull gray. The eight-man troop was ready to dress and put on disguises for the Pierre adventure. Fake mustaches, beards, eyelashes, plastic noses, hats, and sunglasses. They'd be in black tuxedos–after all it was a Big Apple soiree. Comfort, one who did not overlook the smallest detail, looked over his

Argonauts. He studied Al Green, the designated chauffeur. "Man, you couldn't find a better hat?"

Green, lanky with a mild afro and a razor-short mustache, was an African American who worked for a numbers bookmaker from Harlem. His daily wardrobe seemed as though it was inspired by the 1970s character Super Fly. Green turned the hat this way and that way and asked, "What's wrong with it, Bobby? I mean, y'all wearin' real crazy shit, and you're comin' down oun me!"

"What's wrong with it?! It looks like a Halloween prop." He snatched it from Green's hand and waved it for all to see. "Look at this. Does it look like a *real* chauffeur's hat? Remember, Al, you're supposed to be a chauffeur waiting outside in the limo. Which means that if anybody walks past you, it can't look like you're on a trick or treat."

"I think I got somethin' better," Nalo said. He rummaged through an old steamer trunk and groped at an actual chauffeur's cap.

"Good," Comfort said. He looked Nalo up and down and shook his head. "And you, why don't you put on a shorter wig that doesn't make you look like a circus clown?"

Everyone laughed, and Comfort drew on his cigarette. "Look at yourselves in the mirror, and if you still look ugly it means you're recognizable."

Nick Sacco tried on a black fedora, sunglasses, a plastic nose, and a pencil-thin mustache. He was a towering, imposing personality and had the build of a cruiserweight. A defined, square jaw and a thin but slight Roman beak lessened his Mafioso inclinations. "What're you think of this, Bobby?"

Comfort and Nalo nodded in approval, and Bobby Germaine said, "Nick, I say you should have some kind of a wig under your hat."

Everybody was busy attaching the final touches to his masquerade, and the moment for the drill that would redirect the course of these eight, bold adventurers had rung. One by one, they stepped through the door of Nalo's hideout, stenches of urine in the common hallway, climbed down the narrow stairway, and walked out onto the sidewalk. Men in tuxedos and patent leather shoes grouped in front of a dilapidated tenement, overfilled garbage bins hindering the entryway, was the picture of an odd scene.

They moseyed nonchalantly two blocks east, where the getaway vehicles were parked. A 1970 black Cadillac limousine, a green Ford Torino, and a black Chevy Impala. At 3:45 A.M. Sacco, Comfort, and Nalo piled into the limo, Al Green at the wheel. Furnari's car rustlers had stolen the limo and the two swing cars. Ali-Ben and Germaine as the driver boarded the Impala. And Frankos and Al Visconti were in the Torino. The three-car motorcade, the limousine leading, was off to the Pierre.

Cleverly, Comfort had set on this night to storm in because banks had been closed since Friday afternoon, the day of New Year's Eve, through 9:00 A.M. on the following Monday. Hence, throughout the holiday weekend the Pierre guests had no choice but to secure all valuables in the hotel deposit boxes.

The sky was starless, the temperature extremely frigid, breath vaporizing from the mouths of the limo's passengers. They were traveling north on Park Avenue, and Nalo asked, "You guys got your guns loaded?"

Comfort said, "We're not shooting anybody, Sammy. The weapons are just for show." He lowered his window three or four inches and flung his cigarette butt into the darkness, red sparks flickering on the asphalt.

The hour for the sortie was fast approaching, unspoken misgivings taming the brigands into sullenness. The Impala and the Torino turned westward onto 60th Street, and both cars parked on the corner of Madison Avenue, the limo staying on the northbound course on Park Avenue to 61st Street. Germaine, Frankos, Ali-Ben, and Visconti walked west for one block to Fifth Avenue and swung right. Hands in the pockets of the tuxedos, arms snugly at the sides to retain body heat, the subfreezing air made the chilling wind feel as if it were slashing at their faces. The walk was challenging, and at this ungodly hour the Big Apple was not dazzling and unanimated.

"We should've been wearing overcoats. This is too cold for me," whined Ali-Ben.

"This is the way Bobby and Sammy wanted it. I guess they figured the coats would've been another thing to stash once we got up to the Pierre," said Germaine.

They were four hundred feet from 61st Street and Fifth Avenue; a police cruiser was idling, white exhaust pouring from its tailpipe. "Shit!" Visconti cried out.

"Just stay cool and keep strolling," Germaine said. "We're carrying heat and sure don't wanna get a pat down."

"Yeah, we'll get locked up before we even do the job," Frankos said. "We look kind of odd walkin' around at four in the mornin' in twenty-degree weather without any coats."

The two police officers in the cruiser saw the four men in tuxedos and strained to make out the moving silhouettes on the unlighted sidewalk. "This is strange. What are these guys doin' walking around in this cold without overcoats?"

CHAPTER 12

3:53 A.M.

A hundred yards east of Fifth Avenue, Al Green steered the limo close to the curb fifty feet from the 61st Street entrance of the Pierre Hotel. "Germaine and the others should be gettin' here any minute," Green said, peering out the windshield, his jaws flexing as he chewed gum.

Around the corner on Fifth Avenue, the doors of the police cruiser sprang open, and the two officers came out.

Inside the limousine, a minute had passed; Comfort, Nalo, and Sacco wondered why the rest of the gunmen weren't here yet. "It's only a three or four minute trot from where they parked the Impala and the Torino. And until they cut left on 60th Street, they were right behind us."

Not too distantly, trouble was looming. Walking cautiously toward the four coatless chaps, one of the cops hollered in a baritone voice, "Everything okay with you fellas?"

The foursome didn't slow their stride, and Germaine said, "Uh . . . yeah. No problem."

"Kind of cold to be out with no coats on," the officer said cynically.

Ali-Ben explained in his Turkish accent, "Eh, we was in one of the Aitalian restaurants on 56th Street. They havin' a New Year's party, and we just gettin' some fresh air." In the seventies and early eighties, 56th Street was a venue of Northern Italian restaurants, so Ali-Ben's story was plausible.

And before the officers might question the obviously phony whiskers and wigs, Germaine, quick thinking, touched his chin. "That's why we got on these stupid beards and mustaches."

At that very moment, grave concerns were festering in the limo. "What the fuck happened to those guys?" Nalo asked no one in particular. He leaned forward and looked out far ahead of the limo's hood. "Maybe we should drive around the block and see where they are."

"If we do that and then come back again, it's gonna look suspicious to the guard manning the side entrance here. He already saw us from behind the glass door." Comfort said. "We'll give them another minute."

"Somethin' is wrong," Sacco muttered. "Somethin' ain't right."

Indeed, the pair of policemen glanced at one another, and the one with the low voice asked, "What are your names?"

"Joe King," Germaine answered.

"Don Sullivan," Visconti said.

The cops nodded at Ali-Ben. "And you, what's your name?"

"Khaled Mustafa."

Frankos didn't wait for the cops to ask him and said jokingly, "I'm Burt Reynolds." The Greek did have a remote resemblance to that famous actor. "I'm only kiddin'. My name is Mike Hunt."

Again, the patrolmen gazed at one another, mulling whether these crazy, inappropriately dressed pedestrians were up to foul play. They stared suspiciously at the four for fifteen to twenty seconds, Germaine and Ali-Ben shivering. The second policemen said,

"I guess there's no harm done. But you guys better get back inside somewhere before you catch pneumonia."

Anxieties stirring inside the limo, Nalo banged irately on the back of Green's headrest. "Al, drive around the block, and let's see where the fuck they are."

Green put the limousine into drive, switched on the headlights, and suddenly four shadowy men came into view, trotting side-by-side toward the limo. "There they are."

"All right, we're back on track," Comfort said, running a hand across his brow.

Sacco, Nalo, and Comfort bailed out and hid on the sides of the Pierre's entryway. Comfort, donning a longish wig and hat, the lapels of his black wool coat buttoned up to the neck, partially masking his face walked to the door, and pressed the bell button. If one were to look out from inside the doorway, his accomplices could not be seen.

CHAPTER 13

4:03 A.M.

In the hours between 1:00 and 6:00 in the morning, the Pierre is closed to outsiders, and the only access into the building is from the secondary 61st Street entrance, where a security officer admits only guests and people who have room reservations. He sees Comfort and asks through the intercom, "How can I help you?"

Comfort answers, "I'm Dr. Forster. I have a reservation."

From behind the glass door, the guard mouths the words, "I have to call the front desk for verification, Dr. Forster." The security officer picks up his telephone handset and punches in the extension to the front desk. "This is Jules. I need confirmation for a Dr. Forster." He winks at Comfort as if to say, *I'm sure everything is okay.*

Out on the sidewalk, all eyes are on Comfort, and he glances subtly at his mercenaries, who remain unseen on the sides of the doorway under the light-brown awning advertising *The Pierre.*

"He's checking my reservation," Comfort says in a hush, shifting from one foot to the other, rubbing his gloved hands together.

They nod, cold breath spewing from their mouths, feet stomping to circulate blood, anxiousness stamped on everyone's faces. Peering through the glass door, Comfort has a full vision of the lobby, the décor exuding opulence.

In less than twenty seconds, which seemed an eternity, Jules dips his head up and down, verifying the reservation. He unlocks the door, the latch clanking, and waves in Comfort. "You're all set, Doctor."

"I sure am." Bobby Comfort charges the unsuspecting Jules and shoves a gun in the poor man's chest, pressing him face-first against a wall. "Don't make a sound, and nothing will happen," Comfort hisses.

"I won't . . . I won't," utters Jules, hysterically rocking his head.

"What's the number to this extension phone here?" Comfort asks him.

"Uh . . . 113," Jules gasps, terror pumping through him.

With precision-like dexterity, Comfort handcuffs and gags the guard. He then pushes him into a broom closet so no one in the lobby will see what has just occurred. Nalo and four of his cohorts walk casually eighty feet into the lobby and across the reception area, handguns concealed, a ploy not to scare the clerk behind the desk into activating the distress signal. Frankos is monitoring the 61st Street door on the lookout for possible incoming residents of the hotel. Al Green is on standby out by the curb in the limo. Germaine is standing unobtrusively, not far from the vault room. And Visconti bolts down the wide marbled stairway to the lower level and turns left into the Security Office, a tobacco-smoke scented space. A guard in a black suit, no tie, is at a desk, coffee cups, newspapers, and hand-held two-way radios strewn on it. He's attempting a crossword puzzle. A second one is lounging on a black leather couch, riveted into a raunchy magazine, *Hustler.* The sudden appearance of the gun-toting Visconti stiffens the security officers into a frozen gape, and they stare at him in a baffled look. The armed intruder, his fake beard, and bushy eyebrows are signs of trouble. His revolver pointed at the one on the couch, Visconti says, "Get up. Don't do anything stupid, and you won't get hurt." The guards' hands fly up in the air, surrendering unconditionally. "What're you gonna do to us?" asks the shorter guard, blinking fitfully and cowering in fear.

"Like I said, my man, no need to worry. Right now, we're gonna stay put down here." Visconti nods at the stairway. "We're stayin' here until my friends upstairs give me the green light to take you two up there."

On the ground floor, Ali-Ben is walking offhandedly in the corridor that leads to the Pierre's main entrance on Fifth Avenue. He absorbs the elaborateness of the tray ceiling and the brass, pyramid shaped chandeliers that bear understated lavishness.

Sacco, the fedora low over his forehead, strides fifty paces into the same hallway and stops near the elevators. The black operator, rotund and chubby, is slumbered on a bench. He hears Sacco's steps, and as if he's an ever-ready sentinel, ups to his feet. "Goin' up, sir?"

"No, not yet," Sacco answers, averting eye contact. At this stage, except for the one security officer, Jules, no one in the lobby is conscious of the impending invasion. To the casual observer, all is normal, and the ambushers' priority is to restrain the reception clerk, preventing him from setting off the emergency warnings. It's 4:10 A.M., and the atmosphere in the Pierre's expansive, extravagant vestibule is one of complacence. *The calm before the storm.* But in a split second, Nalo fast-steps to the front desk, and with the snap of a lisping snake leaps over the counter, simultaneously drawing a Smith & Wesson revolver from his waistband, and tackling the receptionist, restraining him so he can't press the alarm button under the desktop.

"Please don't hurt me. I'll . . . I'll do whatever you want. Please!" pleads the attendant. On the night shift, only one person covers the front desk, and Nalo is now straddling him. Within seconds, the agile mugger overpowers the wheat-blond-haired clerk, moistness in his eyes. Swiftly, Nalo handcuffs Blondie, whose face has whitened, and tapes his mouth.

"THIS IS A ROBBERY. EVERYBODY DON'T MOVE. Do as we say and nobody will get hurt," Nalo announces loudly, but as pleasantly as his gruff voice allows him to.

EVERYBODY DON'T MOVE is the cue, and in concert the buccaneers draw guns and spring into action, each deploying his rehearsed tasks.

The Pierre personnel and the guests who are scattered here and there freeze on the spot. At first, some don't register that command, but the vigorous commotion of the bounding gunmen lights the reality of this eddying maelstrom.

"Oh, my God! It's a holdup!" a redhead says in a scream. She's in her early thirties, eyes wide in angst, hands sandwiching her cheeks from sheer fear. "Somebody call the . . . Oh!" She sees Germaine lunging in her direction, wielding a silver pistol.

She raises her hands, and Germaine winds his arm around the woman's waist. "Stay put, girl. I'm not gonna hurt you. Please lemme cuff your wrists." And she does, his Old Spice cologne suffusing her nostrils.

Ali-Ben, too, has a customer. He spotted a bellhop lugging a brass-framed luggage cart. He rams his pistol into the baggage handler's spine, and turns him over to Visconti. Ali-Ben then dashes to the foyer of the side entrance; there Comfort pulls Jules out of the closet and relegates him to his reliever. "You got him?" he asks Ali-Ben.

"Yeah, I got him." And Ali-Ben takes the guard by the bicep.

Comfort calls out to Frankos, careful not to use his name for the hostages to hear. "Everything okay?"

"It's all cool. It's all cool." Frankos said. He had taken Jules's gray uniform sweater, and the Greek was now wearing it. The pullover had a full-length zipper and a gold and black patch bearing the inscription, SECURITY OFFICER, lending the Greek the appearance of authority.

By the elevators, Sacco aims his gun at the African American operator, who gasps and drops to his knees, hands stiffly stretched out in the air, his egg-size eyeballs popping out. "Mah man, don't shoot me. Oh Lord, please don't shoot me. Look here, I won' say nuttin' to nobody. No sir."

"On your feet, pop. We're gonna take a short walk. Just for exercise. Looks like you don't get enough."

"Where yoh takin' me, mah man? I never done nobody no wrong. I got lil' gran'kids to look after," the black man babbles on.

Sacco marches him to a semi-secluded alcove snuggled to the right of the vault behind the front desk. Ali-Ben is already there with the handcuffed Jules, and so is Nalo who's prodding Blondie into the alcove. "All right, everyone get inside and sit on the floor facing the walls," Nalo barks.

The pandemonium is rising.

Not far from the entrance of the now closed Café Pierre, Comfort spots a male in his forties in an ill-fitting black suit, and assumes him to be a security officer. In a quick but composed walk so not to tip off the presumed guard, Comfort, gun behind his back, nears him and presents the weapon he had kept concealed. "Sir, put your hands up. Are you one of the security people?"

"Hey, what the hell is this," says the guard, eyebrows arched on his forehead. "What is this, a holdup?"

"You guessed it, sir," Comfort answers kindly, his pistol in the man's flabby belly. "Now please, won't you open your jacket? I want to see if you're armed."

The security officer unbuttons his jacket and flaps it open. No weapons. "Good, good," Comfort says. "Sir, if you will, let's walk into the alcove." And this accounts for the four-man night security force. The first was Jules; Visconti had surprised the pair down in the security office; and now Comfort apprehended the fourth one.

The stickup men move on to corral a few stunned guests, who at this wee hour of the night, for one reason or the other, happen to be milling about on the ground level—six in all. Also among the unfortunate are eleven Pierre employees, the night skeleton crew. Sacco and Ali-Ben herd the detainees into the alcove, and one by one Germaine and Nalo fetter everyone's wrists. Ali-Ben seals the captives' mouths; tough Comfort insists on exercising kindness and good manners. And the holdup men do not handcuff or gag the frail and the elders.

The alcove is now secured, and Comfort goes down to the subterranean floor, where Visconti has been holding the two security officers. "Okay, you can bring these guys up to the alcove."

Visconti nods at Comfort, and revolver in hand marshals his prey one flight up and into the makeshift holding pen.

The invaders confined the hostages inside the niche, a space now reminiscent of a POW paddock. The raiders have cleared the entire lobby and foyer zones, and Sacco and Ali-Ben spread out into the labyrinth of hallways, supply storerooms, utility closets, and employees' lunchroom in search of anyone still at large. Bobby Comfort puts on the concierge's dark red jacket and takes charge of the phones. The white telephones are reproduction classics from the 1920s art deco era outfitted with brass hardware.

Nalo and Germaine return to the side entrance and the latter says to Frankos, "Open the door. We gotta get the tool boxes and the valises out of the limo."

Frankos browses outdoors through the glass and spies for any pedestrians. "It looks clear." He unlocks the door, and Nalo and Germaine rush out, a mass of cold air stinging their faces. In the limousine, Al Green notices his partners exiting the Pierre and pops open the trunk. "Everythin' awl right in there?"

"Yeah, it's goin' good. *So far.*"

Green helps move the tool box and the Louis Vuitton luggage to the hotel door and runs into the warm car. Why the exorbitantly expensive Louis Vuitton pieces? Who might think of burglars transporting stolen jewels in such suitcases of status?

Nalo and Germaine hustle back into the building, hurrying across the lobby, readying to rip open the safe deposit boxes in the vault. As Comfort had observed in the course of his reconnaissance, due to the constant traffic in the vault room, the management seldom shut its cast iron door. And tonight is no different.

Comfort is at the front desk, overseeing his team at work; Sacco and Ali-Ben, toting revolvers, are roving throughout the premises, patrolling for anyone and anything amiss. Visconti is in the alcove guarding the hostages, and Frankos the Greek is at his post at the 61st Street entrance. The stickup men are all in place, and Comfort nods at Nalo and Germaine, a signal to begin ransacking the safe deposit boxes. Nalo is lugging the heavy tool box, and Germaine lugs the valises into the safe room. Inside there, Germaine says to Nalo, "We gotta keep the door closed, otherwise the hammering and prying is gonna wake up the whole joint." Twenty minutes into this process, a logistical problem arises; in the vault are hundreds of deposit boxes, and the majority of these containers is empty or have odds and ends of no value. The marauders must abscond before the 7:00 A.M. morning shift, and haven't time to rummage through every one of the boxes. An unanticipated glitch.

CHAPTER 14

Though it was strictly business on his part, and not a love affair, Comfort's extramarital folly with the Pierre's assistant book-keeper, the loose brunette Mrs. Glenda Atkins, was about to pay off. In part, in his daily surveying of the hotel he romanced Glenda, who soon warmed to Bobby Comfort but knew him as Professor T. Phillip Pickens. And the cozy chitchats in bed produced invaluable information. She unwittingly told him specifics of the day-to-day management of the hotel. For example, the records and entries of items the guests keep in the deposit boxes were recorded on index cards filed in a metal receptacle. Recalling this, a thought occurred to Comfort. He asked Sacco to have Nalo come to the front desk.

Nalo craned his neck around the vault door. "What is it?"

"Stop banging in there for a minute and come here," Comfort said.

"Hold up," Nalo hollered to Germaine and jogged to the front desk. "Somethin' wrong?"

Comfort said, "There's no point in going through every damn box. Remember I told you that the hotel auditor keeps track of every single thing the guests put in the safe deposit boxes?"

Nalo nodded. "Yeah, that's right."

"Are you thinking what I'm thinking?" Comfort touched his temple, eyebrows doing a devilish dance in wonderment. "We'll make the concierge give us the index cards, and you'll only open the boxes that are worthwhile."

Nalo rocked his head, but his brooding trait did not brighten. "That'll make it a lot easier." He raced to the alcove and said to Visconti, "Bring the concierge out here."

The concierge, a short, freckled man with a boyish face and carrot-red hair, was shaking from head to toe, believing he was in the final minutes of his life. Perspiration was bubbling on his brow, his hair sticking to it. "Please don't harm me. I got a wife and three kids."

"We're not here to hurt you," Comfort said. "What's your name?"

"Uh. . . Rusty."

"Rusty! That's a nice name," Comfort said as if he truly liked it.

Nalo didn't find any humor, and his severe expression never wavered.

Comfort felt Rusty's manacled wrists and to mollify him asked, "Are the cuffs too tight?"

The concierge's breathing calmed a bit, and he shook his head. "No."

"Good. Here's what we want you to do, Rusty. We need the metal case with the index cards that list the things inside the safe deposit boxes. We want you to give us those cards."

Rusty stammered uncontrollably and said, "I . . . I don't know where the auditor keeps them. I'm . . . I'm not lying."

Comfort cocked his head and smiled. "Now, now, Rusty. I'm a nice guy and wouldn't think of hurting anybody." He thumbed at Nalo. "But my friend here isn't so nice."

Rusty's face was drenched in sweat, and Comfort saw his knees vibrating. The concierge side-glanced Nalo, who stood in a stance as though he were about to pummel him. Time was passing rapidly and this bantering could not continue. Comfort peeked at his watch and rested his hand on the petrified concierge's shoulder.

"Look, Rusty, as long as you're dealing with me nobody will hurt you." He pointed at Nalo. "But my pal doesn't care who lives or dies here tonight. See, he's a Muslim, and if he kills you, he thinks he's doing you a favor because he believes he'd be sending you to a better place." Comfort paused. "Besides, there'll be no skin off your back. These people we're robbing got more money than they can count, and whatever we're taking they won't miss."

Rusty's glances pranced from Comfort to Nalo. "I . . . I think the auditor keeps the index cards in one of his drawers. But I'm not sure."

"Well, let's go have a look," Comfort said.

Rusty led his captors to where the metal container was kept. Nalo opened it and scanned the cards. Eureka! The data in each card included the safe deposit box number, the name of the current holder, the date it was last accessed, and a description of the stored valuables. Comfort walked Rusty to the alcove, and some were moaning and sniffling inside there. Nalo hastened into the vault and said to Germaine, "We got what we needed. Take a look at this." A scarce smile sprouted on his lips. "Box number 233 is loaded with jewelry." And he and Germaine pinpointed that box and pried it open.

In possession of the inventory cards, the production of emptying the high-value boxes was now as easy as picking apples, and Nalo and Germaine were feverishly pillaging the safe room, stuffing one of the four Louis Vuittons with millions in diamonds and cash.

CHAPTER 15

The burglary had been progressing, and progressing it was. The hostages, a mix of aristocracy, middle-class workers, and lowly laborers, were now less ruffled and somewhat resigned. Understandably, two or three of the women were sniveling, though Comfort and his brigade were bending over backward to be polite, treating the imprisoned considerately. The phone rang at the front desk, and Comfort lifted the receiver. "Hello, how may I help you?"

An irate voice belonging to a South American male complained, "This is Meester de Montejo. I ring for elevator ten meenutes ago, and it no come."

Comfort contrived an excuse and explained in his polished enunciation, "Sorry sir. We only have one elevator operator at night, and he's . . . well he's indisposed in the lavatory. But I'll send someone else. He'll be there in a minute. What floor are you on, sir?"

"Twenty-four," answered Señor de Montejo.

Comfort moved the receiver away from his ear and stared at it. *Twenty-four!* "Mr. de Montejo, did you mean you're on the twenty-fourth floor?"

"Yes, yes, that's what I said. Hurry up."

Comfort waved at Ali-Ben and Nick Sacco. "Come here you guys," he said. "Listen, take one of the elevators to the twenty-fourth floor. A Mr. de Montejo has been waiting there."

Ali-Ben, his Turkish accent thick and unintelligible, reminded Comfort, "That's Nick's specialty." A guest calling for an elevator at 4:00 A.M. seemed unlikely; nevertheless, Nick Sacco had trained for this improbability. The Cat had asked a friend, an apartment building superintendent, to teach him how to work a manned elevator. Indeed, this company of jewel thieves had devised the means to overcome any crisis. Hopefully.

Sacco gave Comfort a reassuring look and pulled Ali-Ben by the arm. "No problem. C'mon."

Comfort urged, "This guy up there is getting impatient. Hurry. I don't want him calling someone on the outside. If he's got anybody else in his suite, bring them all down here."

Ali-Ben and Sacco sprinted into the nearest elevator. Sacco pressed a black pushbutton. Bingo! The elevator and shaft doors rolled shut. Beside that black button was a brass throttle lever that stemmed from the floor to a height of thirty-six inches. This was the rheostat that controlled the movement and speed of the elevator. Sacco tilted it to the right, and in a jerky jolt the elevator jettisoned upward at an ear-popping speed. "And away we go."

Ali-Ben felt queasy. *Did Sacco really know how to run this thing?* It was accelerating at the velocity of a rocket, and Ali-Ben feared that *for sure* this wood and brass contraption was going to blast through the roof. Sacco was watching an electronic panel of illuminated numbers, each corresponding to the approaching floor, and lighting in succession as the elevator ascended. In forty seconds, the twentieth number blinked, a warning to slow the lift for the twenty-fourth floor landing. "Slow it down, man. Slow it down!" Ali-Ben said, panicking.

"Relax," Sacco replied in a cool whisper. He eased the throttle back to the left, and the elevator slowed. In five to six seconds it would come to a full stop on the twenty-fourth floor.

But the phone rang again at the front desk. "Hello, how may I help you?" Comfort asked.

"Thees is Meester de Montejo. What ees takeen so long for elevatore to come?"

Comfort put on a smile to sound collected and agreeable. "Oh, sorry, sir. It should be arriving any moment."

"I donn know. Sometheen is feeshy. Sometheen is feeshy here."

CHAPTER 16

The elevator door opened, and the two burly men in tuxedos emerged, guns in hand.

"What took you so goddamn long?" Señor de Montejo demanded, belligerence in his voice. But as he saw the cannon-like revolvers, his hostility tempered. "What . . . what's goeen on?"

"We apologize for your inconvenience," Sacco said in his husky voice. "But there's more inconvenience to come." He gently backed Señor de Montejo into the hallway wall.

This was a total surprise to de Montejo; here he was on his honeymoon at the most famed and exclusive hotel in the world, less than twenty hours after his wedding ceremony, and two armed hooligans were holding him at gunpoint. *It must be a dream.*

"Who else is here with you?" Ali-Ben asked.

"Eh . . . my wife and . . . mother-in-law," de Montejo answered, indicating the direction of his suite.

"Let's go get them," Sacco said.

"What do you want with my wife and mother-in-law?" asked the Brazilian, who, not believing that a couple of loco *Americanos* could order him into submission, seemed more frazzled than scared.

"We have a black tie party going on downstairs, and you're all invited," Sacco said.

"Thees is a joke. Please go away." De Montejo, tall and slender, his black hair combed back *a` la* Julio Iglesias, was startled beyond words, and turned to walk down the hall to his suite as though he were free to do as he pleased.

"Sir, this is no joke. Stop and do as we say," Sacco warned, severity in his voice, advancing to tackle de Montejo if necessary.

Ali-Ben took hold of the man's arm, and they escorted him to his room. On entering, Señor de Montejo, a well-to-do ranchei, led the two gunmen to the bedroom where his bride was sleeping. Sacco motioned to wake her. The Brazilian tiptoed to the side of the bed, shook his wife, and uttered in Portuguese, *"Lilliana, Svegli . . . svegliano."* Wake up, wake up.

"Uh, *non ora Diego,*" she said. *Uh, not now, Diego.*

"Lilliana, sveglia, por favor." Lilliana, wake up, please.

"In esso vive, Diego. Lo abbiamo fatto soltanto molti teamses poiché siamo andato voi base." No more, Diego. We did it so many times since we went to bed.

"Lilliana, non è quello. Là ara due banditi qui con le pistole. Gli facciamo andare abajo con loro." Lilliana, that's not it. There are two bandits here with guns. They want us to go downstairs with them.

Lilliana, still sore from the rupturing of her hymen, her virginity, and the excessive workout her vagina had endured over the past several hours, was faintly awake in the darkish bedroom. "Diego, go to sleep," she mumbled in Portuguese, her voice gravelly.

Sacco groped for the light switch on the wall. Seeing her groom in a suit, not a hair misplaced, and a scent of fresh cologne, she widened her drowsy eyes. She said, "Diego, why are you dressed at four o'clock in the morning?" A moment later, she saw Sacco and Ali-Ben, her jaw dropping. "Who are these men? And why are they in our bedroom?"

De Montejo crouched near the edge of the bed and also spoke in Portuguese. "I'm trying to tell you they're forcing us to go . . ." He pointed at Sacco and Ali-Ben as if they were aliens. ". . . These bandits are taking us to the lobby." He helped her off the bed and pulled her pink nightgown down to her ankles. "Put on something and go wake up your mother." Lilliana stumbled past Sacco and Ali-Ben. She went to the second bedroom where her mother, Señora de Lago, a petite lady weighing less than one hundred pounds, was already awake and standing in her doorway.

In a white night robe, Señora de Lago's bluish-white hair neatly coiffed as though it were permanently plastered, had on a menacing stare. In Brazil, it was a commonality, if not a tradition, for the mother of the bride to chaperone the newlyweds on their honeymoon. Señora de Lago, a spunky matron, who did not speak a word of English, wished for someone to explain this rowdy disturbance. And she, too, was questioning why her son-in-law, the dapper, permanently tanned Diego de Montejo, was decked out in his best suit in the middle of the night.

The two ladies dressed, and Lilliana asked the stickup men if they'd permit her time to apply makeup and brush her long, black tresses. Sacco looked at Ali-Ben, and they assented. It was a mistake. To the ire of her captors, Mrs. de Montejo consumed fifteen minutes getting herself ready, her husband and mother's nerves fraying by the minute.

At last, Sacco and Ali-Ben were set to take the horrified Brazilians down to the lobby. Señora de Lago's foggy eyes were misty, and she asked her son-in-law, "Where are we going?"

He shrugged. "I don't know. Just do as they say. These gringos mean business."

Lilliana was weeping, and shuffling along she clutched de Montejo's arm, her head lying on his slumped shoulder. *But why, at four o'clock in the morning, was he doused in cologne, and in his finest Italian-made suit, and silk yellow tie?* This gnawed at her.

In oblivion to what was happening, Señora de Lago was prattling loudly, protesting and damning the burglars, her voice echoing in the hall. Ali-Ben said to de Montejo, "Hey man, tell the old lady to quiet down. We don't wanna wake up the whole floor."

Lilliana let go of de Montejo's arm and moved to her mother's side, winding an arm around the matriarch's waist. "Don't cry, mama. Everything will be okay. I don't think these *Americanos* want to hurt us."

"Please get in the elevator," Sacco said.

The elevator, though one of the finest specimens built, wasn't too spacious, and the five passengers had to stand awkwardly close to one another. The doors closed, and the lift plunged faster than a lead balloon, sucking the breath from Señora de Lago's lungs. And not knowing her fate, the bespectacled septuagenarian yelped a shrill cry, her voice more piercing than that of a Chihuahua. Sacco cringed and spoke through his teeth, "We don't want anybody hurt in any way, but you gotta keep your mother-in-law quiet."

Consolingly, Lilliana hugged her mother. At last, they were on the ground floor, and Sacco and Ali-Ben guided the de Montejos through the lobby and into the growingly crowded alcove. One of the victims in that den, the thirty-one-year-old redhead, as soon as she saw Mr. de Montejo, began writhing and screaming through the duct tape as if she wanted to castrate him.

CHAPTER 17

Hearing uproar inside the alcove, Comfort ran in there, and seeing the redhead in distress he removed the duct tape from her mouth. "What's the matter?"

Wrists trussed behind her back, she disregarded Comfort. Instead, she lunged at Mr. de Montejo, wrath in her eyes. "Who are these women you're with, Diego?!"

The new Señora Lilliana de Montejo was flabbergasted, as was her mother. Diego de Montejo had nothing to say and looked nervous, seeming guilty of some wily underhandedness. The redhead, Visconti holding her by the arms, was kicking him in the shins, intent on hurting Señor de Montejo, if only she could break free. Her face flushed to a candy-apple red, teeth in a canine snarl, her brown eyes as feral as a leopard's. "Diego, you better tell me who these women are."

Lilliana, befuddlement imprinted on her face, glanced around the room, expecting someone to shed light on what on earth she was not privy to. *Who's this woman yelling at my husband, wanting to know our personal affairs?*

Diego de Montejo hung his head as Ali-Ben handcuffed him; Lilliana, the mother-in-law, and the redhead were staring at him, waiting for enlightenment. Adding to the madness, Lilliana was resisting Visconti cuffing her and spat in his face. She came face-to-face with de Montejo, noses two inches apart. "Diego, I'm only going to ask you once more." Huffily, she gestured at the redhead and said in some form of English, "Who's this Chiquita . . . this *Americana* who's talking like she knows you? She . . . she looks like she lost her reputation when she was twelve."

The redhead expanded her chest, protruding the breasts, and sneered, "I may have lost my virginity, but I still have the box it came in. It looks to me like all you got left is a hole with a rat trap in it."

Señora de Lago, too, stepped in close to de Montejo and chimed in but in Portuguese, "My daughter has the right to know who this *Americana* is. And so do I. She looks and dresses like a *puta*. And in the morning I'm going to call the family lawyer. My daughter deserves better."

The redhead, in a skimpy, skin-hugging red dress that wasn't much more than a hand towel, did not understand the Portuguese *rat-ta-ta* of the feisty mother-in-law, though she surmised the gist of her slur. "Who are you callin' a prostitute, you old, shriveled-up spic?"

The trading of insults went on and on, puzzling everyone in the holding pen, who were clueless to the issue at hand, and Comfort stepped in to end the bickering. But clarity soon prevailed; the redhead, Joanne Rinaldi, a stunning woman whose temper was as ignitable as gasoline vapors, was Señor de Montejo's mistress. When Comfort & Company had invaded the hotel, she was the pretty young lady whom Germaine shackled and hustled into the alcove.

Before her capture, Joanne had been waiting in the lobby for her boyfriend to sneak away and whisk her off to a second room he had rented on the seventeenth floor. Unbeknownst to his wife and mother in-law, Señor de Montejo was partaking in two honeymoons. But his dalliance was thwarted, and the catfighting between the de Montejo ladies and the sexy Joanne was raging on. "Ladies, please let's be civil. I . . . I can explain . . ." Diego de Montejo said over and over, though no one was listening to him.

His wife, fighting off Visconti, spat at Joanne, though the spittle fell short of the target. "You're nothing but a *puta*."

Humiliated, Joanne's jaw fell open, her delicious mouth gaping. "What did you call me?"

"Yes, you're a lowlife *puta*," Mrs. de Montejo reaffirmed. The scorned bride was puffy-eyed from crying, the mascara damp and rolling down her cheeks, simulating the legs of a spider. The verbal brawling was beginning to entertain everyone, who had no idea if it had been purposely scripted or it was spontaneous.

Diego de Montejo's marriage, less than eighteen hours old, was on the rocks. His mother-in-law was instigating her daughter to file for divorce at daybreak, and the female hostages were rallying for her, caressing and consoling the former virgin. The speechless and besieged Mr. de Montejo, a multimillionaire, owned cattle ranches in Marianópolis do Tocantins in central Brazil, and a divorce settlement might yield his eighteen-hour bride approximately $1,800,000, an amount equating to $100,000 per hour. Not a bad day's work for the brief Mrs. Lilliana de Montejo.

Unmindful of the quarreling in the alcove, Sammy "the Arab" Nalo and Germaine were hammering nonstop at the safe deposit boxes, metal shrapnel flying in the air. They were using three-foot crowbars with curved and thin bifurcating ends and flat-top shafts. Each break-in necessitated six to eight dead blow hammerings before the crowbars could be wedged into the crevices of the cast iron frames that encased the boxes. Nalo and Germaine had been pummeling relentlessly, laboring into a dripping sweat. "Sammy," Germaine said, "so far we filled two of the four suitcases."

Rapt in smashing a twelve-inch by twelve-inch box, Nalo ignored him but closely worked his crowbar as if he were a sculptor wielding a chisel. This box had been assigned to a socialite, Aleksandra Petranovic, a self-proclaimed princess from Yugoslavia, who was often the starry subject of the Page Six gossip column. The forty-four-year-old trendsetter, an impressive presence of voluptuousness, was a frequent guest at the Pierre. She was popular and esteemed among the prosperous, and when in the company of men, especially the older private at another time. He thought for a while, and then said, "Hey, you guys are making a hell of a racket. Keep the goddamn noise down. We don't wanna wake up the people on the second floor."

Pounding the hammers, Nalo answered sharply, "Yeah, no problem." This abruptness heightened Comfort's keenness that his partner was in business for himself. Sammy Nalo's conscience was so tainted that not even bleach could've brightened it, and Comfort knew it too well.

Germaine saw Comfort's troubled look and laid his tools on the floor. "What's the matter? Is there something wrong, Bobby?"

Comfort didn't answer for a few seconds, wondering if Germaine, too, was lining his own pockets. "Is there anything wrong? I don't know *yet*. For now, just keep the noise down."

THE PIERRE HOTEL AFFAIR

tycoons, she readily engaged the ancient geezers. Million-dollar jewelry, conviviality, and wheat-blonde hair, were the attributes that shone the spotlight on Ms. Petranovic, and she was the sparking flame of the evening. In another life, in the period of her impoverished years as an immigrant, she was a prostitute. Years later, at a select gentlemen's club the seductive temptress targeted with her amorous glances a brittle octogenarian mogul. Ms. Petranovic's unnatural sensuality, *and* her endearing Slavic accent inebriated him. And thinking with the wrong head, as males often do, the old dog took the high-class hooker as his bride. As she had foreseen, he died shortly thereafter, and she fleeced his multimillion-dollar estate. Having succeeded in her fraudulent marriage, soon after the obligatory thirty-day mourning period Ms. Petranovic married a second octogenarian magnate. And then a third, hence her rise to respectability and prominence.

As Nalo pried open Ms. Petranovic's safe deposit box, his heartbeat raced. He couldn't believe his luck. Inside a blue jewelry case was a sixty-to-seventy karat diamond necklace. *This gotta be worth 750 grand!* He glanced in Germaine's direction, who was ripping out boxes on the opposite wall of the vault, unaware Nalo had been watching him. Glimpsing at him, Sammy Nalo took the necklace in his hands, and was about to sneak it into his inner jacket pocket. Just then, Comfort was by the vault's door to warn Germaine and Nalo to cut down on the noise. But the moment froze in Comfort's mind, and Nalo's slyness unveiled itself in slow motion, though Comfort wasn't sure what he had seen. *Did that son of a bitch Sammy slip something into his damn pocket?*

Noticing Comfort, a curious look on his face, Nalo reacted with an involuntary shudder, gulping a sigh of surprise. But he wasn't certain his partner had snagged him. Comfort's eyes, though, stayed trained on Nalo's as if to ask, *Did you just shove something in your pocket?* Unfazed, Nalo shunned Comfort's stare, and restarted the hammering of the boxes, the banging rumbling through the lobby.

Comfort, still standing by the vault's door, was undecided whether to confront Nalo right here and now, or to have it out in

CHAPTER 18

T he phone was ringing at the front desk, and Comfort hurried back to it. He was perturbed over Nalo's deviousness, but managed to put on a formal tone. He answered on the fourth ring. "Hello and welcome to the Pierre. May I help you?"

A mousy woman's voice said, "I want to make a reservation for tomorrow evening. I'd like a suite high up and facing Central Park."

"I'm sure we can accommodate you, Madame. But at this time of night, one reservation clerk is on staff, and if you give me a phone number where he can reach you I'll have him call you in twenty minutes." Comfort was on edge, and his eyes reverted to the vault room as if he could spy on Nalo from where he stood.

Inside the alcove, aside from minor complaints and murmurs of discontent, thanks to the civility of their warden, Al Visconti, the captives were resigned that all would end well. The de Montejos and Joanne Rinaldi had suspended the bickering, and the rowdiness had quieted.

Sacco and Ali-Ben were patrolling the first floor; so far, no sign of trouble, and they hoped things stayed that way. Nalo and Germaine were blissfully dismantling the safe deposit boxes, and the commotion was now less noisy. Frankos the Greek, who had been guarding the 61st Street entrance, hadn't spotted anything abnormal outdoors, and because of this late hour, and the extreme subfreezing wave that had befallen the Big Apple, traffic was virtually nonexistent, and the whole block lay in tranquility. Complete stillness. All was quiet, and the seas were calm. But the minutes ticked away, and Comfort and his crew could not waste time; it was 4:45 A.M.; the brigands had to clear out before the seven o'clock morning crew mounted.

Just as the inactiveness of his post was lulling him into boredom, out on the sidewalk Frankos saw a man of about sixty-five with longish hair whiter than snow. His appearance made the Greek think of the character Geppetto, Pinocchio's father. Geppetto rang the intercom buzzer. "Who are you, sir?" Frankos asked, tightening his lips so not to laugh.

On prior occasions, Geppetto never saw this guard. "I'm Jordan Graff, a resident of the hotel. Please let me in. It's freezing as hell out here."

The Greek allowed him in and stuck a .38 Colt at Graff's temple, terrorizing him into a state of incoherence. He then walked Mr. Graff to the lobby, at which point the horror-stricken chap began moaning and wailing, his legs buckling.

"Who's this?" Bobby Comfort asked. "He doesn't look too good."

Frankos was propping up him so he could stand. "He's a resident. His name's Jordan Graff."

A surge of blood blushed Comfort's face. "What's wrong with him?"

"He was fine until I let him in and put my gun to his head," Frankos said nonchalantly.

Graff, his complexion now as white as his hair, was gasping for air and mumbled through his clenched lips that he might be suffering a heart attack. Comfort placed his palms on the sides of his head, but tried not to panic. "Stay with him, Greek." Comfort ran into the alcove, and speedily cut the duct tape off the reception clerk's mouth. "Blondie, you know if a doctor is in the house?"

The clerk saw Graff and recognized him. "Uh . . . uh, that's Mr. Graff. He . . . he has a heart condition. What's wrong with him?"

"I don't know. I'm not a doctor. That's what I wanna ask you. Is there a doctor in the house that you know of?"

"Oh, no! He . . . he looks like he needs one badly," the clerk muttered and began panting.

Comfort shook him by the shoulders. "Blondie, that's not what I asked you. Is there a doctor here tonight?"

The clerk, scared for Mr. Graff, answered, "I . . . I don't know offhand. I have to check the registry."

"Let's go look," Comfort said, pulling Blondie by the arm.

Frankos felt as though he jumped into a tub of scalding water. "Bobby, if this dude gets a heart attack and dies, we'll have a murder rap on our hands. What're we gonna do?"

"Right now, I wanna see if we can get a doctor to check him out."

Although Frankos's day job was killing for hire, and normally his complicity in a murder wouldn't bother him, his morals forbade him to take part in a homicide unless he was compensated. And tonight, if this Geppetto look-alike died, and the Greek were to be held accountable, he couldn't possibly justify the punishment.

"You better do it fast," Frankos said. "This guy's lookin' worse and worse by the second."

CHAPTER 19

Hands fumbling, the reception clerk opened the registry, warily flipping page after page, Comfort hovering over him. Blondie, wheezing, scrolled down the last page that had been filled out and pecked it with a finger. "There. Dr. Joseph Thomas Houllahan is in suite 4122. He's an Irishman visiting from Dublin."

Comfort, his pulse slower, said to Frankos, "Go back to the side entrance and keep watch. I'll handle this."

Frankos returned to his post, and Comfort phoned Dr. Houllahan's room. "Hello, who's this?" the physician answered in an Irish brogue, his voice croaky.

"This is the front desk calling. Sorry to bother you at this time, doctor, but we have a medical emergency."

"A what? I'm here on holiday. I'm not here to treat patients." Dr. Houllahan sounded drunk, or maybe he slurred because was half asleep. Maybe.

"Doctor, as I said we have an emergency down here in the lobby. I urge you to please throw some clothes on, and I'll send someone to bring you down here."

Graff, his chest expanding and retracting at a rapid rate, had slumbered in a club chair not far from the front desk, and Blondie shouted to Comfort, "Hey, hey, I think he's passing out. He's passing out!"

Comfort covered the mouthpiece. "Make sure he doesn't fall off that chair." He had a second thought and flailed his arm in a panic. "No, no. Better yet, lay him out on the floor." In a swell of fear, he held a clump of his hair and spoke into the phone. "Doctor, we have someone with a heart ailment who needs medical attention."

A slight pause, and Dr. Houllahan garbled out, "Eh, why . . . why are you calling me? You, you should be calling the emergency medics."

Good point.

Comfort hadn't foreseen this and had to think on his toes. "At this time of night help won't get here before a half hour. And as a physician, aren't you under oath to be of assistance to anyone who's in need of medical attention? I don't know about your neck of the woods, but that's how it is in America."

Dr. Houllahan coughed and hacked, phlegm swamping his throat. "Oh, awl right, awl right. I'll get ready. I can't even have a bit of rest on me bloody holiday."

Comfort was fairly sure that this doctor, wherever he came from, at very least had been nipping at the spirits, or he might be totally drunk. And would he be coherent to resuscitate the near-comatose Jordan Graff, whose skin was darkening to a purple? Comfort knew every passing second took away a fragment of hope for the patient's survival. "Go to room 4122. A Dr. Houllahan is in there," Comfort said to Nick Sacco and Ali-Ben. "Get this quack down here faster than fast."

The Irish physician heard the knocking and, half-dressed, opened his door. As soon as Sacco and Ali-Ben saw him, they knew he had more alcohol in his blood than a liquor store. Dr. Houllahan, a freckled man whose bushy brown hair and a handlebar mustache looked cartoonish, wasn't too steady on his feet, and reeked of whiskey. Sacco and Ali-Ben eased him out into the hallway, and walked him inside the elevator. "What in the bloody world is this? Uh, who . . . who are you two hooligans?"

"Nothin' to worry about, Doc," Sacco said. "We got a sick guy in the lobby, that's all. Sorry to wake you up, but you're the only doctor in the house."

Though his kidnappers were civilized and well-mannered, Dr. Houllahan seemed unnerved, and couldn't shake out the cobwebs in his whiskey-sodden mind. "I don't know who you really are, and I should call the police."

Sacco and Ali-Ben grappled his arms. "Like I said, nobody's gonna hurt you. We simply want your help, and then you can go back to sleep. Or drinking," Sacco said.

Down at the front desk, they brought Dr. Houllahan to Comfort, who looked at him and exclaimed, "Oh, that's just great. One doctor in this whole place, and he's a drunk."

"I beg your pardon," the doctor said in his Irish brogue, his weedy eyebrows rising, eyelids blinking. "I'm one of the most respected physicians in Dublin, young man." He burped, a blast of stale liquor emanating from his mouth. "Eh, where's the person who needs treatment?"

Despite the alcohol, Dr. Houllahan rose above it, and superficially examined Mr. Graff, who was suffering with chest pains. The doctor stood straight, swaying faintly, burping again. "This gentleman is in grave danger. I detect a coronary thrombosis that will surely lead to a myocardial infarction. He should be *supine* on a bed." He nodded solemnly and fell into a green upholstered divan.

Comfort hadn't understood the doctor's medical jargon and bent over the now dozing Irishman. "What the hell did you say?"

Dr. Houllahan, eyes semi-closed, sighed impatiently. "He's about to have a heart attack, me lad." He waved lazily. "You must transport him to a hospital. Immediately! Give him an aspirin right away." his whispery voice trailing off into sleepiness.

"And what's this about a supine position?" Comfort asked, but it was too late; Dr. Houllahan was snoring on the divan.

Sacco nodded at the unresponsive Jordan Graff and said to Comfort, "This guy can go any minute. What're we gonna do?"

Comfort pinched the bridge of his nose. "We have to call 911 and get this man to a hospital before he dies."

"Call 911?!" Ali-Ben blurted out.

"Yeah, we gotta get the EMS here," Comfort said. "Go tell Germaine and Sammy to stop hammering in there and come out here right now."

"I don't understand," Sacco said, puzzlement in his eyes. "We can't call the cops."

Comfort petted his chin and glanced at Graff. "We have to call 911. Get everybody out of the alcove and put them somewhere they can't be seen. Let's move fast."

Ali-Ben, Sacco, and even Blondie, who was beginning to feel as if he were one of the gunmen, thought Comfort had gone mad.

CHAPTER 20

N alo and Germaine were at it in the safe room, smashing and prying, ignorant of the Graff crisis. Sacco walked in there to update them on the developments in the lobby. Nalo, electrified at the harvesting of millions of dollars in gleaming diamonds, wasn't cognizant of anything, and clanged on. Sacco grabbed his wrist and stopped him. "We got a problem out there, Sammy. You guys gotta come out 'cause there's a change of plan."

"What's goin' on?" Germaine asked, beads of sweat on his forehead, a fuming cigarette stuck on the side of his mouth.

"Both of youse stop and come out. And close the door to the vault room. We gotta make a move," Sacco said.

Out in the lobby, Comfort was devising an impromptu strategy. He moved close to the reception clerk, who was still manacled. "Blondie, listen and listen good. You gotta help us. Okay?"

Blondie, thankful not to have been harmed, nodded willingly, his ears red from fright. "What . . . what do you want me to do?"

Speaking as if he were coaching a Little League pitcher, Comfort said to him, "We're gonna untie the porters and the maids in the alcove, and I want you to tell them to take Mr. Graff to a vacant room, and lay him on a bed." He patted Blondie on the shoulder. "Do you understand?"

Blondie tipped his head in agreement and couldn't have been more obedient. Comfort said, "After you bring Mr. Graff into a clean room, we're gonna take the rest of the hostages, you included, to somewhere else on the ground floor. Got it?"

Nalo and Germaine knew nothing about the sudden change, and they were thrown off balance. "What the fuck is goin' on?" Nalo asked.

Comfort informed him of the Graff emergency, and that they had to phone for an ambulance. Nalo objected. "Call 911! Have you lost your marbles? We're in the midst of a robbery, and we got two dozen hostages. And you wanna call the cops?!"

Germaine was also opposed.

Comfort inched in closer to his compatriots. "You guys wanna deal with a murder rap? Because that's what's gonna happen if this guy dies on us. Now let's get busy."

Nalo was in a stunned stare, and Comfort asked him, "What?"

Nalo motioned toward the vault room. "Why don't we put the hostages in there? Once you shut the door, it's soundproof. And if anyone o' them makes any noise, no one will hear the fuckers."

Germaine and Comfort chortled. "Great idea, Sammy," Comfort said, slapping Nalo on the side of his arm.

Sacco and Ali-Ben were commandeering the relocation of Mr. Graff to a suite on the third floor. As prescribed by Dr. Houllahan, one of the maids had shoved an aspirin into the patient's mouth. Nalo, and Germaine went into the alcove and told the captives they'd be placed elsewhere.

Visconti, who hadn't yet known about Graff, asked Nalo, "Why do we gotta move everybody?"

"I don't have time to explain. Take off everybody's duct tape."

"Why?" Visconti asked, a bemused look on his face.

"Just do it," Nalo cracked.

Dreadfulness was daunting the hostages. "Where are you taking us?"

"Why can't we stay here until you finish doing your thing?"

"Oh, Jesús, Maria, y José," shrilled the old Chihuahua, the de Montejo mother-in-law, her palms together in prayer. "They're taking us to be killed like a herd of sheep. Oh, Jesús, Maria, y José." This prompted hysterics in the alcove, and Mr. de Montejo's party and his paramour, Joanne, whose sexiness was steamier when mad, were still kicking one another, annoying the other victims.

"Please don't kill us," the black elevator operator beseeched, saliva wetting his rubbery lips. "I tell yah, we won't be sayin' nothin' to nobody. No siree, no siree. Please don't kill us."

"All right, everybody calm down," Visconti said. "Calm down. We ain't killin' nobody."

A wide grin blossomed on the black man's mouth, his teeth resembling the keyboard of a piano. "See, I knew you wouldn't do us harm. Oh, may the Lord bless you. He goin' bless y'all. Uh, uh. He goin' bless y'all." He said to his co-hostages, "Don't worry everybody. These good people here ain't gonna hurt us. The Lord be watchin' over us. I feel it."

"Thanks for your sermon, pop," Germaine said.

"Okay, everybody up and let's start movin' out," Nalo said.

The heartening words from the elevator operator did not dispel those terrible visions of slaughters and tortures. Instead, one of the four security officers stood chest out and chin high. "We're not leaving here. If you wanna kill us, you'll have to do it here." This heroic decree triggered moans and cries from the women, and another guard resonated, "That's right! We're staying right here."

"Speak for yourself, you fool," Joanne Rinaldi said.

Nalo walked out to consult with Comfort. "They don't wanna leave where they are. They think we're gonna take them somewhere and kill everybody."

Comfort looked confounded. He could not and should not delay calling for help; Graff must be stabilized without wasting another minute. "I'll talk to the hostages." He went into the alcove, Nalo trailing him. Comfort put out his cigarette butt in a crystal ashtray lying on a maple bureau and smiled cordially at the prisoners. A pitiful sight. "I'm here to appeal to you. First, I want to say how sorry I am for inconveniencing you. I wish for nothing more than for you to be absolutely comfortable. But we have a medical emergency. A man who came into the hotel a while ago might be having a heart attack. A doctor, one of the guests here, wants him hospitalized immediately."

"Oh, poor man." Everyone sighed and listened attentively as though they couldn't wait to hear more. One of the brave security officers asked, "Who is this man? Is he a guest?"

"I don't know, but we can't waste time. I have to call 911. And this is the reason we have to move you into the vault room." Comfort glanced at the captives for a reaction; everybody seemed to feel compassion for the sick man, whoever he might've been. And Comfort implored, "Please, let's all go into the vault room as fast as possible. Okay?"

The hostages rose on their feet, and shuffling and groaning, wrists cuffed, marched in a single file to the vault room. Ali-Ben woke Dr. Houllahan, who was startled, propped him off the divan, and led him to the new holding pen. Nalo, Visconti, Ali-Ben, and Germaine stayed there with the detainees, shutting and locking the vault door from the inside. No sooner had everyone settled in, the de Montejos and Joanne resumed the squabbling, hissing at one another.

The phone rang at the front desk, and the call was from Suite 8336 belonging to Mrs. Henrietta Randall, widow of billionaire J. Arnold Randall III. She was a plump dowager, her bluish hair coiffed and glued in a coating of hairspray. Her stout, overly rounded shoulders brought to mind a humpback whale. Mrs. Randall wanted fresh bath towels, and Comfort gave this task to Sacco.

Everything appeared normal as if all was calm and peaceful. Comfort phoned 911 and reported that a guest may be suffering from a serious illness, and to please send an ambulance. The 911 operator's voice was monotone. "What is your name and location?"

"I'm James Young, and I'm at the Pierre Hotel on 61st Street between . . ." Comfort said.

"I know where the Pierre is. What is the name of the patient?"

Comfort thought for a moment, deciding whether he should give the 911 operator Graff's name. "I don't know who he is."

"I'll dispatch a cruiser and an ambulance. They'll be there shortly."

Up on the eighth floor, Sacco gave Mrs. Randall the towels, and she questioned his tuxedo. "Umm! You're so handsome in a tux," she said in a lustful hiss. "But I never saw any of the hotel personnel in a tux."

"Oh, I'm not part of the hotel staff. They have a temporary shortage on the night staff, and I'm fillin' in."

Mrs. Randall found Sacco appealing. "I see. Won't you come in?" She touched her chin as if a thought came to her. "Actually, my toilet isn't flushing from time to time. Would you mind checking it for me? I'll take care of you."

He obliged her, but nothing was wrong with the flushing system, and bid her good night, rushing through her suite door.

Frankos was stepping out to forewarn the limo driver, Al Green, not to be alarmed when ambulances and police cruisers would be swarming in. But as the Greek was about to exit, a man and a woman rang the buzzer. Frankos pushed the intercom button. "Are you guests here tonight?"

The man, bundled in a three-quarter length black coat and a gray beret, stared awkwardly as though he were trying to recognize Frankos's face. When he couldn't, he answered, "We're residents here. Mr. and Mrs. William Goetz. Aren't you supposed to know us?"

The Greek couldn't believe this coincidence. The police could be here any second, and this couple had to come just now. Incredible! He unlocked the door, and skipping the standard protocol of confirming residency, allowed the couple in. The Goetzes found this breach of security odd, and the husband noted, "This guard doesn't seem to know us. Why would he let us in?" The answer came in a moment; Frankos deftly jammed his pistol in the middle of Mr. Goetz's shoulder blades. He resisted and made a foolish attempt at outmuscling the Greek until Mrs. Goetz, a bleached blonde, begged him to surrender—though in the scrap she scratched Frankos's cheeks. When the tussle fizzled, Frankos, hanging on to Mrs. Goetz by the arm, his gun pressed against her husband's spine, shepherd the latest arrivals to the vault room. There they were shackled beside the other sorry souls, whose stares were bleak and wary. Thankfully, the police cruiser and the ambulance hadn't yet come.

CHAPTER 21

S acco was in the suite watching over Mr. Graff, whose symptoms were worsening. He had been struggling to breathe, and was lapsing in and out of a coma. Sacco believed Graff was on the verge of heart failure. Uneasiness was enveloping the Cat, and when this would be over he was envisioning a police dragnet hunting him and his Pierre coconspirators. They'd be sought for murder. Life imprisonment. It is a widely assumed misunderstanding that a murderer sentenced to twenty-five to life is paroled after serving the minimum bit. Wrong. It's a rarity for a parole board to free a killer. The only circumstance under which someone convicted of a homicide ever leaves his or her prison is in a pine box. This unthinkable outcome bubbled perspiration on Sacco's forehead. Fretting, he phoned Comfort at the front desk. "Hey, this guy looks like he's gonna go any minute. Where the fuck is the ambulance?"

Within a minute, three police officers were at the 61st Street entrance, ringing the intercom. Frankos unlocked the door and let in the policemen and two EMS technicians who were tailing hastily behind. Al Green in the limo didn't know what was happening, as

cruisers, ambulances, and even a fire truck—flashing lights and strident sirens—were teeming into the quickly congesting street. He was in the dark as to the sudden fleet of emergency response vehicles. Mr. and Mrs. Goetz had interrupted Frankos from warning Green of the expected swamp of police action. The late night serenity had turned the block into a turbulent site, police radios chattering loudly, the fire truck's loudspeakers blaring, cruisers parked haphazardly on both sides of 61st Street, and a dozen cops and firefighters walking about aimlessly. All this for a sick man who basically had to be placed on a stretcher and wheeled into an ambulance.

Green, a rush of panic flooding his stomach, was fretting if he should scram from there or stay put and wait for instructions from Frankos. Green peered in the side view mirror. *Shit!* He saw a cop nearing the limo. He rolled down his window and grinned goofily, milk-white teeth seemingly iridescent against his eggplant-toned skin. "What's goin' on, Officer?"

The officer, a short, stout South American, waved him on. "It's a medical issue. You gotta move this boat. The ambulances have to get closer to the doorway of the hotel."

A medical issue! What the hell is goin' on in there? Did one of the guys shoot someone? Overlapping thoughts deluged Green's mind, his pulse beat racing. "All right, Officer." And he drove the limo a few hundred feet to the west, re-parking it on the north side of 61st Street.

Inside the Pierre, the three policemen and the EMS technicians had crowded the front desk, where Comfort was acting as if he were in charge. He represented himself as the night manager, James Young. He was carrying on his person proper ID for a James Young. He said to Visconti, "Show these gentlemen to Mr. Graff's room."

No one suspected anything wrong, so far.

Mrs. Randall phoned again. This time she wanted tubes of skin moisturizing cream. *What is this old goat going to do with body lotion at 4:30 in the morning?* Comfort marveled. He phoned Sacco, who was guarding Graff in the suite where they had placed him. Sacco answered the ringing, "What's up?"

Without mentioning names, Comfort said, "Come to the lobby as soon as one of us gets there with the cops and the EMS techs."

Visconti ushered the response personnel to Graff's room. The paramedics began working on the patient, and Sacco returned to the lobby. Comfort asked him, "Everything under control with Graff?"

"Yeah, they're gettin' Graff ready to take him out to the ambulance. Do you need me to do somethin'?"

Comfort said, "You won't believe this. That old broad, Mrs. Randall, wants moisturizer." He laughed. "At 4:30 in the morning, no less. The world is full of weirdos. Anyway, go to the supply room, find the moisturizer, and get it to her."

The seventy-six-year-old widow, a promiscuous relic, invited the tall, striking Sacco into her suite, engaging him in small talk. She spoke in a slight British accent, lending sophistication and the unspoken aura of nobility. Mrs. Randall made it known that today was her birthday and she intended to celebrate every minute of it. Daylight hadn't yet peeked over the horizon, and she already had a bottle of expensive champagne on ice. The old boot snuggled up to Sacco and tickled him under his chin. "How about the first toast of the day with me, big boy?" Although Comfort and his thieves had run through every possible contingency, they weren't prepared to neutralize an insistently flirtatious guest—a late septuagenarian, no less. Sacco, a man in his early thirties, desperately wished to free himself of Mrs. Randall's advances. He had to patrol the first and second floors to ensure that any strays whom they might've overlooked earlier wouldn't pop up while the police were in the hotel. And this horny great-grandmother was craving a tumble in the hay with someone the age of her grandson.

Mr. Graff, unconscious on a stretcher and deteriorating by the minute, had to be loaded into a freight elevator on the extreme east end of the hotel. An oxygen mask, the clear plastic fogging, covered his mouth and nose. The EMS techs were wheeling him out and into an ambulance. The police officers filled out forms, which they required Comfort to sign. He scanned the paperwork as though he would not sign it unless nothing therein might pose

a liability for him. One of the cops spurred him along and said, "Don't worry, nothing is gonna come back at you personally. This is standard bullshit."

Comfort, ever the actor, said, "Easy for you to say. Anything goes wrong, and it's my ass on the line." He pretended to reread the fine print, and the boys in blue, New York's finest, were growing restless. One of the three cops, his tour of duty about to end, was anxious to clock out and go on to his second job. Not uncommon for NYPD police officers to moonlight off the books.

"C'mon, sign the damn papers. We ain't got the whole night," grumbled the officer who had been doing most of the talking.

At last, Comfort, sneeringly, scribbled a signature on the report forms. The same cop took the paperwork, and motioned his two coworkers to head for the exit. The police departed, and Comfort called Nalo on the phone extension inside the vault. "Sammy, the coast is clear. The fuzz left."

Nalo and his companions began breathing easier. "Whew! It worked," Germaine said, passing a hand over his hair.

"Thank God," Visconti said, making the sign of the cross.

Ali-Ben chimed in, "My faith is always in the Almighty Allah."

They sprung open the vault's door, and shuffled the lamenting hostages back to the alcove, complaints about the heat and stuffiness inside the safe room filling the captors' ears. The black elevator operator seemed genuinely concerned about Mr. Graff. "How that man be doin'?"

Visconti said, "He's in good hands. He'll be fine."

The black man looked up at the ceiling, and praised, "Oh, bless your soul. You done the right thin' by callin' the powleece. Bless your soul."

And Nalo and Germaine restarted tearing out the safe deposit boxes.

CHAPTER 22

Nick Sacco had been in Mrs. Randall's suite and hadn't reported to Comfort for fifteen minutes. Worried that something might've gone wrong, Comfort called him at her room. "Mrs. Randall, this is the front desk. I'd like to speak with the person who delivered your moisturizer, please."

She handed the phone to Sacco. "Hello."

"What the fuck are you doing up there?"

Sacco, in coded terms said, "She won't let me go." The champagne had made her giddy. She was behaving as foolishly as a sweet sixteen on her prom night.

Comfort said, "The Graff problem is over, and the heat is off. Get down here, I may need you."

Sacco stepped away from Mrs. Randall and said in a hush, "I'm tellin' you, this crazy old broad won't let me go. It's her birthday, and she wants me to have breakfast with her."

"Have breakfast with you?!" At a loss, Comfort said, "Hell, take her down to the alcove—at gunpoint, if necessary."

"All right." It was time for Sacco to jar Mrs. Randall out of her fantasy. "Look, ma'am, I don't know how to tell you this, but I'm really a burglar. See, there's a robbery goin' on in here."

She placed a hand on her chest and gave him an appalled look. "Oh my! You're not a hotel employee? You said you're in the middle of a robbery here in the Pierre Hotel?" Mrs. Randall's neck was wrapped in a ten-karat emerald necklace, her wrists bejeweled in a gold diamond bracelet, and platinum diamond earrings were stuck in the earlobes, tempting Sacco to strip the old sex monger of her status symbols. She shimmered brighter than a constellation, and he knew the worth of those pricey ornaments bordered on the one million dollar range. But he reminded himself that was not the purpose of this mission. Stripping Mrs. Randall of her personal property would be a first-degree assault, and this did not coincide with his modus operandi. Not to mention that he would not want to treat her any differently than if she were his own grandmother.

"Now that I told you the truth, I'm gonna have to take you to where the other hostages are."

Sacco, the suave boy-toy she'd been longing for, was abducting her. "Oh no, no. You will do no such thing. Do you know *who* I am?" Her gray, murky eyes widened, and she made haste for the phone. In three long steps, the long-legged Cat had his arms around Mrs. Randall's waist, and contained the kicking grandma. "Stop, stop, you brute! How can you do this to me? I'm old enough to be your grandmother."

Oh, so now you're old enough to be my grandmother. And just a minute ago you were ready to take my clothes off. Handling Mrs. Randall gently, he had to carry her because she wouldn't go on her own, legs thrashing wildly, her slippers hitting the hallway walls. Her designer glasses fell to the floor, and he accidentally stepped on the spectacles. There went $1,500. Sacco covered her mouth with his free hand, and she tried to scream, though only muffled sounds stemmed from her nose.

Exiting the elevator, Mrs. Randall's blue chiffon skirt was rumpled high on her thighs, a pair of dairy-white legs with scrolls of purple veins. Sacco, still carrying the rich widow, lost his grip, and she slipped away but didn't get far. Ali-Ben had been watching, and he scrambled to recapture Mrs. Randall. He and Sacco jostled her into the alcove, where she was scandalized when she saw eighteen to twenty people, most of whom were hand-bound, silvery duct tape over their mouths.

Visconti was surprised at the addition of another victim so late into the robbery. "Who's she?"

Sacco said, "This is Mrs. Randall, everyone. She's upset, but I'm sure you'll make her feel at home." The Cat then indicated Visconti and assured his elderly admirer, "He'll look after you. If you need anything, he'll take care of you."

Mrs. Randall's new company assessed her gold and diamonds and platinum and emeralds, and saw she dripped of wealth *and* snobbishness. But in this den of captives, the brilliance of her accessories incited envy and wistfulness. Mr. de Montejo's bride, Lilliana, was resentful that her groom hadn't lavished her with more extravagant jewelry as a wedding gift, but the sure-to-follow divorce would be lucrative for her, and she'd buy herself any size diamond she wanted. Maybe a ten-carat pear-shaped one.

De Montejo's girlfriend Joanne Rinaldi, too, longed to be pampered, and perhaps, she figured, if he did divorce his twenty-four-hour wife, he'd make her his queen. And the philandering Diego de Montejo, known for his generosity when wooing women, might very well do that. At least until he tired of the luscious Joanne.

On the other hand, the working class people in the alcove, the black elevator operator, the kitchen workers, the maids, the bellhop, the clerks, and the four security officers—whose monthly salaries couldn't even buy a half carat of the fifty or so Mrs. Randall was flaunting—had no conception of her wares' worth, and couldn't visualize that if an individual possessed just the jewels she was wearing, that person would be rich.

On another front, Frankos sprinted alarmingly through the lobby and told Comfort that a young man delivering the morning papers was at the 61st Street door asking to come in. He was twenty-two years old and had a black goatee and a pageboy ear-length hair cut. He was skin and bones, and his head and face bore the outline of a flesh-less skull. Comfort motioned for the Greek to allow in the malnourished newspaper boy before he panicked and drew the attention of passersby. The Greek scampered back and unlocked the door. The intruder, shivering from the cold, stepped into the entryway, newspapers in a canvas bag strapped over his shoulder. He said distrustfully, "Hey, man, where's the dude who usually guards this entrance?" The razor-sharp winds had whipped his cheeks into a purplish red, his lips colorless and dry.

Frankos produced his handgun, and pushed him toward the lobby. Wild-eyed and writhing to slip away, the paper boy, agile and dicey, whizzed in the direction of the door, shouting, "What the fuck is this?"

Frankos dove at the runaway, and after a minor joust tied him into a full nelson hold. "If you try that again, I'll blast a slug in your ugly head." Frankos was breathing hard from the skirmish, and turned him over to Ali-Ben, who had come just in time. Ali-Ben took the newest prisoner by the wrists, and he yelled, "Lemme go, you scuzzy Arab. Lemme go. What're you think you're doin'?"

As Ali-Ben was handcuffing the bristly man, he saw a revolting disfigurement on his face. The paper boy had a severe harelip that suggested a sinister personality. Ali-Ben paid no attention to the unsightly scar and hauled him into the alcove. And the detained group expanded to twenty-four.

One of the hostages, Ms. Amanda Jefferson, an aspiring black model, signaled to Al Visconti, who had been subtly eyeing her. He gladly walked to where she was sitting, crouched in front of her, and loosened the duct tape on her mouth. "What's the matter, are the cuffs too tight?" His voice was whispery, as if he didn't want anyone to hear his comfy conversation with the ebony beauty from the South.

Ms. Jefferson gestured for Visconti to lean closer, and ashamed, she despaired that her menstrual cycle had begun. "I need to go to mah room and take care o' this."

He nodded caringly. "Lemme see what I can do."

"But I woun one o' the girls to go with me," she said, her long, thick eyelashes fanning at Visconti.

"All right, all right. I'll be right back." Visconti stepped out into the lobby and knocked on a wall for Comfort to see him.

Comfort asked, "What's wrong?"

"One of the women has to go to her room."

"Why?"

"Well, you know . . . eh, she has to plug her dam. Know what I mean?" Visconti said. "But she won't let any of us take her there unless another lady goes with her."

Comfort was at his wit's end over these incidentals; nonetheless, he told Sacco to handle it. Ms. Jefferson had chosen Joanne Rinaldi to go with her, and Sacco unfettered the two ladies. Joanne wanted to know, "Where are we going?"

Woman-to-woman, Ms. Jefferson confided to Joanne it was that time of month, and needed to go to her suite, and as Visconti had said, "she had to plug her dam." But she didn't want to be in her room alone with one of the gunmen. Joanne, glad to get away from the de Montejo vixens, understood. "Sure, I'll be there in case one of these jocks gets the idea to dip his tool into that hot volcano of yours."

Sacco, his pistol pointed at the floor, walked into the lobby with the two hotter than hot mamas. But Ms. Jefferson, feeling an oncoming accident, darted for the elevator, which by now Sacco was skilled at handling. The lift jettisoned them to the floor of the leaky model's suite. Ms. Jefferson, her panties feeling warm and soupy, hastily unlocked the door and scuttled to the bathroom, where she dawdled for what seemed an eternity. Sacco was edgy, as time was running short. Three clumsy minutes passed, and Joanne and Sacco, alone by themselves, opened a dialogue. "Is this what you do for a living?" she chanced in an expression of fascination.

"Yeah, and it's a pretty good way to make a buck," Sacco answered casually. "Plus, I can make my own hours, and work whenever I want to."

"So is this all you do. You don't have a regular job or anything?" Intrigue in her tone.

"I don't need to do nothin' else," he touted as if he couldn't think of a better occupation. He nodded with his chin at Joanne. "Hey, lemme ask you somethin'. What're you doin' with that Brazilian playboy? Sounds to me like he's playin' you. Stringin' you along."

She tilted her head, slowly swiped her tongue over the lips, and said in a sassy voice, "Why, you offering something better?"

"Maybe."

Joanne was on the king-size bed, her elbow propped on the pillow. She slid to one side and reached for the pen and notepad lying on the nightstand. Not wanting Ms. Jefferson to see her doing this, she scribbled furiously, tore the sheet off the pad, and folded it. She slipped the note between two fingers, winked, smiled solicitously, and gave it to Sacco. She had written her name and phone number on it.

No sooner he had shoved the paper into his pocket, Ms. Jefferson emerged from the bathroom refreshed, her lipstick and eye makeup renewed. "Ready to go."

"I gotta cuff you both before we leave here. Sorry," Sacco said, timidly.

"You gotta do what you gotta do," Joanne said mockingly, looking at her pink-lacquered nails and joining her wrists for him to cuff. *Was she letting out the hook and bait to have him arrested?*

NICK SACCO

I really liked this girl, Joanne. She had a certain look; everybody has a preference when it comes to physical attraction. Know what I mean? But I said to myself: one minute she happens to be this rich and good-looking Brazilian's commara, *and the next minute she's making a play for me. Could it be she was attracted to me, or maybe my being a jewel thief turned her on? Or did she have other plans that could've gotten me in hot water? Nonetheless, I still wanted to get to know her. Throughout my life, I had two addictions: gambling and women. And an addiction to women can be as bad as any other vice. A subconscious fear was rippling in my gut that maybe I should forget about this Joanne.*

CHAPTER 23

6:18 A.M.

The seven o'clock shift was fast approaching, and Sammy Nalo, determined to rip open every deposit box, doggedly disregarded how late it was. Through gritted teeth Comfort yelled, "Sammy, that's enough. We gotta get out of here." But Nalo was unstoppable. "Goddamn it, Sammy, stop and let's get ready to go. NOW!"

Under a spell of greed, Nalo was orgasmic, and Comfort said to Germaine, "C'mon, help me yank him out of here."

And Germaine told Nalo, "Sammy, for Christ sake we gotta go."

Comfort signaled Germaine, and together they grabbed Nalo by the arms and manhandled him away from the boxes and into the lobby. "Wait! Wait! One more box. One more box," Nalo pressed as though he were in a state of incoherence.

"No way," Comfort said. "You damn well know we can't waste another minute."

Nalo did rise above his stupor, and he and Germaine zipped shut the four brown-patterned Louis Vuittons chock full of jewels, bearer bonds, and cash. They gathered the burglary tools and white gloves and did one final check to ensure they had collected every piece of their equipment. "I think we got a sizable haul, Sammy," Germaine said gleefully, affectionately patting one of the signature bags.

"Yeah, we sure did," Nalo remarked coldly. He walked in a jog to the front desk area and said to Comfort, "We cleaned out the safe room. You can bring everybody back in there."

According to the perpetrators' strategy, before evacuating the Pierre the hostages had to be, once again, moved to the vault room, and Comfort knew this would upset and cause the captives anxiety. He said to Ali-Ben and Sacco, "We gotta get everybody into the safe room. Let's do it now."

Sacco and Visconti peeled off everyone's duct tape, and Ali-Ben instructed the prisoners to stand and file through the alcove archway.

Of course they protested. "Where are we going?"

"Yeah, where the hell are you taking us this time?"

"I'm not leaving here."

The head security officer stood as if he were about to charge Visconti. "What kind of games are you playing with us?"

"We're not playin' any games with you people," Sacco said. He calmly looked at his audience. "We wanna go as soon as possible so we can leave you alone and in peace. But for now, please do as we say and nothin's gonna happen to you. Trust me, okay?"

Joanne, winking at Sacco, knew no harm to her or anyone else was in the cards. The others weren't too persuaded. But minus any choices, with trepidation they complied and peacefully walked to the vault room. As they resettled in there, Comfort, still donning the concierge's burgundy jacket, came in. He had scripted a short farewell speech and pumped his palms in the air to douse the chatter. "Ladies and gentlemen," his recitation began, "I thank you for your cooperation, and we hope we haven't caused you too much of an inconvenience. If anyone here has a deposit box we broke into, we will mail back to the hotel anything that belongs to you." Comfort had a pencil and a small black notepad in hand. "Please give me your box number." He looked at the sullen faces before him and saw heads shaking. "I guess none of you has a deposit box in here. Well, good!"

The hostages didn't know if this spiel was genuine or hinted of sarcasm, their looks nonplussed, eyes squinting, lips twisting. But as solemn as a monk, Comfort preached on, "We ask of you to tell the police that you hardly remember anything and would not know what we look like; you were simply too scared and nervous. There's no law that says you have to be a witness, and I feel I can trust you to do the right thing. And as a token of gratitude, we're giving you each twenty dollars as a gift."

Comfort's act of good will was an astounding absurdity; this had to be some kind of a joke. "Are you jivin', mah man?" the elevator operator asked. "'Cause if you're for real, the Lord goin' guide y'all to health and prosperity. And He goin' reserve a place for you in Heaven. Oh yes indeed, The Lord goin' be with you."

And no, Comfort was not fooling, and followed through with his gesture of good will. Except the four security guards, he slipped a crisp twenty-dollar bill in the pockets of those who were hand-cuffed. "You security boys, who look like undertakers in those cheap black suits, are not getting any gifts because you all got cop mentalities."

Understandably, the black man's appreciation for the twenty-dollar gratuity was immense, considering that in 1972 a laborer without any skills earned approximately thirty-five dollars per day. Likewise, the three chambermaids, who tonight were part of this improvised societal blend, grossed twenty-two dollars per day, and the kitchen helper's wages amounted to twenty-six dollars for a nine-hour shift. But this assemblage in the alcove was an unnatural and infrequent happenstance. For two and a half hours, destiny had thrown together elements from different ranks and brands of society in an enclosed space not larger than twenty feet by fifteen feet. And under such wicked conditions, those two and a half hours must've seemed longer than two and a half years. Moreover, in gross disproportion to the income of the Pierre menial workers, Joanne

Rinaldi, a kept woman, spent hundreds of dollars on exotic skin lotions. Mrs. de Montejo wasted more money on worthless mud facials than the chambermaids' salaries; and the debonair Diego de Montejo spent just as much for shoe shines. Not to mention the extravagant Madame Randall, the heiress to a fortune. On Tuesdays and Fridays she purchased wine and champagne at a cost of two hundred dollars.

The security officers, another class of citizen whose monthly take-home pay was $960.00, were not as appreciative as the elevator operator. This breed of people was inclined to mistrust anyone and everybody. They detested the likes of Comfort & Company—who tended not to earn "an honest livelihood"—and vowed to work with the authorities in apprehending and bringing in those "blood-sucking maggots." In actuality, the guards' dislike for the Pierre raiders was the product of envy. The more verbal of the four garbled under his breath, "I'm gonna make sure we get you bastards."

CHAPTER 24

Sacco severed the telephone lines in the lobby and those in the adjoining corridors. Nalo and Germaine were struggling to carry the four bursting suitcases overstuffed with the loot. "By the weight of these, we've done pretty good," Germaine mused, the veins in his neck enlarged from the heavy lugging.

"It looks that way," Nalo said indifferently.

Visconti and Ali-Ben packed the miscellany of burglary tools and other paraphernalia in a green metal box on rollers and wheeled it out onto the sidewalk. Working in unison, Germaine and Nalo stacked the luggage into the trunk of the limo. Comfort lagged behind, guarding the victims, and Frankos the Greek stayed at the 61st Street entrance to thwart any newcomers to come into the hotel. Sure enough, just as he and Comfort were about to exit the Pierre, two policemen, who had been walking the beat, buzzed the intercom, seeking refuge from this frosty night. Sacco, Nalo, Ali-Ben, Germaine, and Visconti had piled into the unusual getaway vehicle seconds before the pair of patrolmen had appeared. "Holy shit!" Sacco groused, his reflexes going for the pistol grip in his pocket. A tremor of panic rippled through the robbers' guts, as they watched helplessly from inside the limo.

The Greek mouthed to Comfort that two NYPD cops wanted to come in. Comfort thought about this for two or three seconds. "Let them in."

Frankos put on a quizzical look. "Did I hear you right? Did you say let them in?"

"Well, what should you tell them? Come back later? We're not done robbing this place yet. If we turn those cops away, they'll think something isn't right. So let them in."

Frankos braced for the worst, opened the door, and waved in the two officers, striving to be hospitable. "C'mon in fellows. C'mon on in. It's nice and warm in here."

Shifting from one leg to the other, and necks withdrawn into the collars of the uniform overcoats, one of the officers griped, "Uh, cold as a bitch tonight." He rubbed his gloved hands together, teeth chattering.

As this was playing out, the gunmen in the limo thought for sure that in a matter of seconds Frankos would be shooting these two flatfoots at point-blank range. And that would've been a shame; they just happened to be in the wrong place at the wrong time. The line of sight from inside the limo, though, did not open to a full view of where Frankos and the policemen were talking. Several moments passed, and relieved that they didn't hear any deafening gunfire, wondered in suspense what had gone down. Did the cops overpower and subdue Frankos? Or had Comfort and Frankos taken the unwitting interlopers at gunpoint? Neither. Frankos's sharp wit had saved the day, in this case the night. He suggested to the two half-frozen officers to go to the lower level stairway. "In the basement you'll find a coffee pot and hot chocolate. That'll warm your innards."

"Thanks, thanks. We'll help ourselves." As the two cops were stomping down the stairs to the subterranean floor, the Greek locked the door, and he and Comfort went out, ducking into the limo, essentially imprisoning the two policemen inside the Pierre. "Those two flatfoots had to show up at the last damn minute. Incredible!" Frankos grumbled.

"No harm done, Greek," Comfort said. "Right now, those two guys are having a free cup of coffee and anything else they can steal in the food pantry down there." Comfort shooed at the air with a palm. "By the time they figure out they've been had, we'll be off the streets."

Nerves began slackening in the limo, Nalo, though, wasn't totally at ease. "What if in the next couple of minutes these two Keystone Cops figure out what just happened and radio for help?"

Comfort, already upset with Nalo over the likelihood he had taken a handful of gems back in the vault room, glowered at him. "Don't jinx us, man." He loathed to dwell on that thought, and said to Al Green, "Step on it. Let's go before the devil makes something else go wrong."

Sacco swiveled to look beyond the limo's rear window, sparse snowflakes dancing in the darkness. All was quiet.

Green accelerated for roughly six hundred feet on 61st Street and turned left at the corner of Fifth Avenue, the eastern border of Central Park that at this hour was as dark as a desert on a moonless night. One block south, and the limo swung left again on 60th Street, which is one-way going east. In the middle of that block, Green could see the Ford Torino and the Chevy Impala where they had parked them earlier, the densely overcast sky low and whitish with falling snow.

He slowed the limo and maneuvered it toward the curb behind the Torino. The Impala was a hundred yards up ahead. His parking was sloppy, and the passenger side front wheel scraped the curb, the hubcap screeching loudly. Nalo pounded the back of Green's headrest. "What're you tryin' to do, man, attract attention? Watch where you're goin'."

"Sorry. Shit happens," Green answered offhandedly, riling Nalo.

The Pierre hit squad cleared the smoke-filled limousine, and Green was to drive it to an auto wrecking yard in Canarsie, Brooklyn. There the manager of that facility was to crush and bale it. Comfort, Nalo, Germaine, and Visconti hoisted the Louis Vuitton luggage from the trunk of the limo, and transferred that highly valuable

cargo to the Torino and the Impala. Everyone shed their facial disguises and hid them under the rear seat of the limousine. And Green sped off to Brooklyn.

The others had to drive to Nalo's safe house as stealthily as possible. Nalo said, "It's startin' to get light, and it's freakin' me out. Let's get in the cars and get out of here." But in the scope of reality, Murphy's Law is ever consistent; one of the backup cars didn't start. The extreme low temperatures had frozen the battery. "Fuck!" yelped Visconti, banging the steering wheel. He was the designated driver of the Chevy Impala, and Ali-Ben was to be at the helm of the Ford Torino.

"What's the matter?" Nalo asked.

"Battery's dead as a doornail. Hope we got booster cables in this darn car."

Nalo pummeled his left palm with the right fist. "Damn it!"

CHAPTER 25

At 6:43 A.M., the early January dawn was gaining daylight, a faint violet-tinted sky. The traffic, though sporadic, was on the rise, sounds of car horns and swishing tires breaching the silence of the night.

Germaine opened the trunk of the Impala. "I found a pair of jumper cables." He untangled the jumpers from under a pile of trash, empty liquor bottles rattling and reeking of alcohol, Sacco and Nalo nervously standing by.

Comfort, Ali-Ben, and Frankos, who were about to get into the Torino, saw the hood of the Impala open, and hastened toward the disabled car. "What's wrong?" Comfort asked.

Visconti didn't go into details but said, "Tell Ali-Ben to turn the Ford around and nose it right up to the Impala here." He buttoned his jacket and raised the collar, the shearing winds increasingly stronger. "We gotta jump-start the engine off the Ford's battery."

"Shit, this is gonna make a scene. I can't believe this," Comfort bitched bitterly, slapping the fender of the Impala. He rushed back to the Ford Torino, pointed at the aged Chevy Impala, and said to

Ali-Ben and Frankos, "The goddamn Impala won't start. Battery's dead. Or maybe frozen."

"Damn," cried out Frankos. "We got suitcases full of swag in the trunk of these cars. If a cop shows up and starts . . ."

"Right now, let's not worry about that," Comfort said dismissingly.

"Yeah, let's just do what we gotta do to get that piece of shit started," Ali-Ben said.

Sacco said, "Let's not stand around like a bunch of ducks stranded in the pond. We look too conspicuous in these tuxes. The rest of us should get in the cars."

"Good idea." Comfort waved his index finger in circles, and said to Ali-Ben, "Make a U-turn and nose the Ford up to the Impala. The booster cables are not that long, so pull up close to that goddamn clunker." He backed away from the Torino, and Ali-Ben began the illegal U-turn, a traffic infraction.

As the Ford Torino reversed direction on the one-way 60th Street, to Ali-Ben's consternation a police cruiser traveling in the opposite course was on a collision path with the Torino. Ali-Ben, though aghast, deftly evaded the cruiser and aligned the Ford parallel to the curb grill-to-grill with the Impala. The harrowing near-miss scared the burglars; they thought this was the beginning of the end. Surely the driver of that police cruiser wouldn't overlook Ali-Ben's illegal U-turn that had just about caused a head-on collision; and what could happen next?

An option was to shoot it out with the lone officer, and the odds of outshooting him were high; after all, it was seven against one. Frankos, a sharpshooter, was capable of aiming a bullet to only wound and not kill the cop. But what if the Greek missed and murdered the policeman? No, that was not an option Comfort would approve. As an alternative, they could all jam into the Torino and make a run for it before the policeman came face-to-face with the Pierre stickup men. But the cop would radio for assistance and a reckless chase might ensue, a dragnet, roadblocks, and helicopters pursuing the runaways until they'd be trapped. This, too, was not a viable choice. Comfort and Nalo's Pierre plot had underscored not to hurt anybody, even if it meant surrendering. But the heavens would stop the rains before Nalo and Frankos would succumb peacefully.

The cruiser skidded to a halt, the emergency lights atop the roof now flashing, strobes of red beacons bouncing off the pavement and the neighboring buildings. The wintry, early morning daylight was suddenly ablaze, highlighting the Ford and the Chevy as if they were under a brightly lit circus tent.

"Keep your cool, you guys. Keep your cool," Comfort said in a hush as the policeman, hand on his sidearm, started making his way in the direction of the Torino. Pretending not to be in fear of the certainty of an arrest, he told Germaine, "Hook the booster cables to the Impala's battery terminals."

Ali-Ben picked up the other end of the boosters from Germaine, and tightened the clamps onto the Torino's battery. He signaled to Visconti, who was behind the wheel of the Impala, to turn the ignition key. He did, and the engine rumbled to life as the cop, guarded and unsure of what he was in for, saw Comfort making eye contact as he accosted him. "I know my friend shouldn't have made that U-turn, but we have an emergency of sorts," Comfort said forthrightly.

His placid demeanor unknotted the patrolman's tension. "What's the emergency?"

"It's a little embarrassing, Officer," Comfort said in a contrived shyness, scratching his earlobe. He gazed at the Ford Torino and the Chevy Impala. "Eh . . . three of us in those two cars are due to be at a breakfast speech engagement at NYU." Smilingly, he ran a hand over his jacket and pants. "That's why we're in these monkey suits." Comfort meant the tuxedos.

"So," the cop remarked rudely.

"Well, Professor Dupree—he's the one sitting in the back of the black Impala—oh, by the way, I'm Professor Hagan. Anyway, Professor Dupree," Comfort covered his mouth as if to be discreet, "he . . . he's got a severe case of diarrhea. Must've been some shellfish he ate a few hours ago. And we have to get him to a clinic before he goes all over the car seat."

The policeman's reddish eyebrows drew together, his brow pleating. "But why did your pal in that Torino have to make a U-turn?"

"The Chevy wouldn't start, and we had to boost it. But if we don't rush Professor Dupree to a doctor, we're going to have a hell of a mess in that car." Comfort laughed lightly so not to let the cop think he was lying.

They were twenty feet from the two vehicles, and though Nalo couldn't hear their conversation, knowing Comfort's acting skills and his ability to improvise, felt heartened that they'd skate away from this hair-raising mishap. His accomplices weren't too sure; they could feel their own bowels liquefying. "What the fuck is Bobby doin' with this cop?" Sacco asked, his head shaking at the thought of a SWAT team storming in.

"Relax, man. Relax," Nalo said. "Bobby's done this a thousand times. He knows what he's doin'."

"It's not easy to relax right now, Sammy," Frankos countered, his right hand on the gun in the jacket pocket.

"Look, all of you shut the fuck up and keep your cool. Damn it!" Nalo whispered angrily.

The patrolman studied Comfort, the flashing lights of his cruiser luring onlookers. "All right, tell your buddy, the jerk who made the U-turn, I'll let it go this time. And get Professor whatever his name is to a clinic where they can plug his asshole." And the police officer returned to his green and black cruiser.

"Thank you, Officer. Thank you," Comfort said reverently. He wiped his forehead of humidity and rejoined his collaborators. "Let's get in the cars and go." The two-car convoy rolled west to Nalo's Tenth Avenue apartment. In those same moments, Al Green, driving the limousine, was in the westbound lanes of the Belt Parkway entering the Canarsie section of Brooklyn. He wasn't far from the auto-wrecking yard owned by a "friend" of Lucchese consigliere Christie Furnari. There the owner of the scrap yard was readying the compactor to crush and bale the limo. By now, the light of day was in full bloom, and Green, not to chance that the highway patrol might stop him, resisted speeding, though a minute wasn't too soon to be inside the fenced property of the scrap yard. Within a half hour, at 7:30, he saw the twenty-foot-long, red and yellow sign advertising Ralph's Auto Wrecking. Green turned into the greasy, frozen-muddy driveway of this obscure establishment. The proprietor, Ralph Milano, in coarse brown coveralls and a black leather hat with furry earmuffs, directed Green in, pointing to where he should park the condemned automobile. "Shut off the engine and leave the keys in the ignition," Milano said in a gravelly, hostile voice, a wet, spent cigar bobbing on his chapped lips.

Green removed his chauffeur's hat, bow tie, and jacket, tossing the garments on the floor of the limo. He took a navy-blue parka coat from the trunk and put it on. In one of the pockets he felt folded sheets of paper, his customers' numbers bets he had forgotten to leave behind at his bar in Harlem. Milano, a brusque type, edgy with impatience, watched Green switch clothes, and kicked the left front tire, mud shaking off his oversize black rubber boot. He pointed to a younger man, also in coveralls and boots, and hollered to Green, "Mikey here will bring you back to the city." Ralph Milano, short, his back curved, the chin jutting and looking like a shovel, a fur of hair in his ears, could've passed for a troll. He said to his worker, Mikey, "Drive this *mouleenian* to the Westside in midtown."

This *mouleenia*! That was an Italian slang for eggplant, a derogatory calling to African Americans, and Green was offended. *That greasy guinea.*

"Midtown where, Ralph?" Mikey asked as if he'd been told to go to Mars.

Milano, his skin as leathery as a reptile's, took the cigar out of his mouth and spat brownish phlegm on the grimy ground. "How many midtowns do you know of, you yo-yo? You want me to guess for you! Manhattan, where else?" Head shaking, he walked into his office, a junked school bus without wheels that over time had sunk a foot into the muddy soil.

Mikey, long, unruly blond hair sprouting from under his baseball cap, was stout and paunch-bellied. He twirled a toothpick in his mouth, and his face seemed as though it were darkened with a coating of black soot. He opened the driver's door of a blue Pontiac Grand Prix. "Get in this car." And Al Green was on his way to Nalo's safe house, but was still brooding about the scrap yard operator's slanderous remark. He couldn't believe this Milano character, a junkyard dog, a white trash of a caricature, had the nerve to call him a *mouleenian. I goin' make him pay for that.* In so far as the limousine, well, the cigar-chomping Milano was to crush it into a bale of scrap metal not much larger than a bale of hay.

Mickey calculated that the best route to drive to Manhattan from Brooklyn was by way of the Belt Parkway westbound to the Brooklyn-Queens Expressway, leading to I-495, and ultimately to the Midtown Tunnel. But Mickey's fast, erratic driving and weaving through the morning rush-hour traffic was spiking Green's afro. He was holding on to the armrest of the passenger's door so tight that his brown knuckles were whitening. "Hey man, slow down before you get us killed." No sooner Green had made that prediction, Mickey swerved from the center lane to the left one. He had failed to first look in the side view mirror, and bumped into a white Buick Skylark barreling at seventy-five miles per hour, sideswiping and shoving his car into the right lane, where another oncoming vehicle broadsided it. Mickey's Pontiac flipped, rolling over, sheet metal sparking on the asphalt, then sliding on its roof, and clanging to a gradual halt. It settled at rest upside-down, the rear wheels spinning wobbly. And the crunching and crashing ceased to a silent stillness. The stream of traffic in all three lanes stopped, and the motorists, who had been driving immediately behind the out-of-control Pontiac at the moment of impact, could not see signs of survivors.

CHAPTER 26

At the safe house, Comfort and Nalo almost ruptured their hernias lifting the heavy Louis Vuittons onto a folding table, an unsteady fixture that could barely withstand such weight. A white, bell-shaped porcelain lamp hung low over it, casting a dimness of light. Comfort, his posse of buccaneers watching hawkeyed, emptied the luggage and methodically sorted and spread the jewelry on the flimsy tabletop, separating and grouping the items into categories. In haste, he and Frankos got into counting the cash. They were amused at peeling through hundreds of five-hundred-dollar bills, a rare denomination of US currency. When they finished the count, it totaled $2,920,000. "Wow!" Frankos said. "Wow!"

On the opposite side of the table, Nalo, a loupe wedged beneath his eyebrow, was immersed in assessing the gems, discerning for cracks and carbons. "Um, I see a lot of flaws in some o' these," Nalo said mournfully, downplaying the quality and uniqueness of the stones.

Frankos the Greek, Ali-Ben, Bobby Germaine, and Al Visconti had little knowledge about jewels. Neither did Al Green, who hadn't yet returned from his errand in Brooklyn. Sacco glanced at his watch. "It's eight o'clock. Wonder what happened to Al?"

"Yeah, he should've been here by now," Visconti said. "When it comes to collecting money, you can make book that the most unreliable asshole will be on time. And if Al ain't back here to get his piece, I betchu somethin' is wrong."

Germaine flopped a hand at Visconti's negativity. "Nah, he probably got jammed in traffic. This is the height of rush hour."

"Hope you're right," Sacco said, rocking his head in doubt.

But what about these jewels they were looking at? Besides Comfort and Sammy Nalo, the Cat was the only one of the Pierre prowlers who had expertise in gems and stones. He felt in his pocket, pulled out a loupe, and reached for the diamond bracelet that Nalo had dispraised. Through the magnification of the loupe Sacco scanned those diamonds for more than thirty seconds. He put away the loupe and scowled at Nalo. "Sammy, what flaws are you talkin' about? This ain't costume jewelry. These are Asscher cut diamonds with a high color grade, man. I mean, they got almost no color at all. I bet they're three carats each, and I'd say they got a damn good clarity grade, too."

An Asscher cut diamond is square-shaped, and its facet cuts are rectangular, radiating an exceptional brilliance. And what Sacco meant by the near absence of color was the limpidness of the gem as if it were a pristine drop of water, the ideal characteristic of a stone. "So I don't know what the fuck you're talkin' about, Sammy."

Indeed, Sacco knew his apples, and Frankos looked at him to read his thoughts whether Nalo was having an impulse to cheat his partners. "Sammy, don't even think about trying to fuck us," the Greek warned, a mean sternness in his voice. "And I'll tell you right now, I gotta get more than two hundred and fifty grand."

Comfort diffused the building tension. He lit a cigarette and put on a friendly grin. "Most of you don't know much about this. Right?" Everyone other than Sacco nodded in agreement, and Comfort swept a hand over the piles of cash neatly stacked in rows on the table top. "We got about $2,900,000 in cash, so why don't we each take two hundred and fifty grand, and we also give the same cut to Furnari? Eh!"

It seemed simple, but it wasn't. Frankos demanded a larger share because, as he reasoned, he had introduced Comfort and Nalo to Sacco and Furnari. And frankly, without the Lucchese consigliere's blessings, the armament, and the three *duped* vehicles he supplied, the Pierre job couldn't have been exacted. Moreover, Furnari had arranged for Ralph's Auto Wrecking to rid of the *duped* automobiles, and loaned his three most competent burglars, Nick "the Cat" Sacco, Bobby Germaine, and Al Visconti. Ali-Ben and Al Green were acquaintances of Nalo.

Incidentally, a duped car is a stolen vehicle with the serial number tags of a legitimate automobile that had been wrecked or burned. Sacco also felt he was due more than a $250,000 share. After all, Christie "the Tick" Furnari was his connection, and their bond was as strong as a dam. Sacco could've persuaded *or* dissuaded Furnari to either sanction the Pierre proposition or to reject it. "Lemme have a look at some o' these things," Sacco said, scooping a handful of jewelry and shoving it closer to him on the table.

Ali-Ben, who so far hadn't done any talking, seemed disquieted. "I'd like to know what the hell happened to my brother-in-law." The reference to "my brother-in-law" was Al Green, who had married Ali-Ben's sister. And understandably, Green's lateness was nerve-racking. Ali-Ben began pacing as if he were in a cage.

Comfort placed his hands on the hips, elbows winged. "I'm kind of thinking myself if something might've gone wrong."

"Yeah, me, too," Nalo said without looking up, averting eye contact with Sacco and Frankos.

Was it likely that a witness might've reported the limo to the authorities, and Green had been stopped and arrested? At this very moment, Green might be handcuffed in a police precinct lockup, and soon to be interrogated. Al Green was not a hardened felon, and if pressured, well who knew if he could withstand charges of armed robbery? And what if he would readily name his coconspirators? These catastrophic scenarios were buzzing in Ali-Ben's mind and, as the minutes clicked, the same poignant thoughts sprang inside everybody else's heads.

Nalo got busy removing the gems from the settings, and Sacco concentrated on gauging a variety of jewelry pieces, selecting the most unique and larger gems. To his advantage, he was keenly aware that the size of a stone impacts the grading and market value, as do other factors. The key elements, known as the *four C's*, are color, clarity, the carat weight, and the type of cut. And one ingredient of great importance is the density of *inclusions*, which are microscopic particles and blemishes that can only be seen under magnification.

Using a vague mathematical formula Comfort and Nalo approximated the worth of the jewels at $2,000,000. But Sacco's estimation differed significantly; he was at a total of $20,000,000 to $22,000,000 (present value $225,000,000). "Nobody's gonna tell me that what we got here is only about two million. Fuck no!" Sacco, a foot taller and seventy-five pounds heavier than Comfort and Nalo, and backed by the alliance with Frankos the Greek—a feared contract killer—wielded the dominant force of this disagreement.

Nalo held his ground and said to Sacco, "Nick, I don't know where you see twenty to twenty-two million here."

Tenseness was thickening, an aura of malice and deceit in the air.

Comfort, more honorable and sensible than Nalo, did not wish to tangle with Sacco and his ally. "Hey, whatever you guys want, take it." This was not agreeable to Nalo, though he chose not to contradict his partner.

Comfort's magnanimous offer didn't appeal to Frankos. "Man, I don't wanna have to deal with jewels. Fencing them and all that shit, just ain't my thing. I want my cut all in cash, and it's gotta be more than two-hundred and fifty grand. A *lot* more. Period."

"All right, Greek," Comfort placated, a burning cigarette in his hand. "First, let's split the cash, so everybody can go home, and you and I can talk about this later."

"Whatever you say, Bobby," Frankos said but not meaning it, raising his palms at chest level to intimate, *In the end you better satisfy me.*

Counting the two hundred and fifty thousand dollar shares, eight for Team Pierre, and one for Furnari, consumed two hours. As this was going on, Nalo plucked a considerable portion of the gems and set aside the settings, and Sacco centered on selecting roughly two million dollars of the glittering stones for himself. "When all is said and done," he said, "Furnari has to get his thirty-five percent of whatever we got here."

Everyone took his money and concealed it in brown grocery bags. Ali-Ben saw that his stacks of cash, which Comfort had pushed across the table to him, were the same height as the others'. "What about Al Green's end?"

Comfort bent over into the table, and stared at him without lifting his head but with an upward movement of the eyes. He said dryly, "When we know he's safe and sound, *he* can come and get it."

Ali-Ben, his Arabic hook nose twitching involuntarily, glanced around the table, looking for a hint of backing, but didn't find any. Amid everyone's uneasiness over Green's sudden disappearance, speculations of a worst-case scenario were growing faster than a fungal virus. And it was decided that Bobby Comfort, the most righteous of these thieves, would retain in escrow Al Green's proceeds. The troops seemed satisfied, for now, and except Frankos, disbanded, departing one by one. He, Comfort, and Nalo stayed behind at Nalo's safe house to negotiate the Greek's "due share."

They were all richer than a few hours ago, and going home with bundles of unmarked cash, this new day should've been a merry one; but not knowing what had happened to Al Green made it a stomach-churning morning.

NICK SACCO

I couldn't believe Sammy Nalo was trying to pull the wool over my eyes. He had never imagined that I knew more about gems than most jewelers. But as he watched me pick out the best shaped stones, he figured I knew what I was doing. I took for myself a few Marquise, Oval, and Emerald-cut diamonds. These are the most brilliant gems money can buy. But the rest of the guys had no clue as to what anything in this hodgepodge of jewelry was worth. And Nalo took advantage of that.

But something else was bothering me. By the time I got home, I thought for sure Al Green must've gotten pinched.

CHAPTER 27

JANUARY 3, 1972

The day was in full bloom, steel-gray clouds smothering New York City, and the Pierre debacle had been registering top billing on TV and radio news stations, headlining in newspapers across the country. As far as any headway in solving the case, the prognosis among the NYPD investigators was bleaker than bleak. At the first press conference, the sad-faced detectives were hiding an outlook of pessimism. The nervy Pierre pirates had not left an iota of a clue; the hostages were unclear as to the physical descriptions of the gunmen, and didn't remember a hell of a lot, or so they said to anyone who inquired.

Because the odds were that the criminals responsible for the heist might transport the stolen merchandise across state lines, the FBI was poised to claim jurisdiction of the case. The agents spearheading the investigation, though, had wisely chosen to stay on the sidelines for the initial confrontation with the media. They had nothing to tout, no witnesses, no suspects, no informants, no fingerprints, and no evidence whatsoever. The supervising agent,

Jack Goodwin, reasoned, why stand there empty-handed before a bank of cameras, microphones, and cranky reporters, looking as baffled as a zookeeper after the animals have escaped? The FBI understood it's best to skirt the media than to host a press conference dodging an onslaught of questions, offering lame responses, and ducking hand grenades. No, those pestering journalists couldn't be fooled into believing the good guys were winning; it'd be obvious that the authorities were at point zero.

NYPD detectives, though, were known suckers for cameras and microphones—and gluttons for punishment. NYPD Lieutenant Don O'Neil, a tall, long-necked, tough-talking Irishman, directed the onset of the investigation. The tint of his skin, by nature beet-red, some said, "He was born that way." But inside the walls of the NYPD, the rumor mill had it that Lieutenant O'Neil, known as a hardline crime buster, "nipped at the spirits," though to a stranger his alcohol-sodden brain was unnoticeable. In his day-to-day duties, he functioned with effectiveness and behaved perfectly normally. Remarkable!

And here, O'Neil, clean shaven and in his crispiest shirt and black tie, stood shakily behind a podium. He was inappropriately dressed for the weather. The white uniform jacket displayed a shiny gold badge, and the ornate embroidery on the visor of his hat looked like scrambled eggs. Amid a mob of frenzied reporters, mouths billowing cold breath, an NBC journalist in curious apparel—a safari vest with a dozen pockets—raised his hand. "Lieutenant, can you give me a summary of what happened? How many thieves were there? How much did they steal? And how quickly do you expect to make an arrest? Or, in view of the fact that several other hotel burglaries in New York City remain unresolved, do you anticipate ever getting to the bottom of this one?"

As O'Neil pondered that grilling bombardment—which he saw as "harassment rather than unbiased journalism"—a long-haired CBS correspondent interrupted the Lieutenant's thoughts.

"Do you believe the Pierre Hotel burglars are the ones also responsible for the Sophia Loren job? If so, do you know who they are?"

O'Neil gulped, his face darkening to a purplish red, and couldn't process the fusillade of queries. Stalling, he tapped the microphone as if he were testing it. And a third reporter dispatched by Channel 5, brandishing a fur-covered mike, hollered, "Lieutenant, word has it that while the robbery was in progress your precinct sent police officers to the Pierre in response to a hostage with a failing heart. If that's so, how could your men not have realized that armed bandits had the entire hotel under siege?"

How the hell does he know about that? O'Neil's mortification was swelling, a rattled look in his sapphire-blue eyes. The Lieutenant rankled inwardly, closing his eyelids, and wishing for the obnoxious journalists to vanish in some magical way, and that he'd be in a cozy bar, cooling his throat, sipping an icy gin and tonic.

The Channel 5 representative, a seasoned wisecracker, was riding on a good wave. "My understanding is that your men were at the Pierre for almost twenty minutes. How was it possible that they did not notice the hostages?"

O'Neil held his palms at shoulder height, as if to excuse himself for this utter failure to enlighten the press corps. But he was so tongue-tied that his lips quivered soundlessly without forming words. And in those intense seconds of weariness and stress, the highly-decorated NYPD lieutenant, ever the publicity monger, was now wishing he could've waved a magic wand and no longer be in this goddamn line of fire, taking heat from a pack of runaway media savages. O'Neil, feeling a moistening in his armpits, tried to disconnect from the badgering, and concentrated on composing a few sentences that, hopefully, might deflect the verbal bashing.

Just then, a female crime writer for the *New Yorker*, dark-haired and round-faced, her nose tiny and as pointy as the beak of a bird, to be spotted waved a blue bound notepad in the air. In her nasal, squeaky voice, she asked, "Lieutenant, do you have any comments about the two patrolmen whom the perpetrators locked inside the Pierre? Evidently, they weren't on guard while on patrol. How else could the thieves have lured those two officers inside the hotel?" The chirpy, little woman then put on a solemn aspect. "More importantly, is that kind of ineptness representative of the state of affairs within your station house?"

Shit, she knows about that too! Who is this wiseass bitch? Exacerbating O'Neil's embarrassment, his audience roared in laughter. The lieutenant's innards were churning acid. *And whose idea was it to call for this damn press conference?* It had been humiliating. *And for what, just to be in the spotlight for ten minutes?* The strategy was catapulting into a public relation disaster. Maybe he should've barricaded himself in the sanctity of his office at the 19th Precinct in midtown Manhattan. Had O'Neil shied away from the media, "those heckling hyenas" could've only speculated where this whole situation stood. Instead, his witless babbling confirmed that the brazen Pierre gunmen had executed a flawless crime, so far.

To be clear, the FBI too was in constant pursuit of publicity, no less than Lieutenant O'Neil. The difference was that the bureau's agents—polished and of a higher degree of education, and customarily in conservative, well-tailored suits—were less flagrant when courting the press. Also, agents did not call on the media purely to make meaningless headlines. Their objective was to speak to the press only if they could disclose publicly truthful statements—minus the tap dancing—and not for the sake of filling TV screens with owl-eyed faces.

And the jousting to win the dominating role of the Pierre probe would soon begin. The contestants were the FBI, the NYPD, the Manhattan DA, and the US attorney for the New York Southern District.

NICK SACCO

I knew that before midday what we did at the Pierre was going to be all over the news. I was glad to hear the cops hadn't found any clues, but that wasn't necessarily true. The detectives might already know who we were; one of the hostages could've recognized us from police mug shots.

After all, except Nalo, we all had records. And if the cops were on to me or any of the other guys, they'd keep it quiet so to catch us off-guard. To play it safe, I had to get out of town for a while. But first I had to see Christie Furnari and tell him where I had stashed his cut of the robbery. I had rented a room at a hotel in Manhattan and left his cash there in the safe inside a closet. If anybody was tailing me or Furnari, we'd have nothing on us.

CHAPTER 28

Nick Sacco didn't want to meet Christie Furnari at the 19th Hole; it might've been under surveillance. Instead, they met at an Italian café, Mille Luci, on the corner of 18th Avenue and 73rd Street in Brooklyn. The specialty of this bistro was authentic Italian pastry. It was patronized by Italian imports from southern Italy who frittered away time there from morning to night. They drank espresso, played *scopa*, a game with the forty-card Italian deck, and gossiped endlessly. It seemed that for the most part Mille Luci's customers were not gainfully employed.

Italian Americans of dubious connotations, loansharks, bone-crushing enforcers, bookmakers, Mafia underlings, and general pretenders also loitered in the restaurant. And the eatery's frontal façade, bearded by a growth of ivy vines, had tables on a second floor balcony reserved for the VIPs of the underground.

In his early years, Sacco was raised in a turn of the century tenement across the street from Mille Luci. And today, seven hours after the Pierre escapade he was at a table in the café when Furnari walked in. Sacco stood, and they hugged. Furnari shed his black wool coat and sat, the hissing espresso machine steaming an aroma of brewing coffee.

"Right about now I'd love an espresso with some anisette." Relishing that cocktail, the Lucchese consigliere smacked his palate.

"Me too," Sacco said. He waved at a waitress, a cute brunette who didn't speak a word of English. She was "fresh off the boat" and probably "hadn't even had the chance to unpack her suitcase." Sacco held up two fingers and said to her, "Two espressos with anisette and two cannolis."

She smiled, her teeth even and bright, and spoke in Italian: *"Ah! Si, si, ho capito. Lei vuole due espresso con anisette e due cannoli. Vero?"*

Sacco and Furnari shrugged. They didn't understand what the girl had said, but assumed she had confirmed the order, the ceiling speakers belting out Mario Lanza's tenor voice singing a popular Neapolitan song of the fifties.

> *O Sole Mio*
> *Sta` brond' a te*
> *O sole mio*

"Ritorno subito." *I'll be right back,* she said, stepping away, a sexy bounce in her walk, steaming the air.

"The girl's round ass looks like a pair of hot buns," Sacco said to Furnari. "A hot little Sicilian. Ain't she?"

Furnari moved on. He hunched forward into the table and hushed, "How did it go last night?"

"I'm here, ain't I?" Sacco winked. "No problem. None at all, Christie. I don't wanna go into it here. A lot of ears in this joint." Sacco pushed a key and a piece of paper across the tabletop. "I left your package at the Algonquin Hotel on 44th Street. Room 6672. In the closet safe. The combination is on that paper."

Furnari placed a hand over the note and the key, and scooped them in his fist. "Where's that hotel again, Nick?"

Sacco was about to answer, and the waitress reappeared balancing a tray. She had refreshed her lipstick. *"Ecco. Due caffé e due cannoli."* *Two coffees and two cannolis.* She rested the hot blue demitasse cups and the pastry on the table and backed away.

"Is this girl ever gonna learn English?" Furnari remarked offhandedly.

Sacco sipped the espresso and bit into his cannoli. "Um, good!" He chewed for a few seconds and said, "The Algonquin is on 44th between Fifth and Sixth. It's a couple of hundred feet west of the Harvard Club."

Furnari, too, chomped on the creamy cannoli, and with a mouthful said, "I'll find it." He slurped the demitasse, and signaled Sacco to lean in. The Lucchese consigliere said, "I got a message from the 19th Precinct. In a nutshell, they're watching Comfort and Nalo. They think those two are behind the Pierre job. And I was told the cops are gonna ride Comfort and Nalo 'til they pinch them."

Sacco grunted, "Uh! I was afraid of that."

"We're gotta keep our ears open. Meanwhile, you should take a powder until everything cools. Go somewhere warm. Know what I mean?"

Sacco swiped his lips with the tongue. "I plan to. I'm gettin' the fuck outta here tonight."

"Good move, kid. Good move."

"I think we're done here. Let's go, Nick."

They stood, and Furnari picked up the check that the waitress had written out. It totaled $2.50. "I got it, Nick." And he chucked a five-dollar bill on the table.

Sacco reached in his pants pocket and put a ten-dollar bill on top of Furnari's five. Furnari whistled. "You're a big tipper these days, Nick." In 1972, ten dollars was equivalent to $115.00. "Ten bucks plus my five for a $2.50 tab?"

Sacco veered his lips downward. "Eh, what the hell! That girl's sweet. Maybe she'll save some money and take English lessons."

"Never mind the girl," Furnari said. "Just make sure you leave town tonight." He finished buttoning his coat. "I don't like what's gettin' back to me. I got a feelin' they're gonna get Comfort and Nalo, and I hope those two don't crack when the cops put them under the hot lamp."

CHAPTER 29

When the car he was in had rolled over on the Belt Parkway, Al Green lost consciousness for less than ten seconds. As he came to, finding himself lying on the inside of an upside-down vehicle, understandably he was disoriented, to say the least. His forehead was bruised, and he had a bleeding gash on the right temple. His head had bumps and ached, and he rubbed it. "What the fuck happened?" Green asked Mickey, the driver, who was in a sprawl of arms and legs, though unconscious, his hair bloodied. The traffic in all the three lanes had stalled, and more than a dozen motorists bunched near the wreck. One of the onlookers suggested that someone should walk off the parkway to find a pay phone and call the police.

"The white man looks like he's badly injured. Somebody call an ambulance."

On hearing this, as Green was trying to regain his bearings, an awful thought occurred to him. He was a numbers runner by day and a thief by night. And he recalled he had on his person the sheet, a bookmaker's pages of entries listing the numbers combination his customers had played. If the police found the sheet,

Green would be arrested for illegal gambling. It'd be his fourth such charge, and a judge might lock him up and hurl the key into a shark tank. Tearing the sheet and ditching it in the bushes on the side of the Belt Parkway was a bad idea; he'd have no record of his bettors' picks. And if Green were to admit he'd lost the sheet, when the winning numbers would be publicized in the papers, every one of his customers would surely swear it was the combo they had played. And it'd be impossible for him to dispute those claims. This is a bookmaker's worst nightmare. Green had to flee the scene of the accident. But that's also a felony; a half-dozen bystanders had seen him and could identify him from police mug shots. Green was in a catch-22 situation. Since he was a boy, his mama had been telling him that white people said, "All blacks look alike." And if it's true that whites can't distinguish one black from another, he thought, it'd be wise for him to bolt before the police cruisers would be barging in. And he did, making a run through the bramble on the south side of the highway and onto the service road.

A witness hollered, "That black dude is gettin' away. Somebody go after him. He must've been the driver, and he's probably drunk. That's why he's takin' off like a rabbit."

That set off the adrenaline for Green to run even faster, cutting between houses, jumping over cyclone fences from backyard to backyard. But as he climbed a wooden divider, a sixty-pound pit bull, eyes red and feral, fangs exposed, clamped onto his ankle, a bite as strong as a crocodile's. The dog growled as if he were a rabid animal, saliva drooling from his mouth, and Green fought desperately to break loose. In a matter of seconds, his sock and shoe were drenched in blood, and the pit bull wasn't letting go. In a moment of dread, Green, holding on to the fence with one hand, stretched out his right arm to reach for a shovel lying on the grass a few feet away. If he could grab it, he'd wallop the mad canine good and hard, but the shovel was too far, and he wasn't able to latch on to it, the dog tearing ragingly at his leg and foot.

Green realized he was in South Jamaica, Queens, a black neighborhood.

"Damn those niggers and their pit bulls," he said, teeth gritted in pain.

Suddenly, a solid thump and a yelp from the dog, and Green's ankle was free. Ten feet to his right stood a man, presumably the owner of the property.

"Get back into the shed," the proprietor said to his dog. And no, he wasn't an African American, as Green had surmised. He was Caucasian and had a shotgun trained at Green. "What're you doing prowling around my yard, boy? Put your filthy hands up."

Stunned, Green obeyed, his ankle throbbing and gushing blood. "I . . . I can explain."

"You'd better, and you better do it fast, 'cause my wife is in the house calling the police."

Green pleaded, "No, no. Tell her to hang up. Like I said I can explain. We can work this out."

"I don't know about that."

CHAPTER 30

T rue to the forewarnings of the tipsy Dr. Houllaghan, Jordan Graff had suffered a coronary thrombosis at Lenox Hill Hospital. He was in critical condition, and his physicians weren't optimistic. Three nurses and an intern were preparing the patient for quadruple bypass surgery. Piped in symphony music was playing softly in the background.

A scraggly, thin-to-the-bone *New York Post* writer assigned to the crime beat walked stealthily into the reception hall of the hospital and shuffled down a narrow corridor to a stairway. He looked here and there; no one had noticed him. He avoided the elevator and climbed the stairs to the fourth level. He snuck into the operating-prep section of that floor, a forbidden zone. With the likeness of a raccoon, the gaunt reporter had dark circles around his black eyes, or depending on one's imagination, of a ghost. He accosted a female intern in blue scrubs. "Ah!" she heaved a sigh, spooked by the ghoulish trespasser, whose tall, skinny frame and curved protruding chin brought to mind the fictitious character Don Quixote. The nurse's aide's hand flew to her mouth. "Who . . . who are you? How . . . who let you in here?"

He pointed to the green laminated photo ID on his chest and stooped low into her, almost mouth-to-mouth. "I'm with the *Post*. I didn't mean to startle you, Miss."

"Leave right now," she said in a frightened tremor, stepping back, her arm stretched stiffly toward the swinging doors.

His teeth misaligned and as yellow as cheddar cheese, Don Quixote smiled kindly. "I'm not here to make trouble. I just want to ask you a couple of questions about the patient from the Pierre. That's all."

The intern's tension eased. "Uh, you're talking about Mr. Graff, Jordan Graff?"

"Yes, him. What can you tell me?"

"All I can say is that he'll be going into surgery," she said tentatively.

The area was encumbered by large medical equipment, rolling oscilloscope machines, an X-ray apparatus, two or three IV stands, and three gurneys, and Don Quixote could smell pungent odors of disinfectants and antiseptics. White built-in wooden cabinets and a Formica counter were encased on a wall, and glass flasks with liquids of various colors were lined on the countertop. The crime reporter, his stomach intolerant of this environment, was becoming nauseous. He slipped a paper tissue out from a box lying on the countertop, covered his mouth, and coughed. "Sorry. I feel queasy. I gotta get fresh air before I puke all over the floor. Just tell me what's wrong with Mr. Graff. Does it have to do with the robbery?"

The intern saw his complexion turning whiter than a few seconds ago. "His symptoms have nothing to do with the robbery."

Repressing a rush of vomit in his throat, Don Quixote said in a gurgle, "Oh shit." He winced and gulped harshly. "You can't give me any details at all?"

Nauseated by his impending regurgitation and foul breath, she distanced herself. "Look, you better go. I can't help you with anything else."

"Just one thing . . ."

He persevered, and she rebuffed him. "You'll have to go, now."

But Don Quixote dashed to a sink, and vomit gushed from his mouth as though it were a turbulent waterfall, the strangling sound of which was heard throughout the hospital wing.

Graff's heart arteries were ninety percent clogged, an accumulation of plaque over decades of poor diet, smoking, and drinking. But the Pierre incident might've saved Mr. Graff's life. On that night, he had come to the hotel to organize the luggage in his room. He was to travel on an Amtrak to Washington for a speaking engagement. But had he been on that trip, tracts of which were isolated and inaccessible, by delaying first aid to his slated heart failure, he would've returned to New York in a pine box. Ironically, Jordan Graff was a professor of criminology at John Jay College.

The six-hour surgical procedure to replace Graff's heart valves was a success, and on Monday afternoon, as the Pierre poachers were savoring the magnitude of their spoils, he was recuperating comfortably in the recovery room at Lenox Hill Hospital.

At the Pierre, TV camera crews, reporters, and freelance photographers had amassed to a throng. The usually subdued lobby had become a congested cave of murmuring people, filming and lighting equipment, the ambiance of a movie set. And the investigators were sifting through the crowd, interviewing the captives, sleuthing and doggedly talking to anyone who consented to cooperate. But to the detectives' frustration, the victims were not too obliging. Mrs. Randall was forlorn and couldn't erase from her mind the dashing and manly young gentleman who had fooled her into believing he was a hotel employee, and hoped she'd someday meet again, somewhere. In short, Mrs. Randall didn't care that he was a jewel thief. A NYPD rookie detective, Dennis Landers, was assigned to question her. But she only said, "I was so upset that I can't possibly remember what the man looked like."

The young, attractive African American, Amanda Jefferson, whom hours earlier her premature menstrual cycle had inconvenienced and embarrassed her, was a former Miss something or the other from a hillbilly town in Alabama. This morning at ten o'clock, she had a potential career-making appointment. A television advertising producer, who had booked and paid for Ms. Jefferson's stay at the Pierre, had scheduled her to screen test for the commercial of a leading tampon brand. Talk about ironies. And Ms. Jefferson would not under any circumstances miss that golden opportunity. She didn't have time to be interrogated by Joe Perillo, another detective whom Lieutenant O'Neil had dispatched to the hotel. Perillo showed Ms. Jefferson his gold badge. "I'm Detective Perillo. I need to ask you a few questions."

The black beauty was tense as she sat on a chair under a bright chandelier, her auburn afro ablaze as if it were a glowing reddish ball. "I got some business to take care of and don't need to be here dealin' with this mess."

The average-height, slender Detective Perillo, his hair wavy and black, resembling the actor Tony Franciosa, later made an admission to a reporter: "As soon as I saw that black broad, I had a thing for her."

And Ms. Jefferson had known it. She fluttered her long lashes and smiled flirtatiously at Perillo. "You're a handsome dude. Are you Aitalian?"

"Eh, yeah," he answered shyly. "Well, I mean my grandparents were from Italy, but I was born in Brooklyn." Looking at Ms. Jefferson, her legs perfectly shaped and honey-toned, the skirt tight and short, barely covering those mouth-watering thighs, Perillo gulped, his Adam's apple bobbing up and down. In two or three seconds, he felt his penis swell and press against the zipper of his black polyester trousers. "Uh, lemme just ask you a couple of questions. May I call you Amanda?"

"Uh, uh." But Ms. Jefferson swatted a hand at the air, her fingernails purple-lacquered, silver bracelets jingling on both wrists. "Look Detective . . ."

"Call me Joe, please."

"Okay, Joe. Ah like that name," she said sheepishly. "But ah can't really help you 'cause ah don't even remember what them robbers looh like." Perillo had been ready to write in his yellow pad, and Amanda, ever so lightly, placed her hand over his, a tingle shivering up the love-struck detective's spine. "You know, Joe, I'm a model, and today may be the biggest day of mah life." She tilted her head in a pleading way. "And ah gotta git ready to git outta here, otherwise I'm gonna blow mah thing."

His penis now back in its cage, Perillo flashed a grin. "I figured you must've been a model or someone in the entertaining field. That's cool." Undecidedly, he took the liberty to caress Amanda's bicep. "Well then, I won't keep you. But just for the record, I gotta have your address."

Amanda gave Perillo her contact info, and he said, "Thanks. If something comes to mind, be sure to call me. All right? Here's my business card."

She looked at it, and then gazed at him invitingly, her eyes a pair of large chestnuts. "You *know* Amma gonna call you." She waved at him teasingly and walked away, her round buttocks bobbling side to side, and he couldn't remove his eyes off her.

But Amanda was a dead end for Perillo. As an Italian, how could he bring "this mouleenian" home to his old-fashioned mother? Out of the question. And he knew it. The poor old woman would be so shamed that it'd kill her. In those days, an Italian mother wished for her son to marry a "nice Italian girl," who was a good cook, could sew and iron, "make plenty of babies," and spoke Italian. And if a daughter-in-law fit that mold, though she could otherwise be a brainless moron . . . that would be just fine. "But these modern girls, who wanted careers, were nothing but *puttane*, whores. Forget about the ones who were actresses, models, or beauty queens. They were altogether the devil's daughters."

On a different note, Lilliana de Montejo and her mother were eager to consult a divorce lawyer, and couldn't be bothered with the investigation of the heist, stonewalling the investigators. Joanne Rinaldi was still badgering her boyfriend. Throughout their fling, Diego de Montejo had repeatedly assured her he was an eligible bachelor, and in the near future they'd live happily in Brazil on one of his ranches. But those visions had set sail and were no longer. And now Joanne, to protect her new prospect, Nick "the Cat" Sacco, the gunman whose name she didn't know, wasn't helpful to the police sketch artist, either. *Will that good-looking, warm-hearted thief call me?* She'd be thrilled if he did. As she viewed it, the likes of Sacco, criminals tied to the Mafia, were fascinating personalities. By nature, she was enraptured by mystique and intrigue, as are females of adventure.

But the New York City police commissioner didn't share Joanne's fascination. Fuming, he phoned the captain of the 19th Precinct. "I can't believe those perps had the gumption to call 911, and the responding officers weren't aware that an armed robbery was underway right under their noses." *How was that possible? What a bunch of idiots.*

"Sir, I know it's beyond bizarre, but I don't have an answer." The captain's collar was suddenly too tight, and he loosened his black tie. "Eh, one of my lieutenants will soon be briefing me on the details."

"I want you to update me the minute you have additional information. I'm getting political pressure from the mayor's office, and I must have answers."

"Yes sir. You'll hear from me within the next few hours."

But the victims couldn't wait to rise above the mire of this horrific experience; and in fear of reprisals from those charming thugs, the hotel night staff opted not to be heroes, the tight lips frustrating the authorities. Moreover, five or six employees of the Pierre, the cleaning staff, were illegal immigrants, and this was a period in which the US government strictly enforced immigration laws, deporting illegal aliens. Thus those who didn't have a green card, afraid of severe repercussions, were equivocal and nebulous in describing the robbers.

Another issue was tormenting the hotel guests who had incurred huge losses: the dreadful day of reckoning whereupon they might've had to tangle with the IRS and explain how they'd obtained hundreds of thousands of dollars in jewelry and cash. For this reason, the majority of the victims chose to understate their losses, and some even denied they were victimized. Hence, they skirted the investigators' chafing questions, stalling the investigation.

Meanwhile, the media wanted answers, and Lieutenant O'Neil was not about to be subjected to a second humiliating press conference. He said to his captain, "Hell, those pricking reporters have no mercy. And I'm ducking all journalists until I have something concrete to say." A sound decision.

But the lack of progress in solving this high-profile crime upset the captain; after all, he had to appease the commissioner, who was pressed to placate the politicians at the mayor's office. This chain of relays, though, had broken links, and all because the victims, motivated by different concerns, were uncooperative. What was O'Neil to do? He sure as hell couldn't torture anyone into assisting his investigators. Or could he?

CHAPTER 31

B obby Comfort and Sammy Nalo, coupled as jewel thieves for several years, were an effective team. On a personal note, their friendship had survived many bumps and scrapes. On this early morning, though, in the wake of the Pierre escapade, rather than rejoicing and celebrating his largest heist ever, Comfort was disturbed by the nagging suspicion that his pal Sammy might've defrauded him. But he wasn't sure; he thought he'd had a glimpse of Nalo shoving a diamond necklace into his pocket, then again maybe he hadn't. Feeling grimy and exhausted, Comfort lit a cigarette. "Sammy, you and I have been through hell and back. And you know that no matter what you can trust me. But I need to know something, and I want you to be straight with me."

Nalo blinked nervously. "Sure, Bobby. I'm always straight with you." An outright lie.

Comfort disregarded that falsity and spoke in a tone that implied he knew the truth: "Back there at the Pierre, did you swipe any of the jewelry for yourself?" Nalo didn't answer promptly, and Comfort, head cocked, raised his hands, palms outward. "Think it out, Sammy, 'cause I don't want you to lie to me."

"Bobby, are you sayin' I'd steal from you? That's ridiculous, man," Nalo said indignantly. "I can't believe you'd even think that."

Comfort expelled a cloud of smoke. "If you didn't, you didn't. I'll accept that." He pointed at Nalo. "But if I ever find out otherwise, you and I are gonna have it out. Understand?"

How could he ever find out? Nalo thought. He looped his arm around his friend's shoulders and laughed. "Bobby, you're a real gas. Like you just said, you and me have been through thick and thin. I'd *never* cross you."

Comfort thrust his arm for a handshake. "All right, I'll take your word, and this whole thing is forgotten."

They shook hands and parted company. But did Bobby Comfort in fact bury the hatchet? A trace of suspicion skulked in his mind, and he was determined to find out if Nalo, who was always under threats because of his gambling debts, had snuck a handful of diamonds for himself. For the moment, though, that would have to wait.

Customarily, after a job they assumed a low profile; no shopping sprees, no extravagant purchases, and no partying. Comfort drove home to Rochester, New York, where his faithful wife and daughter, a family whom he adored, awaited him. Sammy Nalo lay low his apartment in the Bronx, a disheveled one-bedroom flat where he cavorted with a variety of transients, topless dancers, shameless cocktail waitresses, and aspiring actresses who double-dutied as prostitutes. At the same time, he was married to a semiretired hooker, for whom he rented a house on the south shore of Long Island.

Bobby Comfort's westbound drive on Route 90 to Rochester was a monotonous six-and-a-half-hour journey. During the trip, his chain-smoking burned almost two packs of cigarettes, engulfing the interior of his metallic blue 1969 Plymouth GTX with air-choking smoke. But it soothed his nerves, and the New York City–Rochester run allowed him to think without distractions. The circumstances on this particular drive, though were precarious, and he, wound with tension, was keenly mindful of maintaining his speed below the limit. If a highway trooper were to stop his high-powered automobile, well, Comfort had much to worry about; behind the door panels of the Plymouth GTX he had tucked ten satchels of gems, a varied assortment of extraordinary stones. He tuned the radio to an FM station that played rock songs from the sixties.

Riders on the storm
Riders on the storm
Into this house we're born
Into this world we're thrown

The 1971 melodious Doors hit calmed Comfort. He glanced at the speedometer and the needle was at the 65-miles-per-hour mark, the speed limit on Route 90. The Plymouth was purring along, the gas-guzzling 426 cubic-inch hemi V8 hardly laboring.

At this segment of the trip, Comfort's mind went to what he had stored in the trunk of the car—toys for his little girl, Nicole, gifts for his nieces, and a special present for his wife, Millie. He had purchased at wholesale a gold bracelet with rubies totaling fourteen carats. Comfort gifted Millie with jewelry he purchased, which he could prove with a paid receipt. Astutely, he never gave her anything he had stolen. If the police ever searched his home, no incriminating gems would ever be in the house. And now he was floating in a daydream, imagining his daughter, brown pigtails and all, hugging the three-foot teddy bear he'd surprise her with, a cuddly stuffed animal she had longed to have. And Millie, too, was sure to marvel at the beauty of the ruby bracelet, a gleaming trinket she'd wear proudly when she and Bobby would socialize and dine at restaurants. He had been away from home for six weeks and was pining to be with his cherished wife and daughter.

On the highway, the green overhead sign read: ROCHESTER 12 MILES EXIT 45. In twenty minutes, the Plymouth GTX pulled into Comfort's driveway. He opened the trunk and took out the teddy bear. After settling in, he'd unload his clothes and drive the car into the garage; there the GTX and the millions of dollars in jewels hidden in it would be safe. In the late sixties and early seventies, hemi-powered Plymouths were a top preference of car thieves. His garage, though, was secure and equipped with a state of the art alarm system. And Comfort thought of leaving the satchels of gems in the GTX overnight. In the morning, he'd go to his bank where he rented three safe deposit boxes.

The teddy bear behind his back, he unlocked the front door of his home and pushed it open. "Millie, Nicole. Daddy's home. Hello everyone, where are you?"

The little girl emerged running in the hallway. Comfort smiled lovingly and crouched down to her height. She dove into his arms, and he embraced her with the teddy bear. "Mommy, mommy, look what daddy got me!"

Millie walked in short, quick steps toward Bobby, and on seeing him spread her arms. "Oh, you've been gone so long." She kissed him passionately on his mouth, forehead, and neck, Nicole's arms wrapped around her daddy's legs.

All three were clumped together, and Comfort caressed Nicole's cheek. "Well, I'm back, and this time for good."

Millie loosened her grip on Bobby and regarded him, her hazel eyes moistening. "Is that a promise? Do you really mean it?"

"Of course I mean it." He lit a cigarette, and Nicole towed the teddy bear to her room.

"I'm so afraid when you're away on these jobs," Millie said, a lonely tear rolling down her rosy cheek. She gazed into her husband's eyes, nodding in the direction of Nicole's nursery, and said through sobs, "That child needs you, and God forbid something goes wrong. What would I do without you?"

Bobby tugged her into him. "Here's the good news I've been dying to tell you." He cupped her chin in his hands. "This last job was a big one. A real big one. And I'm not doing any more. How about that? Does that make you happy?"

Millie stepped back, pushed her black bobbed hair behind the ears, and gave him a snarling look. "I hope you're serious about this, Mr. Comfort."

He sprang into a generous smile and winked at her. "Hey, hey, hey! I got something for you. Close your eyes." He pulled a small, blue box from his pocket and opened the lid. "Okay, you can look."

"Oh, wow! Bobby, it's beautiful. I can't believe it. It's . . . it's so different." And she threw her arms around his neck, kissing him over and over. She clasped the ruby bracelet on her right wrist and admired it, her countenance bright and happy. "Are you sure it's all right for me to have this?"

"Sure, it's legit. I bought it at a jewelry store in the Diamond District."

That night, after tucking Nicole into bed, Bobby and Millie noshed on tidbits, and skipped a full meal. In these reuniting hours, Millie and Bobby's appetite was only for one another. They scurried to the master bedroom like squirrels chasing one another and rolled into passionate lovemaking.

In the late dawn, the gray, wintry daylight was dispersing the darkness, and the phone rang, startling the couple. "Who the hell is calling this early?" Bobby pressed the phone receiver to his ear, overnight mucus clogging his throat. He coughed and said in a raspy voice, "Hello, who's this?"

"Bobby, it's Sammy. I hate to bother you so soon. But I got a big problem."

"What kind of a problem?" The instant Comfort said it, he realized these sorts of conversations were off limits by phone. "Never mind."

"All I can tell you is that you gotta get down here as soon as possible." Nalo paused as if he was undecided whether to say more. "This problem I'm talkin' about has to get straightened out within the next two days." His speech accelerated, and he was breathing heavily. "Otherwise, I don't even want to think about what's gonna happen. Please Bobby, come down as soon as you can. I'll tell you what it is when you call me back from a pay phone. Call me at ten o'clock at the usual phone booth on the West Side. You know which one I mean."

Comfort sighed, Millie listening with a look that opposed her husband returning to Manhattan. Comfort turned to see if his wife had wakened, and whispered into the mouthpiece, "I know which phone booth you're talking about, Sammy. I'll call you later at ten." *What kind of hassle did Sammy get himself into this time?*

CHAPTER 32

Bobby Comfort and a Rochester Mafia made man, James "Rene the Painter" Piccarreto, had set an appointment at La Volpe, a southern Italian bistro on the east end of Rochester. This restaurant was controlled by Piccarreto, a mobster with a hair-trigger temper. He was at a table in the private catering room of the eatery, holding delicately a porcelain cup half filled with espresso coffee, his pinkie finger extended rigidly. He slurped on the rim of the cup and laid it down. Ever so slowly, Piccarreto raised his eyes at Comfort. "Have a seat, kid."

Loud rock music from the sixties was blaring from a Wurlitzer jukebox.

> *Hey Joe, where you goin' with that gun in your hand?*
> *Goin' down to shoot my ol' lady*
> *She'd been messin' with another man*

Comfort thrust forward the right arm for a handshake, and the Rochester gangster shook his hand limply as though he had no use for pleasantries. Comfort said, "How're you doing, Rene?"

Piccarreto, short, neck-less, and barrel-shaped, his bloated face pockmarked, looked at Comfort's briefcase. "What're you got in there for me?"

"I have some high-end things I want to consign to you," Comfort answered as he sat opposite from Piccarreto, placing the briefcase on the chair next to his.

The kitchen help was preparing for the anticipated lunch crowd, aromas of fried calamari and hot red sauce infusing Comfort's sense of smell. He scanned around him, and satisfied that no unknown persons were in proximity he rested the attaché on the table, and opened it. He untied a brown velvet satchel, and spilled samples of the high-luster stones onto the white tablecloth.

"What I've got in my briefcase are all of the same quality as these, and retail for about six and a half million."

$6,500,000?! How was this possible? At Nalo's safe house, hadn't he and Comfort said the Pierre loot was in the range of $2,000,000? Was that a misunderstanding or perhaps an honest mistake? Or did they dupe their partners in crime? Indeed, they did. But this indiscretion would never surface. Or would it? Time might tell.

Piccarreto, his eyes beady and steely, swilled his espresso. "And what're you wanna get for all of this?"

Comfort was not happy showing his wares in this busy restaurant, his head darting side to side. He gathered the samples off the table and closed the briefcase. "Rene, a good part of these stones are four carats and up. Many are Marquise and Asscher cuts. All top notch VVS2 clarity grades. The best." Comfort put his thumb and index finger together and kissed them, underlining the superiority of the gems.

"Bobby, get to the point. What's your bottom line?"

Comfort inhaled on his cigarette. "I want two and a half million."

"That don't leave much room for me."

Comfort was amazed at the volume of lunch customers packing the main dining room, the commotion growing louder. He gave Piccarreto a friendly grin. "Look Rene, if you can't move all this so you and I can be satisfied . . . no sweat!" Comfort sliced the air with his palms facing upward. "I'll take everything back, and we'll still be friends."

Comfort slid out a cigarette and gestured at Piccarreto with the pack. "Want one?"

"No, I just quit smoking. As far as this swag, Bobby, leave it with me, and I'll be in touch in a couple o' days."

"Fair enough."

Comfort slipped a sheet of paper in his pocket on which he had itemized the content of the briefcase. He closed the attaché, and pushed it closer to the Mafia made man. They shook hands and Comfort said, "See you in two to three days, Rene."

If he hadn't come to terms with Piccarreto, Comfort's Plan B was to dump the satchels in his bank's safe deposit boxes, and dispose of the jewels elsewhere.

The other pressing chore was for him to reserve two seats on a flight to LaGuardia Airport in New York City, one two-way ticket for him, and one for his trusted friend, Dom Paolino, a stocky, dusky-complexioned Rochester resident who often represented Comfort in dealing with fences. Earlier that morning, from a public telephone Comfort had called Nalo at a phone booth in Manhattan, and they openly talked about the problem at hand. Nalo's bookmaker, to whom he was once again delinquent in payments, gave him seventy-two hours to settle his gambling debts, or else. This meant that Nalo had to liquidate a portion of his loose stones. Hence, Comfort recruited Paolino as the liaison to a prospective buyer, whom a contact in the Diamond District would introduce him to.

"Millie, listen," Comfort began softly, "I gotta go back to New York."

"*Whaaaat???!!!* You can't go back there so soon! What if they're looking for you? You could get picked up." Angst shaded Millie's eyes as she buried her face in her palms.

Hearing mommy cry, little Nicole came running into the den, tears dampening her cheeks.

Comfort looked at his daughter and saw a distraught child. He said to Millie, "Honey, stop making yourself crazy. It's upsetting

Nicole. Everything will be all right. Believe me." He kissed her on the forehead. "I gotta straighten out whatever problem Sammy has. If something happens to him, it could boomerang to me, and the cops might start looking into some of the past jobs we did. Don't you see?"

Millie lowered her head and couldn't be placated. She kept silent and then said, "I sense something is wrong. I feel it in my bones."

CHAPTER 33

C omfort set out to join Dom Paolino at the Rochester Airport. Millie drove him there, and blizzard conditions were blowing, snow blurring visibility. "You had to pick this terrible morning to fly?" she said, glumness in her voice.

Millie's misgivings were warranted; the commuter aircraft of that period were twin-engine prop-driven planes not much more substantial than a tin can with wings. Thirty-eight mile-per-hour winds were already spooling, the temperature plunging below seventeen degrees Fahrenheit. Comfort hugged his wife. "C'mon, get rid of the sad eyes. You're all wound up over nothing." And he kissed her. "I'll be home before you know it."

She pushed herself away from him. "You better, or I'll never forgive you." She waggled a finger at him and said in a looming tone, "And so will Nicole."

As Millie said that, images of the child came to Comfort's mind, melancholy thoughts churning pangs in his innards. He upped out, and slid his luggage from the rear seat. "Bye sweetie. When you get home, give my little honey a kiss for me." He enfolded the lapels of his olive-green overcoat around the neck, freezing winds whizzing past his cold, purple ears, and jogged to the airline passenger terminal. To call it a *terminal* was an overstatement. In practical terms, the interior of this ghostly sheet metal structure was not larger or grander than a railroad station with two ticket booths, a stench of kerosene fumes from a portable heater fouling the air. Six or seven people were milling about, all seemingly uneasy over the deteriorating weather, awaiting announcements about possible changes of the departing flights.

Paolino, his nose squashed as though at some point in time he might've fractured it, saw Comfort walking through the door, and raised an arm. "Bobby, over here."

They embraced, Comfort stomping his feet to revive blood circulation. Paolino looked out a floor-to-ceiling window, through which he could see the tarmac, patches of ice splotching the asphalt. He nodded at the outdoors. "We picked a hell of a day to fly, eh?"

Comfort chuckled, a nervous laugh. "That's just what Millie said." He stared at the window and reflected on Nicole's look of distress over her mommy crying. "Hope we don't go down in this blizzard."

"They might cancel the flight." Paolino sucked on his tongue, snowflakes hitting the glass. "Whatever will be will be."

The flight was not canceled. Instead, they were herded for a hundred yards to a mobile access stairway and into a DC-3. Because of the aircraft's tail-wheel landing gear configuration, it sat in a squatting position. In the cabin were two rows of seats for twelve passengers plus a crew of three. The one stewardess on board fought to shut and latch the heavy door, and soon the two engines ignited to a roar, a burst of black smoke blasting from the exhaust manifolds. The flight attendant, well-rounded, ear-length blonde hair, was demure in a blue blouse and skirt ensemble, and a white, sheer scarf. Balancing herself precariously on high heels, and speaking above the rumbling noise of the eighteen-cylinder radial engines, she said in a trained voice, "Ladies and gentlemen, we're about to taxi onto the runway. Please fasten your seatbelts." She had on a dutiful smile as though the passengers couldn't have chosen a better day to fly.

The DC-3 started bumping along until it reached the apron of the runway. The cockpit had no door, and Comfort and Paolino, who were in the seats side by side in the two rows, watched the pilot shove the throttle levers to full acceleration, and the plane's engines revved deafeningly, transferring jaw-jarring vibrations throughout the fuselage and into the cabin. Comfort was sitting on the starboard side, and peering out the porthole window he saw something that made his pulse race. The wing's top surface had accumulated a sheathing of ice, and what suddenly came to mind was a recent plane crash in the news that had been caused by icing on the wings. He felt a knot the size of a fig in his throat as he recollected reading that ice buildup reshapes the *airfoil*, the wing, compromising its *airlifting effect*. This was troubling, and he found himself murmuring prayers.

Fifteen seconds into the takeoff roll, and the aircraft was bouncing and yawing as though it were in danger of veering off the runway, the pilot fighting the yoke to keep the DC-3 on track. (The yoke is an aeronautical term for steering wheel.) Comfort, his heart in his mouth, was wondering if the wings were about to start flapping. White-knuckled, everyone on board was squeezing the armrests, the endearing stewardess still smiling. The aircraft's speed was increasing moderately, as were the vibrations. An inch of snow had accrued on the runway, but Comfort couldn't see past forty to fifty feet. *Barreling down at nearly one hundred miles per hour, does the pilot know where the plane is headed?* It would've been surprising if this small, vintage aircraft was equipped with state-of-the-art avionics (electronic navigational gear). Thirty-five seconds had passed from the moment the DC-3 began rolling, and the tail wheel lifted off the ground, yielding to more fishtailing. As the airplane advanced three-quarters down the runway, it seemed as though the front landing gear was glued to the asphalt. Comfort looked out his porthole window, and through the near whiteout of snow could faintly make out the line of pine trees not far ahead. Eyes on the fast-growing forest, without turning to Paolino, Comfort tapped his arm. "Dom, holy shit! We're running out of runway. Hope this flying can gets off the ground, like now."

The DC-3 was laboring to overcome the strong head winds, the stewardess's smile withering.

At last, Comfort and Paolino felt the front wheels airborne, but the rickety aircraft's rate of ascent seemed perilously slow, the ominous pines mounting by the second in the short distance ahead.

CHAPTER 34

Comfort and Paolino's coloring had ashened, as did the faces of the other passengers. The floundering plane dipped, sucking the breath of all souls on board, and two or three female commuters yelped out a burst of screams. In the next three seconds, the nose tipped upward, and Comfort heard the swishing of the treetops scraping the underbelly of the fuselage, the left wingtip lowering and still grazing the foliage below, pine needles scattering in the air. The DC-3 banked to the right and, miraculously, maintained a minimal but steadier climb. At last, it penetrated the gray clouds, breathing resuming inside the cabin.

At home in Rochester, Millie was pacing room to room, wringing her hands, worrying about the increasingly inclement weather or some other destined doom. She couldn't guess what it might've been, but a gloomy premonition would not disperse in her head. Was Bobby's flight doomed, and he'd be killed? Or was he about to be arrested in New York? Millie had been disquieted since her husband had mentioned he'd be flying to Manhattan. And her distraught state was infecting Nicole, a love-smothered, sensitive child who was as fragile as an eggshell.

Somehow, the unsteady DC-3 touched down safely at LaGuardia Airport, where the weather, though in the low thirties, was a great improvement over the Rochester whiteout. "That was some flight," Paolino said to Comfort.

"Never again, man. Never! Next time, I drive. I feel like kissing the ground."

They waited for the carousel to spit out their luggage, and Comfort seemed jumpy. He looked at his watch. "As soon as we get our bags, let's find a pay phone. I gotta call Millie. I know she's going nuts."

In the terminal, they found a bank of telephone booths, every one of which was occupied except one. Comfort ran to it before someone else might beat him to it. He fed several quarters into the coin slot and dialed. "Millie, it's me. We just got here at LaGuardia."

"Oh, thank God. Thank God, Bobby. You don't know, I was getting sick."

He could hear his wife's stressed gulps of air. "I know what you must've gone through the whole morning, baby. The flight was a little rough, but everything's okay. Anyhow, I'll call you tomorrow."

"You promise?"

"Sure, I promise. But please don't forget to kiss my little princess for me."

"You know I will. But Bobby?"

"Yeah? What is it, honey?"

"Please be careful. And . . . don't get too confident."

Millie couldn't shake the ill omen lurking inside her, a feeling that had also begun affecting Comfort's subconscious.

CHAPTER 35

Nalo had driven to LaGuardia to meet Comfort and Paolino and take them to the Royal Manhattan Hotel on 45th Street and 8th Avenue. They loaded the baggage in the trunk of Nalo's white Volvo 144S, and proceeded south on the Grand Central Parkway. Paolino and Comfort lit cigarettes, creating clouds of smoke and peeving Nalo. "So what's going on, Sammy," Comfort asked, flicking his Pall Mall in the ashtray on the dashboard.

Nalo didn't turn to look at his passenger, eyes on the road. He sighed with heaviness and said, "Ah, this Joe Longone, the bookie. You know him."

"What about him?"

"He's pressing me. I . . . I owe the bastard about two hundred and twenty grand."

"Two hundred and twenty grand!" said Paolino, whistling in astonishment in the rear seat.

Comfort shook his head. "Sammy, this is insane, man. You gotta curb your gambling."

Rocking his head slightly in understanding of Comfort's advice, Nalo said, "You're right, Bobby. But what can I do? I mean, every-body's got a vice. And . . ."

Paolino cut in, "That's a hell of a vice. Besides the money you're throwin' away, one day someone's gonna do you in."

"Thanks, Dom. I didn't need that," Nalo said sullenly.

"Dom's right, Sammy," Comfort said. "You're risking your life making your money, and you're risking your life in the way you're spending it. More like pissing it away."

"I don't wanna talk about it right now. This is not why I asked you to come down," Nalo shot back.

Comfort raised his palms in surrender. "Fine with me. Anything you say, Sammy. But I wish you'd stop calling me every time you get yourself in a pickle."

"It won't happen again," Nalo guaranteed.

They were now in the westbound lanes of the Long Island Expressway. Paolino didn't join the conversation, and stared out the window, in awe at the Big Apple skyline cropping four or five miles ahead, the East River glistening in the foreground of that unrivaled panorama.

In a downcast tone, Nalo said, "All I wanna do is fence about forty to fifty of my stones, and that'll pull me through *and* get rid of that fuckin' Longone. Those guinea bookmakers are all the same. Pressure, pressure, pressure! Violence, violence, violence!"

Nalo paid the twenty-five-cent toll and aimed the Volvo into the white-tiled tube of the Midtown Tunnel, a one-and-a-half-mile underwater tract trafficked by seventy-seven thousand vehicles per day. On exiting it, he turned north on 3rd Avenue to 45th Street, and left onto 8th Avenue. He parked temporarily in front of the Royal Manhattan Hotel and said to Comfort and Paolino, "You guys check in, and I'll find a parking space."

In the rented suite, which Comfort had already smoke-polluted, they sat in the living room on a pale-yellow linen sofa. Facing it were four mint-green lounge chairs arranged in a semicircle. Inside of ten minutes, Nalo knocked and Paolino opened the door for him. Nalo fell back into one of the chairs and rolled up his shirt sleeves, arms as hairy as a bear. He said to Comfort, "This jeweler we did business with a year ago, Bert Stern, he's got a booth in the Diamond District."

"I remember Stern. We sold him a lot of odds and ends," Comfort recalled, relaxing in his cushiony chair.

"Anyway, Nalo continued, "Stern works with a diamond cutter that knows a banker who dabbles with gold, silver, and gems. The cutter's name . . . I think is Harry Towson."

"You think!" Comfort said as he threw his head back. "You better be sure. And did you check him out?"

"I myself didn't check him out, but Stern vouches for this guy."

"Hope you're right," Paolino said scathingly.

"We're gonna have lunch this afternoon with Stern and the cutter, Towson," Nalo said, looking at his watch. "Matter of fact, we gotta meet them at the Cattleman in about an hour."

"I've heard of that joint up in Rochester. Supposed to be a damn good steakhouse. Where is that place?" Paolino asked.

"Seventh Avenue and 51st Street," Comfort said. "Well then, we better get going."

"I'll go get the car and meet you in front of the hotel," Nalo said, restlessness in his movements.

They rose, donned their coats, went down to the lobby, and stepped through the revolving doors.

The midday traffic was typically in high volume bogged down with automobiles, trucks, and flocks of yellow Checker cabs that through the early eighties weaved from lane to lane, harrowingly dodging other vehicles and miraculously avoiding pedestrians. At the Cattleman, a maître d' welcomed Comfort and company, taking the three to a booth where Bert Stern and Harry Towson were already seated. Stern was in an eye-catching pink jacket over a plum shirt, colors brighter than the feathers of a parrot. An aroma of seared beef was the predominant smell inside the restaurant, a mouthwatering whiff for meat lovers.

Stern and Towson stood, arms ready for handshakes. Nalo recited the introductions, and everyone settled on all sides of the rectangular table, which was full of sparkling glasses and a complement of porcelain dishes bearing the restaurant's logo etched in gold leaf at the center.

"Good to see you, Bobby," Stern said in a strong baritone voice that was incongruent with his short, tubby body. He was bald and made a futile attempt at covering his glossy scalp. He combed the few remaining strands of hair above his left ear over the right side of the head, appearing as though he had drawn those sparse filaments with a black marker. Stern, who chortled at the end of every sentence, patted Towson's sleeve. "Harry here is not only a great stone cutter; he also has a few valuable contacts." Stern winked and smiled. "I'm talkin' about certain parties who are in the market for your merchandise." By "certain parties," he meant fences.

Towson, soft spoken, his salt-and-pepper hair razor cut, closed in to the table. "I represent a banker. This banker is buying a lot of stones and money doesn't seem to be an issue. He's not a *hondler* either." He looked at Stern. "Unlike our friend Bert." Everyone laughed, Stern tolerating the joke in kind. "Anyhow," Towson said, "I can set up a meeting with the banker."

"What's the banker's name?" asked Nalo.

Towson hesitated before he said, "Ronald."

"Ronald what?"

"Uh, I don't know his last name," Towson answered ineptly.

Comfort said in a surprised in voice, "You don't know his last name? How can you be so sure that this Ronald isn't an undercover cop?"

"Simple," Towson replied casually. "First of all, I cut a lot of diamonds for Ronald, and he always pays in cash. Secondly, I know two jewelers who sold him a slew of legit gold and silver." He paused a few seconds. "If he's an undercover cop, why would he be buying jewelry that's not swag? Look, Ronald believes a wild economic inflation isn't too far ahead, and he's converting his cash into gold and gems." Towson pecked his temple. "Actually, that's pretty smart of him."

"But it never occurred to you to find out Ronald's last name?" Comfort belabored.

"Yeah, didn't you wanna know who you're dealin' with?" Nalo added.

"Like I said, he's been buying legitimate items, not just hot material, and he pays in cash. Maybe he doesn't want the whole world to know he's got undeclared money. What's so unusual about that?" Towson reasoned.

Stern interrupted this volleying and said, "Hey, why don't we get some food before we starve to death?" He raised his arm and signaled to a waiter. Everyone ordered the same choice, aged Porterhouse steaks, the specialty of the house. Comfort asked the waiter for a bottle of burgundy, a California brand. Nalo didn't care for wines; he had a penchant for the Greek beverage, ouzo, and Stern might've chosen Manischewitz. But the Cattleman was an American chop house and didn't cater to ethnic palates.

They all ate hardy, the Porterhouse steaks were as tender and soft as a stick of butter, and now it was time to revert to the issue at hand, Harry Towson's shadowy buyer.

Nalo dropped the utensils in his plate, a disruptive loud clanking that turned many heads. He burped and thumped his chest with a fist as he burped. "So Harry, you're okay with this contact of yours. I *do* agree with you on the fact that this . . . eh, what did you say this banker's name is?"

"Ronald," answered Towson.

"Yeah, Ronald. What you said makes sense. If he's a cop or FBI, why would he buy legitimate jewelry?"

Comfort and Paolino weren't too convinced. Across the table, Stern understood their trepidation. "Bobby, what Harry said is perfectly logical. Besides, you or Sammy aren't going to meet with this Ronald. Dom will." Stern nodded at Paolino. "Dom doesn't have a reputation as a jewel thief in New York. And let's say this so-called banker turns out to be undercover, the police won't have nothin' on Dom. After all, Dom will have in his possession only a handful of stones that could've came from anywhere, and don't *necessarily* have to be hot. Right?"

No matter what anybody said, though, Comfort couldn't rid of the intuition that had rooted itself in his gut. He and Nalo were still on the FBI's priority for the Loren job. And even more demoralizing, on the third page of today's *New York Post* was an article pertaining to the Pierre.

PIERRE ELEVATOR OPERATOR WILL WORK
WITH POLICE SKETCH ARTIST

And Millie's words resonated incessantly in Comfort's ears: "Please don't go back to New York. Something is gonna go wrong. I feel it in my bones."

CHAPTER 36

T he following morning, the steaks not yet fully digested, Comfort, Nalo, and Paolino showered and shaved in the suite at the Royal Manhattan and set out to go see Bert Stern, Harry Towson, and Roland with no last name. The location for this tryst was the Market Diner on 43rd Street and 11th Avenue. Stern had chosen a partitioned corner table and had already been there with Towson and Roland. Comfort, Nalo, and Paolino walked in and joined the others. The diner was noisy and the food greasy. A tent of smoke hovered overhead, and the smell of recycled frying oil seemed to be a permanent odor.

Stern said, "You guys have a restful night?"

The new arrivals nodded mutely, and Stern pointed to his right at Roland the banker. "Bobby, Sammy, Dom, this is Roland. Harry you already met last night." Stern then said to the guest star, "Roland, this is Bobby Comfort, Sammy Nalo, and Dom Paolino."

They shook hands coldly and sat. A minute or two of idle talk made everybody feel at ease and less nervous. Roland, tall and slim, wore thick prescription glasses mounted on black frames. Looking proper in a dull black suit, he was all business—a stony face and blondish slicked-back hair—and said little, if anything at all. Up to this point, Towson did all the talking.

Nalo said to the banker, "I want to unload about $250,000 worth of diamonds. Four to eight carats each with mixed shapes. They're all high clarity grades. Can you handle two hundred and fifty grand?"

Poker-faced, his eyes magnified through the glasses, Roland answered curtly, "Uh, uh." He rocked his head almost in slow motion as if to underscore his reply. "As long as an appraisal from a reputable appraiser meets my expectations, we'll have a deal."

"Where do you wanna do this?" Comfort asked, hostility in his tone.

Towson chugged a glass of lemon water, and speaking to the whole table said, "The exchange can take place tomorrow at eleven o'clock at the Summit Hotel on 51st and Lexington. Come to the lounge. That's where Roland and I will be. Roland will have a room at the Summit, and we'll go from there."

"So there are no misunderstandings, Sammy, the retail appraisal of your diamonds has to come in at least at $500,000. Or else we won't have a deal," Roland stated arrogantly.

"That's fine with me. I know what I got, and I know what it's worth," Nalo said.

Comfort asked Roland, "You mind telling us your last name?"

"Yes, I do mind." Roland rapped his chest with a hand as though he were a person of substance. "I'll just say this; I'm a high ranking executive at a financial institution and don't want my side business to be a conflict of interest."

Roland's anecdote didn't satisfy Comfort. Nalo, on the other hand, desperate to liquidate his stones so to be rid of the dog with bared fangs, saw nothing amiss or fraudulent about Roland. Was the urgency of Nalo's problem clouding his thinking? Or was Comfort too skeptical, or too careful, or too paranoid? After all, professionals who are in capacities of prestige, and at the same time delve into an illicit business, tend to be prudent, and even enigmatic.

"If we're set, then we're done here, and we'll adjourn 'til tomorrow at the Summit Hotel," Towson said, searching everyone's reaction for doubts or second thoughts.

Nalo rapped the tabletop in confirmation of the appointment. He looked at Comfort and Paolino. "Are you guys okay with this?"

Comfort lowered his eyes and said in a hush, "Guess so, Sammy. It's your ball game."

Paolino drank water and didn't answer.

"We'll see you tomorrow at eleven," Nalo said to Towson and Roland.

No one else commented, and Roland upped off his chair. "All right. See you all in the morning."

When the banker stood, Comfort, Nalo, and Paolino saw for the first time how tall he was. "Big dude," Nalo said, watching Roland walk away.

"Anything else that we have to talk about?" Comfort asked Towson.

"I don't think so." Then Towson asked Stern, "What're you think about all this?"

"To me, it sounds cut and dry, fellas."

Comfort, Nalo, and Paolino flagged down a cab and returned to the Royal Manhattan. As they settled in the suite, the two Rochester men opened the minibar and had a drink. Comfort dumped ice cubes in his whiskey, and stirred it by shaking the glass. And now was the appropriate time for him and Nalo to hash out where to safely warehouse the bulk of the gems from the Pierre.

Comfort downed the whiskey and said, "We gotta get rid of the rest of the stones."

"You have any ideas, Bobby?" Nalo asked.

"I was thinking of leaving the whole satchel with Al Green."

Green, who in the hours after the robbery had survived the car rollover accident on the Belt Parkway, and the clash with the pit bull, resurfaced, and Comfort and Nalo squared him away in respect to his due share of the heist. Green had proved to be trustworthy, and they decided to trust him with the satchel, a large quantity of high-grade gems stowed in a black double-lined cloth sack. The bag was hidden in Nalo's apartment in the Bronx, but should the Roland rendezvous go awry, Comfort and Nalo were taking steps not to lose it to the authorities. "I'll go talk to Al Green later," Nalo said.

"Why don't you go right now?" Comfort suggested as he poured another three-ounce bottle of Jack Daniel's into his glass.

"Bobby's right," Paolino said, who was on the couch reading, rather viewing, an issue of *Playboy* magazine, a bottle of Miller in his hand. "The sooner you get rid of that stuff, the better it is for all of us."

"What time is it?" Nalo looked at the wristwatch. "It's a bit too early. Al is probably still runnin' numbers."

"By the time you drive all the way up to Harlem, traffic and all, he'll be done with his numbers run, and you'll find him at his bar," Comfort said.

"What's the name of his bar again?"

"Eh . . . what the hell was it? Oh, yeah, the Black Pussycat." Comfort thought for a moment. "It's one block east of where the old Cotton Club used to be on 142nd and Lenox."

"That's it," Nalo recalled.

"Well, then, get going. I'm counting the seconds to get done with this and say goodbye to New York City." Comfort squished his cigarette butt in an ashtray, swigged the rest of the whiskey, and not to break the chain, lighted a new Pall Mall. "I still don't like this whole thing, Sammy." He shook his head persistently. "I just don't like it, man."

CHAPTER 37

"**S**ammy, I don't wanna hold on to your shit," Al Green said. "Uh, uh, man. Damn, if I get busted for any bullshit, and the powleece find all that swag in my crib . . . shit, they be lockin' my black ass up, and I'll never again see the light o' day."

Nalo and Green were at the mahogany bar in Green's darkish Black Pussycat, a reek of liquor vapors throughout the gin mill. A black waitress trending a white-dyed afro and white, thigh-high boots brushed up to Nalo and rested her chin on his shoulder. "Can I git you somethin', Booboo?"

Nalo shook his head no.

"She's a fine sistah, Sammy. Ain't she?" Green said.

She kissed Nalo's neck. "You looh like youh down in the dumps. Some pink pussy might make you feel better, Booboo. Uh, uh."

Nalo wasn't in the mood for sweet whisperings, though had his quandary not been weighing on him, he sure would've loved a romp with the "fine sistah." He said to Green, "Can we go somewhere and talk, just you and me?"

Green nodded at a door next to a glitzy jukebox. "Let's go in there." He shooed away the hooker, and she sauntered to the other end of the bar in a dancing step, the jukebox playing a sixties song by the Four Tops.

Reach out for me, I'll be there.

The Black Pussycat was drafty, the wind howling through the poorly insulated side door, and Nalo, lightly dressed, was forcing himself not to shiver. "Look, Al, I just want you to hold on to my goods for a couple of days. That's all."

Green leaned his shoulder into the wall and looked at the floor, a worn-blackened wooden parquet from the late 1800s. "I don't know, Sammy. I mean, if somethin' goes wrong I don't wanna be blamed."

Nalo pinched Green's cheek to soften him. "Nothin' is gonna go wrong. C'mon, do it for me, Al."

That evening, Comfort and Nalo delivered the satchel to Green's apartment on 110th Street in Harlem. "It's all in here, Al," Nalo said. "When this is all over, we're gonna give you, as you blacks say, a little piece o' change." And he handed him the black satchel.

Green took it and laughed. "You white dudes are funny. You're damn right I goin' want a little piece o' change."

Comfort and Nalo drove southbound on Riverside Drive back to the Royal Manhattan, and all through the ride neither one spoke.

Dom Paolino was chomping on a hamburger in the hotel's lounge and washing it down with a frosty beer. He saw Comfort and Nalo walk in, and they joined him for a dinner of bar food. Comfort ate a Caesar salad, and Nalo ordered buffalo wings marinated in a southern concoction of barbecue sauce.

"How did it go with Al Green?" Paolino asked.

Comfort pointed at Nalo. "Sammy here talked Al into taking our stock for a couple of days."

"That's great," Paolino said, his mouth stuffed and biting into the hamburger.

Behind the dining area of the lounge, on a dance floor were a dozen or so tightly squeezed revelers, arms and legs floundering in convulsive twirls and twists, a strobe light freezing the dancers' movements. The capturing effect of the strobe light made the action seem as if it were a jerky, black-and-white silent film from the early 1900s.

Comfort scratched the tip of his nose. "Yeah, well. Green looked scared, and I hope he's got the common sense not to do anything stupid and get pinched. One thing can lead to another. You know how it goes."

"Tell me about it," Paolino said, emptying his golden Miller.

On finishing the abbreviated dinner and a few anesthetizing cocktails, they went to Comfort's suite. Nalo had been carrying a brown toiletry tote containing a half-million dollars in diamonds. He placed it on the coffee table in the main room. "In there is almost half a mil. That ought to do it for Roland."

"I hope so," Comfort answered dolefully.

Nalo asked Paolino, "What time are you meeting Stern and the others tomorrow morning?"

"At eleven."

Nalo sighed. "All right. I'm goin'. Keep me in the loop. If I don't hear from either one of you, I'll know it went bad."

"Let's pray to God it all ends well. And take it easy, Sammy," Comfort said.

"I don't know what God can do," Nalo answered. "I suggest you guys rely on yourselves and watch your asses. And forget about God."

"All right, Sammy, everybody looks at life differently. You have to learn to respect others' opinions. We'll talk tomorrow."

Nalo stepped through the revolving doors, and stood on the sidewalk beneath the twenty-five-foot awning advertising The Royal Manhattan, surprised by the onset of a snowstorm, white flakes dusting the pavement. The elevator shoes unsteadying his ankles, he started plodding eastward to where he had parked the Volvo. A few seconds into his walk, and he could hear the nerve-racking closing-in of footsteps. Nalo's heartbeat began thumping. He glanced behind him and managed a momentary peep of two fast-stepping, squatty figures in dark coats, the brim of the stalkers' black hats low over their brows.

CHAPTER 38

The two obscured goons sidled alongside Nalo and clutched his arms. "How yah doin', Sammy?" said the one on Nalo's right, his voice raspy and high-pitched. "Just keep walkin."

"Who the fuck are you?" Nalo demanded, wriggling to free his arms.

"Take it easy, Sammy. Stay still. You can't run too far."

"What're you want from me?"

"Your pal, Joe Longone, hopes you're gonna make the deadline. Know what I mean, Sammy? 'Cause if you're not . . . well, he feels it's only right for him to order a nice flower wreath for your funeral. But he wants to know what your favorite flowers are."

"I'll make the deadline. I always do. And tell him he don't need to worry about flowers for me. If anything, he should send flowers to his wife, and maybe she'll stop fuckin' his driver."

"Always a wiseass, Sammy. Ain't yah?"

Nalo tugged his arms from the hoodlums' grips and brushed his sleeves. "Just tell Longone to keep cool for now. Meantime, stay the fuck away from me." Again Nalo was under the gun, and unless he liquidated a portion of his jewels and reconciled matters with Longone, all his problems could be over.

The next morning at the Royal Manhattan, Comfort said to Paolino, "You should leave now and head to the Summit. It's better to get there before everybody else. You know, scope out the place and get a feel of things."

"Yeah, I'm all set to go." Paolino visited the bathroom, brushed his thick, nappy hair and splashed a few drops of cologne on the cheeks. He went to the foyer closet for his tan raincoat and draped it over the shoulders.

Comfort gave him the briefcase with Nalo's stones. "Dom, be careful and always watch your ass."

"No problem. I've done this before. You should know that." And Paolino was en route to the Summit Hotel to dispose of swag gems for cash.

As he shut the door behind him, Comfort slumped onto the couch, lit a cigarette, and fell into somberness. Why did he chance flying back to New York in the immediate aftermath of the Pierre job, overseeing a fencing deal on behalf of Nalo, who was in another one of his pickles, and likely would be in one again? And if the shoe was on the other foot, would Nalo do the same for him? Probably not, Comfort knew.

As the elevator door opened on the lobby level, Paolino had a thought: pay the hotel bill now so that the minute he'd be done with Roland, he and Comfort would avoid delays leaving Manhattan. *The sooner we get out of here, the better it is.*

"Will that be all, Mr. Paolino?" asked a prim and proper clerk at the checkout desk, a glimmering limpidness in her green eyes.

Paolino, always on the prowl for "fresh meat," winked flirtingly at the blonde girl, who blushed. "That'll do it." He glanced at the name tag on her lapel. "I see your name is Jill. Pretty name. I'll see you again." And as he walked away, he winked at her a second time.

Jill, competent in her work, called out to him, "Sir, your receipt."

He backtracked, and in an exaggerated sweep of his hand took the receipt from her. "You're not just gorgeous, but efficient as well." And he blew Jill a kiss, a crooked smile on his lips. "You can bet I'll see you soon."

Jill's efficiency, however, was precisely what Comfort could've done without.

CHAPTER 39

Paolino, enraptured by the prospect of dating Jill sometime in the near future, pranced happily, feeling as though he were floating on water. He signaled a cab and, traffic permitting, he should be at the Summit in fifteen minutes. Paolino strutted through the lobby and went to the lounge, a bar/restaurant that was sparse of customers. A lunch buffet spanned along one wall, scents of broiled seafood tingeing the sleepy dining room. Pretending to be peeking at the vast variety of food, Paolino scoped the surroundings for anybody who might've been spying on him. No suspects in sight, and all seemed normal—a few hotel patrons, bellhops, and two or three black-suited businessmen milling about, everyone minding his or her affairs.

Paolino sat on a bar stool and asked the bartender for a bottle of Perrier. As he sipped the signature water, in less than five to six minutes Bert Stern tapped him on his shoulder. "Hey Dom. How's it goin'? Are we all here?"

Benjamin Fradkin, a gem appraiser at the Manhattan Diamond District, and Harry Towson, a fast-talking character who exuded undue confidence, had come with Stern, who greeted Paolino, "Good morning," and gave him a hearty chuckle.

Fradkin was a short, cross-eyed senior in his mid sixties. Shy and timid, carrying a utility bag, he hardly whispered, "Hi."

Stern nodded at Fradkin and said to Paolino, "Benjamin's got a fair reputation in the Diamond District. He'll do a good job appraising the stones, and the deal will be over before you know it."

"Pleased to meet you, Benjamin," Paolino said. He did an imaginary head count. "Where's Roland?"

"Oh, he's up in his room," Towson replied matter-of-factly.

"Well, what're we waitin' for? Let's go see him," Paolino said.

"Roland doesn't want anybody in the room but you and Benjamin. Understandably, he prefers for no one else to witness the purchase." Towson paused and cocked his head. "And frankly, I don't wanna be present either."

Stern must've felt he had to justify Roland's wishes and said, "Sure, I wouldn't wanna have everybody and their horses to see the deal go down. As a banker, Roland is trained to be extra cautious."

Towson took a piece of paper from his pocket and looked at it. "Dom, he's in room 1032. He wants you and Benjamin to go up and knock on the door . . . and do what you gotta do. Bert and I, we'll wait down here 'til you guys finish your business."

Paolino glanced at Fradkin, whose nervousness would've been apparent even to a person in a coma. "If that's the way it's gotta be, let's get it over with. We'll meet you back here when we're done."

"Sounds good," Towson said. "I'm just going down the block to the newsstand to pick up the *Post*, but I'll come right back here to wait for you."

Back at the Royal Manhattan, Bobby Comfort's stomach was in knots. Roland's perfectly fitting explanations had sounded rehearsed. But from an objective perspective his clarifications were reasonable and certainly plausible. Despite this, no amount of reasoning could set aside an inexplicable sensation that nibbled at Comfort's thoughts.

Fradkin and Paolino walked to one of the elevators and rode it to the tenth floor. They found Room 1032, and Paolino knocked on the door. A cheerful voice from inside the room said in a musical tone, "Just a minute, please."

Fradkin's partially bald head had a sheen of sweat, and at last he and Paolino heard footsteps. But when the door opened, a pink-faced, gray-haired man in a cheap brown suit waved them in. "Who are you?" asked Paolino, surprise arching his eyebrows.

The stranger answered, "C'mon in, c'mon in. Roland is in the bathroom. He'll be right out."

As Fradkin and Paolino entered the suite, the brown-suited person said invitingly, "Meantime, get yourselves set up there by the coffee table."

Fradkin warily placed his bag on the table and unpacked his jeweler's scale and a notepad. He also dug in his jacket pocket for the loupe. Paolino, just as guardedly, rested the briefcase beside Fradkin's scale and opened it. He removed a neatly folded cotton handkerchief from one of the compartments and unfurled it, revealing a layer of diamonds. Paolino realized he and the elderly Fradkin were alone, wondering where the pink-skinned host had gone. And why was Roland in the bathroom for so long? Was he strapping on a concealed listening device?

CHAPTER 40

As they waited for Paolino and Fradkin to finish dealing with Roland, Towson and Stern were in the Summit's lounge in idle talk. Elbows on the bar, Towson, looking sharp in a double-breasted, navy blue blazer, said, "Bert, mind taking a walk with me to the newsstand?"

"I could use some fresh air," Stern answered.

They walked through the lobby, and out onto the Lexington Avenue exit of the hotel. A few steps farther on the sidewalk, four uniformed policemen encircled Towson and Stern. In seconds, two of the cops manhandled Stern and swiftly handcuffed him. They jostled him into a cruiser, folded him into the rear seat, and slammed the door shut, bystanders watching the arrest.

It was an oddity to see the glaringly attired Stern in colorful garments, owl-eyed and frightened as Towson ambled toward 51st Street as if he were window shopping. This was dumbfounding to the cuffed Stern. Why was he arrested and treated as though he were Public Enemy No. 1? And why was Towson walking away from this?

Stern asked what the charges were against him, but the lowly police officers couldn't elucidate on what was in store for him. One of the more sympathetic cops said, "We don't have any information for you. We're just carrying out orders. Once you get to FBI headquarters, they'll tell you everything."

"FBI!!!!!" exclaimed Stern, his pulse beating faster than a drummer.

In Roland's suite the phone rang, and Fradkin and Paolino gazed apprehensively at one another. The individual who had answered their knock reappeared and picked up the handset. "Hello."

The call originated from a phone booth on 51st Street, where Harry Towson was. "Lieutenant O'Neil?"

"Yes. Who's this?"

"This is Harry. A couple of minutes ago, your people got Bert Stern," said Towson, an FBI informant. "You know what to do next."

Unbeknownst to Fradkin and Paolino, NYPD Lieutenant Don O'Neil was posing as a colleague of Roland, who was actually FBI Special Agent Jack Goodwin. In the room adjacent to where Fradkin and Paolino awaited the supposed Roland were O'Neil's four detectives, who had been eavesdropping on the unsuspecting pair. They were also monitoring the phone lines in Roland's suite and knew Stern had been apprehended.

Fradkin and Paolino were growing edgier by the second. Roland's lengthy bathroom visit was becoming a farce. More demoralizing, the pink-faced man, who had purported to be Roland's something-or-other, had disappeared, for a second time, into another part of the suite. Indeed, Lieutenant O'Neil was in the bedroom phoning his men next door, giving the order to proceed with the raid.

"What the hell is Roland doing in the bathroom so goddamn long?" Paolino murmured.

"And where did this other guy go?" Fradkin asked.

The answers came within two or three seconds as the stillness exploded into a whirlwind of action. The door burst open and four men charged in, guns drawn, looking as if they were about to unload a barrage of bullets. At the same time, Roland/Goodwin rushed out from the bathroom, and O'Neil ran in from the bedroom. "Hands up and don't move," Agent Goodwin said commandingly.

Fradkin, a law-abiding citizen, felt his legs as rubbery as worn chewing gum. Hands up high, the bottom of his shirt now loose and disheveled, he said, "I . . . I don't know why you're doing this to me. I'm . . . just an appraiser. I've never been in trouble. I gotta sit, or I'm gonna pass out."

"Maybe you never got into trouble before, but you're in deep, deep shit now," O'Neil said.

"Can I please sit?" Fradkin pleaded.

"For cryin' out loud, let him sit. He's an older guy," Paolino said fearlessly. This wasn't new to him, and he did not cower.

"Where are your partners?" Goodwin asked Paolino.

"What partners?" Paolino remarked stoically.

Goodwin pointed at the briefcase. "Look, we have reliable sources that are in a capacity to attest precisely from where those diamonds were taken. So save yourself and admit it."

Hands still up, Paolino said, "I don't know what you're talkin' about, my friend."

The six law enforcement agents closed in and handcuffed the two suspects. This undercover operation was a joint venture between the FBI and the NYPD. Agent Goodwin, the leader of the sting, told O'Neil to inspect and inventory the gems inside the briefcase, Fradkin's precision scale standing not far from it. O'Neil said to Goodwin, "I don't know much about diamonds, but I'll have a specialist in the department check this out. He'll prove they came from the Pierre."

Lieutenant O'Neil's buoyancy and swagger was the product of his ignorance in the diamond field. First and foremost, no means were available for an expert to identify loose gems. Secondly, the majority of the victims, even if they could recognize their stolen belongings, had declined to file a police report. For personal motives, as previously mentioned, they denied having incurred any losses. As for Fradkin, whom Goodwin and O'Neil viewed as the weak link of this sting, they couldn't intimidate him into informing on Stern, Paolino, and anyone else who was part of this "gang of hotel thieves." The shaken appraiser, who was on the verge of tears, didn't know from where, or how, or who had acquired the stones. He was here simply because he'd been hired to do his job.

Goodwin said to O'Neil's detectives, "Frisk these perps thoroughly."

That drove Fradkin to tears. "I'm not a perp, whatever that means." He nodded at the briefcase, his shoulders heaving. "These people are paying me to appraise those diamonds over there. That's all. I don't know anything else."

Jack Goodwin did not heed Fradkin's appeal and signaled the detectives to frisk him, which produced nothing. But upon poking into one of Paolino's pockets, they found a hotel receipt from the Royal Manhattan that had been paid an hour earlier. The name of the guest listed was D. Paolino. "What's this?" O'Neil asked wryly, flipping over the invoice two or three times. "Who else has been staying with you at the Royal Manhattan?"

The color left Paolino's face. *I wish that damn Jill hadn't reminded me to take the hotel receipt.* "I have no idea what you're talkin' about."

O'Neil passed the receipt to Goodwin. He examined it as if it might've been encoded and printed with invisible ink and shook his head in disbelief. "Mr. Paolino, you gotta stop playing games. How can you say you don't know anything about this hotel bill that has your name on it?" Goodwin waved the receipt close to Paolino's face. "Here, look, it's made out to you."

Paolino strained not to appear frazzled. "Maybe . . . maybe you made it up." He raised his eyelids at the detective who had searched him. "Who's to say that your guy here who just went through my pockets slipped it in there?"

"Maybe this and maybe that," O'Neil said. Then he turned to Fradkin, whose eyes were watery. "What about you, you know who was stayin' at the Royal Manhattan besides your pal Paolino?"

"I . . . I don't even know where the Royal Manhattan is. I told you Bert Stern hired me to do an appraisal job."

Goodwin took the baton. "Mr. Paolino, listen good. Speaking of your associate, Mr. Stern, we already arrested him, and right now he's at FBI headquarters on 69th Street. He told my colleague that you had other accomplices staying with you at the Royal Manhattan." This wasn't true, though it's a typical interrogation ploy designed to frighten a suspect into an admission. This ruse is effective on inexperienced criminals, but Paolino was too seasoned to fall for it, though on learning Stern had been collared a rush of diarrhea was boiling.

At this stage of the inquiry, Goodwin discounted Fradkin as a coconspirator but pressed on interrogating Paolino. To ease the tension, he called him by his first name. "Dom, we're going to get the whole story from Stern. It's just a matter of time before he folds. So why don't you make it easier on yourself and help us? Tell me who was behind the Pierre job, and I'll see to it that the prosecutors go easy on you."

Repressing a surging bowel movement, Paolino said, "If you're so damn sure Stern will tell you what you wanna know, why are you asking me to help you? Let Stern help you."

O'Neil said, "Enough. We'll get the truth. We'll start by snooping around at the Royal Manhattan. How's that?"

"Do whatever you want. But right now, I gotta go to the bathroom before I shit all over the floor."

Two detectives walked Paolino to the bathroom door and unlatched his handcuffs. O'Neil, upbeat at the finding of the hotel invoice, phoned his desk sergeant at the 19th Precinct on East 67th Street and dispatched two cruisers to the Royal Manhattan. He said to the desk sergeant, "Tell whoever you're dispatching that I'll be on my way to meet them there."

Paolino was done in the bathroom, and the detectives re-hand-cuffed him. Outwardly, he upheld his composure, appearing as cool as a block of ice, alluding he hadn't a care in the world. Inward, well that was a different story; Paolino knew O'Neil would surprise Comfort in his room at the Royal Manhattan.

CHAPTER 41

O'Neil consigned Fradkin and Paolino to Agent Jack Goodwin and hastened to West 45th Street for the Royal Manhattan. There two uniformed officers and two detectives were waiting for him in the lobby by the check-in counter. "What's this all about, Lieutenant?" asked Detective Will Bannon, a body-building, hefty young stallion. His coworkers had nicknamed him "Bannon the Cannon."

"We have to search a room on the twelfth floor. Number 12022. It's likely that one of the Pierre's perps might be hiding in there."

"Got a warrant?"

"Don't need one. This is not a residence, and I have sufficient probable cause," O'Neil answered in a cocky way. He talked to the concierge of the hotel, who gave him directions to the manager's office, a spacious two-room workplace deep in the east wing of the lobby. The door was open, and O'Neil stepped through it. Three women were behind desks, two on the phone. The one who wasn't asked, "May I help you, sir?"

O'Neil pecked at the badge pinned to his lapel. "I'm Lieutenant Don O'Neil from the 19th Precinct. Where's the manager?"

The young lady was taken aback with this cop's downright rudeness. "The manager is on a long distance call. Can I be of assistance?"

"No. I need to speak with him. Tell him it's an urgent police matter."

"Uh . . . the manager is a woman, sir," the receptionist said modestly.

O'Neil couldn't have fathomed a female in such a position of responsibility. "Oh. Eh, then tell her I'm here."

The receptionist stepped away and knocked on the frosted glass door of the manager's inner office. And O'Neil muttered in a hush, "A woman as a hotel manager! What's this world coming to?"

Four to five minutes passed, O'Neil pacing and huffing as if he were an expectant father, and General Manager Celeste Hagen, a self-asserting, auburn-haired specimen in her early forties, presented herself and said, "I'm Celeste Hagen. What can I do for you?"

O'Neil wasn't prepared to see a perfectly proportioned, designer-dressed female in this function. "I'm, eh . . . Lieutenant Don O'Neil, and I . . ."

The three hotel employees covertly listening, Ms. Hagen interrupted him and in a smooth monotone voice asked, "May I *please* see your photo ID?"

He flaunted his gold badge. "This is my badge, Mrs. Hagen."

"It's *Miss* Hagen. And despite your shiny gold badge, I *do* need to see your police ID."

She had disarmed O'Neil, ruffling the lieutenant's masculinity and fending his arrogance, as it became noticeable that everyone in the room was reveling in the exchange. He took out his wallet and slipped out the photo ID Ms. Hagen looked at it and batted her curled eyelashes. "When was this picture taken, twenty-five years ago?"

"Eh, no. The department's policy is for all personnel to take new photos yearly," O'Neil said defensively, his voice cowed. "Why do you ask?"

"Because the face in this picture looks like it could be that of your grandson." Ms. Hagen, sharp and witty, had not only clipped the Lieutenant's air of grandeur, but also humiliated him.

When she had had enough fun, she did coordinate for an assistant manager to accompany O'Neil and his underlings to room 12022. They boarded the elevator for the twelfth floor, and Ms. Hagen's aide, using a staff key, unlocked the door. Bannon the Cannon, his muscular biceps skintight beneath the sleeves of his blue polyester jacket, twisted the brass knob, and his leg, strong as a steel ram, kicked the door open. He and the other brawny two-hundred-and-fifty-pounders charged in with the mass of four bulls, arms outstretched, revolvers aimed ahead. O'Neil, not as husky and the oldest on his squad, was the tail of this line. Bobby Comfort, lying on the sofa, feet up on a hassock, was multitasking, watching television with one eye and scanning the *New York Times*. On hearing the loud battering and seeing the door swing open, practically dislodging from the hinges, Comfort sprang off the couch, arms down and rigid, hands balled into fists, his body instantly taut.

O'Neil yelled, *"FREEEEEZE!!! Hands up."*

He and his backup crowded Comfort, Bannon manacling his wrists. The lieutenant patted him down and removed the wallet from his rear pants pocket. Scouring the side pocket, O'Neil found three four-carat emeralds. "What do we have here?" He held one of the emeralds between his thumb and forefinger and raised it up to the light in the window. He stared at it, twisting it this way and that way. "These are mighty fine gems, Mr. Comfort. Guess they belong to the Pierre's guests, eh?"

"Wishful thinking," Comfort said. "Keep dreaming."

The lieutenant gave the emeralds to Bannon. "Put them in a plastic bag. The DA will love to see those." O'Neil then rifled through Comfort's billfold and smiled wickedly as he saw his New York State driver's license. "Well, well, well. What're you know, the slippery Bobby Comfort from Rochester. The famous jewel thief. You did look familiar. But I thought they locked you up a couple of years ago and put you on ice for a long time."

"Yeah, I remember that," Bannon said.

"But this time, Mr. Comfort, you ain't slipping away. We got you good," O'Neil gloated. "Don't we, Detective Bannon?"

Bannon the Cannon had no clue what O'Neil had on Comfort, and answered not too convincingly, "Guess so."

Comfort, his heart palpitating, saw the lieutenant rank on O'Neil's nametag and said in a forced calmness, "You got me good? What *exactly* do you have on me, Lieutenant?"

"We know you and your gang did the Pierre holdup."

"Oh, yes. The only thing I did was to read about it in the papers. What proof you have I did it, Lieutenant? And may I please sit?"

O'Neil placed his palm on Comfort's chest and pushed him into the sofa. "Sure you can sit. Be my guest. As far as evidence, we got plenty of that."

Comfort was looking up at the standing cops. "Such as what?"

In a stab at coercing him into confessing, O'Neil rocked his head as if he were about to bullet-point a lengthy list of witnesses and evidence. He clapped his hands once. "Number one," the lieutenant began, counting, "many of the hostages said they're sure they'll pick you out in a lineup. Number two, you left fingerprints behind. And three, one of your cohorts has given you up." O'Neil gazed at Comfort to read his reaction, but none came forth. "You think we need more than that to send you away for thirty years?"

"I'd like to have a cigarette, please," Comfort said.

"Unshackle him," O'Neil said to Bannon.

Now unfettered, Comfort asked, "Anybody got a cigarette?"

O'Neil gave him one and flicked a lighter. Comfort inhaled deeply and looked at the floor, thinking in silence. He saw through O'Neil's deceptions and contrivances, and understood clearly that most of his claims were outright lies. But he knew something must've gone wrong at the Summit; how else would the police have known he was staying at the Royal Manhattan? Comfort let out a fog of smoke and studied O'Neil's thoughts. "Tell me Lieutenant—not that I'm admitting to anything—but who supposedly ratted me out?"

O'Neil glanced at the others. "Should we tell him? Well, why not?" he said, answering his own question. "How about Dom Paolino?" And he smiled at Comfort in a way to mean he had more compelling testimonies. "You do know Mr. Paolino, right? He happens to be from Rochester, too. What a coincidence!"

At the mention of Dom Paolino's name, a quake set off in the pit of Comfort's stomach, a shot of blood heating his temples. *Could Paolino have confessed to attempting to sell a handful of gems from the Pierre?*

Unlikely.

Assuming it was true that Paolino had been arrested, Comfort deduced, he, Paolino, was not in possession of incriminating items; the loose diamonds in his briefcase couldn't be attributed to the Pierre theft or any outstanding robbery case. Furthermore, he was not a greenhorn petty thief. Dom Paolino—Comfort's longtime, faithful friend and godfather to his child—was a streetwise, leather-skinned wheeler-dealer unafraid of a weekend confinement in the county jail—a worst-case scenario. Because O'Neil and his muscle-bound but brainless detectives couldn't possibly have been armed with evidence to uphold an indictment, the investigators would've had to release Paolino within seventy-two hours. Another flaw in the lieutenant's accusation was the fact that he did not mention Sammy Nalo, nor any of the other gunmen. If Paolino had cracked and confessed, he would've revealed not only Comfort's name but Nalo's as well.

The same theory applied to the possibility that Bert Stern also had been ensnared by O'Neil or the FBI. In addition to Comfort, Stern would've named Nalo. And if the appraiser had been thrown into the mix, he was harmless; the poor man was in the dark about the Pierre siege and, for that matter, did not know Comfort even existed, thus he was not a liability.

In respect to fingerprints, this was a figment of the lieutenant's imagination; Comfort and his robbers had worn gloves throughout the robbery. Lastly, O'Neil's assertions in respect to the hostages nailing him in a lineup, too, were improbable. Comfort did not directly handle the captives, and they never had a clear glimpse of him. Any time he had stepped foot into the alcove, they were sitting on the floor facing the walls.

Those deliberations funneled down to one certainty: O'Neil had lied to try to railroad Comfort into an admission. Although it was probable that Roland or Towson were undercover agents, or informants, and that Paolino, Stern, and Fradkin might've been arrested. If so, Comfort would bet the farm that Paolino hadn't folded under pressure. As for Stern, he was clueless about the Pierre. And though he *surmised* Comfort and Nalo were handling stolen jewelry, he couldn't shed light on their affairs. And Fradkin, he didn't know anything about the robbery or who was behind it. In conclusion, Comfort concluded that O'Neil did not have a prosecutable case.

O'Neil smirked as if he had conquered Comfort. "Now, are you ready to make any statements, Mr. Comfort?"

Comfort breathed in, his jitters unwinding. "I do wanna make a statement. I want to exercise my right to call a lawyer."

Bannon laughed in mock flabbergast. *Exercise my right to call a lawyer!* "Sounds like you know big words, Mr. Comfort. You must've went to college."

"I *did* go to college," Comfort said. "But I doubt you ever got out of kindergarten. 'Cause if you did, you wouldn't have said, 'went to college'. The correct grammar is *gone to college*. You sound like you're well-read but on the toilet."

O'Neil and his jesters leered in amusement, though Bannon the Cannon fell into embarrassed silence, twitching the knot of his cheap, blue tie.

"I think we should smack the shit out of this perp and show him what time it is," said one of the Robocops, smacking his left palm with the right fist.

"Yeah, maybe that's what Professor Comfort needs, some cuts and bruises," O'Neil answered in accord.

Bannon, reeling in the humiliation, leaped at the opportunity to even the score with the much shorter, lighter Comfort. The detective charged forward and seized him by the shirt collar, tugging crazily and ripping off two of his shirt buttons. "Go ahead, rip off my clothes," Comfort said, his face reddening. "Get your fun in now because my lawyer's going to file charges against you assholes."

A sudden anger rearranged Bannon's look, and his coworkers cringed, knowing that Comfort, "a tough customer," could place their jobs at risk. They parted the two men, and the fracas quieted, everybody breathing heavily. Bannon, as if he'd been in a street fight, brushed the sleeves of his gray jacket.

Resigned that Comfort would not incriminate himself, O'Neil said snappishly, "Bannon, cuff this wiseass and read him his rights."

Comfort, his pulse simmering, hair tousled, smiled teasingly, and he placed his hands side by side. O'Neil and his compatriots, clinging to Bobby Comfort's arms, paraded him through the lobby of the Royal Manhattan, people staring curiously. The bruiser detectives squeezed Comfort into the back of O'Neil's black unmarked vehicle and raced off to the 19th Precinct. At the station house, Bannon and a uniformed cop stripped the prisoner of his personal belongings, wallet, money, belt, etc. They confined him in a brightly lit, airless interview pen, locked the door, and left him there. In the center of that room stood a gray metal table and four matching chairs, outdated furnishings that the NYPD must've inherited from Tammany Hall when it ceased to exist in 1967. This interrogation pen had no windows, though it did have an odor of decades of cigarette smoke, and depressing, gray cinderblock walls.

A half hour or so later, Comfort estimated, though he didn't know exactly—in the booking process they had taken his watch— the interview pen door lock clanked and Bannon and O'Neil walked in. A hot coffee cup in hand, a cigarette on the side of his mouth, Bannon stood feet apart in a commanding stance. "Mr. Comfort, you're gonna have to fess up to your crimes. I mean, be smart. Make it easy on yourself."

"I *am* smart. As for you, it's not just education you don't have," Comfort commented, "You have no manners either. You come in here with a cigarette in your mouth, and I would've thought you were about to offer me one. Fat chance! What was I thinking?" He grunted through his nose and taunted Bannon, "My father taught me an old Italian expression. It goes like this: if you have a dumb son, the only thing you can do is to let him be a cop." Comfort had touched a nerve; his insult had stung the two policemen's self-image.

O'Neil, arms across his chest, glared disdainfully at the prisoner. "Listen to me, Mr. Comfort, 'cause I'm gonna *tell you* an old Irish saying: if you have a wiseass for a son, slap the son of a bitch's balls until he screams like a queer who's gotten his dick stuck in a beehive."

Comfort could've ping-ponged with his witty quips, easily out-foxing the interrogators. But not knowing what had *really* happened to Paolino and Stern, he was in no mood for verbal exchanges. Of greater concern, where is Nalo? Was he in custody as well? And even more worrisome, could the FBI or the NYPD have, somehow, tracked down Al Green and confiscated the satchel he was safe-guarding? These possibilities were perturbing, and Comfort knew he had to make contact with the outside world.

CHAPTER 42

Eleven hours had passed since the interrogation began, and O'Neil and Bannon, both continually filling the constricting interview pen with cigarette smoke, finally understood two facts: 1) Bobby Comfort was exceptionally smart: 2) Catholic priests would stop molesting children before he'd answer any questions without the presence of his attorney. The eight-by-ten-foot room was clouded with an oxygen-siphoning haze, and Comfort faked a coughing spell. "Look, I'm not saying another word. Now either book me or cut me loose." Another coughing fit, and he said gaspingly, "I . . . I have emphysema, and if . . . I pass out, my lawyer is gonna hold you two accountable." The emphysema ploy was Comfort's invention to reverse the tide and back Lieutenant O'Neil on the defense. "I'll sue the city *and* you personally."

At that, Bannon winced. O'Neil, less demonstrative at the legal threat, though visibly disturbed at the thought of a lawsuit, nodded for three to four drawn-out seconds in acceptance of reverting to the prescribed NYPD interviewing guidelines. The second attempt to badger Comfort into submission had been fruitless, and the lieutenant ordered Comfort relocated to a holding cell. O'Neil hadn't yet officially charged him and thought it best to first consult with the Manhattan district attorney.

"*Why* do you have to check with the DA before you book me? And when am I getting to make my entitled phone call?" Comfort said in indication that he knew the ins and outs of the law.

Instead of answering, O'Neil said, "I have to put the handcuffs on before we move you to the holding pen." And he secured the shackles. "You can make your phone call in about an hour."

Comfort settled into his cell, a six-by-eight-foot pen, and mired in a spool of anxiety waited to be granted his right to phone his wife, though he wasn't looking forward to that confrontation. He sat on the wooden bunk that was bolted to the one-quarter-inch steel lining of the wall and lowered his head into his hands. Six or seven minutes of sulking in misery, and he stiffened into an erect posture. He thought in wonderment, looking out through the bars of the cell door. It had dawned on Comfort that if Paolino or Stern or anyone else had "ratted him out," O'Neil would've decidedly charged him for, at very least, possession of stolen property without consulting with the district attorney. But whenever an investigator believes a suspect is culpable and detains him in the absence of probable cause, it is the prosecutor who determines whether to consider indicting or releasing the prisoner—the reason why O'Neil hadn't booked Comfort. This was solace to Comfort, and for now all he could do was to recoil into the haven of steadfast denial and retain an attorney. The rest, he trusted, ought to straighten itself out in due course.

Total quietness had fallen in the holding pen, and the ever-present buzzing of the fluorescent light fixture had lulled Comfort into complacency. The door lock jangled, and three new officers grouped into the cell, hovering over the seated inmate. He looked at the cops, and one said impolitely, "All right, whatever your name is. You're gettin' your phone call. Let's go."

The three policemen stepped back as if Comfort were a biting cannibal and led him to a narrow hallway and into the prisoners' processing room. "Use that line on that desk over there," said the rough-edged cop, indicating a wooden desk on which was an old-fashioned rotary phone.

As his custodians surrounded him, Comfort frowned at the three, contempt in his look. "I need some privacy. You mind?"

One of the cops said, "This time, and only this time, we'll let you have it your way. We'll be right outside in the hallway. You got ten minutes."

"I'll take whatever time I need," was Comfort's incisive come-back. "And close the door. You don't need to be listening."

As the door shut, Comfort was at peace, alone without the hounds barking at him. He dragged a splintery chair under him and closer to the table, on which scores of interviewees before him had carved graffiti: *Mike Hunt loves Jeanie Cumminghole . . . Tim fucked Lynn. Cops are pigs . . . Mayor Lindsey is a faggot . . . A queen deserves a king-size dick.* Comfort couldn't help but laugh. He looked at the black rotary phone for a long while and slumped over the tabletop in a whir of thoughts. What would he tell Millie? As Comfort compiled the words in his head, he stuck his index finger in one of the dial's numbered holes and began dialing.

"Hello," Millie's voice, frail and low, came into her husband's ear. At that time, telephones did not have caller ID, though she had "a hunch" it was Bobby. But a murmur in her mind was ringing bad tidings about to thunder into the receiver.

"Millie, it's me," he said in a chirpy voice.

"What's wrong, Bobby?"

Comfort asked, "Who says anything is wrong?"

"I know something is wrong. I just know it."

"I got arrested, Millie." Now it was Millie's sobs and not her velvety voice ramming into his ears. Comfort gulped hard. "But honey, they got nothing on me. They're just fishing trying to break me down. And like I said, they got nothing, baby. Honest."

Millie's bawling spurted a hail of tears, and he could feel her anguish. It pained him. "Everything's gonna be all right. Meantime, get ahold of my sister and tell her to come see me as soon as they let her. Right now, I'm at the 19th Precinct in Manhattan, but I don't know where they're gonna take me."

"Oh, Bobby . . . This is what I was afraid of. Now what?" She couldn't stifle her weeping, saliva bubbling on her lips.

"Baby, they haven't booked me yet, and guess what? They may not because they really don't have a damn thing to charge me with. But if these miserable cops do book me, make sure my sister comes to see me as soon as possible." He paused, hoping she'd compose herself. "No need to tell Nicole anything. This . . . this whole thing will go away. Look, they may let me go tonight . . . if they don't book me. And even if they do, it won't stick. I'm telling you . . ."

"Oh, Bobby, shut up. You always make everything sound hunky-dory." Millie wiped her eyes on her sweater sleeve. "What am I gonna tell Nicole? She's been waiting for you. Oh, this is terrible." More sniveling. "I feel like turning my back on you, and . . . and maybe . . . Nicole and I should move on with our lives."

A throb jolted Comfort's chest as if that last sentence had stabbed him through the heart. "Don't talk stupid, honey. And do me a favor, stop crying."

"I'm tired of living in fear day to day, Bobby. I'm tired of constantly agonizing that you might not come home or that you'll get killed in a robbery. I'm tired!" And Millie slammed down the receiver.

Comfort's eyes pooled; he held the phone receiver at eye level as if he were waiting for it to speak and console him.

The door opened with force, and Lieutenant O'Neil tramped in as though he had this investigation organized and contained, a suited black man by his side. The lieutenant bent into Comfort, the phone still in his hand. O'Neil nodded toward the African American, whose gray wool suit was of slightly better quality than the standard NYPD detectives' off-the-rack outfits. "Mr. Comfort, this is Assistant District Attorney Doug Pope, and he's gonna call the next shot." He regarded ADA Pope, short and mid-height, in his thirties. "Mr. Pope, please have a seat." O'Neil then jerked his chin in Comfort's direction. "This is one of the suspects. His name is Robert Comfort, a known jewel thief."

"Known to whom?" Comfort griped.

ADA Pope inserted a hand into his jacket's pocket, took out a calling card, and gave it to him. "Mr. Comfort, keep that in case you or your attorney need to talk to me."

Comfort looked at the card with indifference. "I don't have anything to tell you, Mr. Pope, so why would I want to talk to you? What I can tell you is that I've been kept here for many, many hours, accused of this and that less any foundation. I've been roughed up by a couple of dumb cops, and I haven't been charged of any crimes. So why are you still keeping me in this smelly chicken coop?"

Pope tilted his head and smiled, revealing fairly white teeth. "That's why I'm here, you see. I've reviewed Lieutenant O'Neil's paperwork and concluded that we have sufficient grounds to indict you for possession of stolen property, and most likely for robbery."

"What robbery?" Comfort asked, a rushing wave of warm blood heating his scalp.

Pope tied shut the manila envelope he had in front of him and looked straight at the presumed thief. "The Pierre Hotel."

CHAPTER 43

The day it had been reported, the assault on the Pierre tempted the interest of the FBI and the NYPD, and buttoning it to closure became the joint effort of these two agencies. Federal agents and New York City detectives incessantly questioned Paolino, Stern, and Fradkin. These last two were older and feeble; it was clear neither had the fiber of an intrepid gunman, and O'Neil eliminated the horror-stricken Stern and Fradkin as accessories. Paolino was a different animal. He had ignored the interrogations, and as a veteran racketeer took shelter in his right to legal counsel. And unable to extract any information, ADA Pope arraigned the relatively unknown Paolino for possession of stolen property. As for Comfort, a much bigger fish, *and* the presupposed Pierre organizer, Pope was contemplating charges of robbery in the first degree—a Class A violent felony carrying a mandatory twenty-year sentence. But could the ebony-skinned African American prosecutor muster material evidence or testimonies of credible sources to cement such a grave charge?

In the interim, daylight was giving way to the January late-afternoon nightfall, and Pope remanded Comfort to the Manhattan

House of Detention, known as the Tombs, a fitting description. White and Centre Streets in downtown New York bounded this dour, dungeon-like jailhouse. It was connected through darkish, dank tunnels to the 100 Centre Street court complex, a multiplex of thirty-three-story buildings flanked by the frenzied Chinatown district and the Federal Plaza government facilities. Four blocks to the north were the colorful, never-dormant SoHo and Little Italy sections of lower Manhattan. Amid these tourist-luring landmarks and magnificent edifices, the Manhattan House of Detention was not reflective of the graveness of its subterranean level. On the contrary, the exterior facade merged seamlessly with the majestic architecture of the vicinity. But confinement in that jailhouse sent an inmate into a resignation of doom.

Bobby Comfort was weathering his detention at the noisy, smelly, and perilous Tombs, an interim jail for criminals of all degrees, varying from the harmless pot dealer to the homicidal psychopath, who were either awaiting trial or sentencing. But the worse part of Comfort's predicament were those answers he so badly craved to know. He was in the dark, segregated from the rest of the world, and he'd give his right arm to learn what Paolino might've told the detectives, if anything at all. Could it be true that his old, trusted friend did give him up? And what about Nalo? Did he run for the hills, or was he even aware of these latest developments? Or did O'Neil and the FBI collar him as well? And last but not least, what became of Al Green and the satchel of jewels? Did he abscond, or was he also apprehended? And wouldn't it be a damn shame if O'Neil's hounds had found those gems wherever Green had stashed them?

A bombardment of thoughts were cascading in Comfort's mind; a deluge of questions and a drought of answers.

What was he to do? Nothing for now. He had to engage a lawyer who would do some digging and legwork that might shed light on where matters stood. Hopefully, some answers might come tomorrow. At the moment, it was six o'clock in the evening, and an ear-piercing announcement booming through the prison PA system disrupted Comfort's concentration. "On the chow, on the chow. Move it, on the chow." This was penitentiary slang for supper time at the mess hall, and the inmates, those who had an appetite for meals that would disgust even sewer rats, were allowed six minutes to walk there. Comfort chose to skip chow, food that looked and smelled as if it were cooked in a dog food factory. Instead, he lay on the hard bed in the cell and covered his eyes with the right forearm, resigned to wait for any news that might surface tomorrow.

That same night, FBI Agent Matt Hammer, square-jawed and tirelessly energetic, was leaning on a gray filing cabinet perusing through a file related to the 1970 Sophia Loren robbery, a storming that took place in her suite at the Hampshire House hotel in Manhattan. It was late in the day, and only a handful of employees were at the FBI Third Avenue office. The ever-clacking typewriters, the humming Telex machines, and the commotion of the staff's pattering feet had waned, peacefulness descending. At this hour, it was conducive for Hammer to pore over that file without disturbances or distractions. He, a tall, svelte masculine type, brown hair and a matching brown mustache, was at his work station, feet up on the desktop, sipping hot green tea. This peaceful hour, though, was shaken when Hammer overheard two agents who were conferring about the Pierre status mention a "Sammy the Arab" as a person of interest. An informant had leaked to Hammer's colleagues that this Sammy, a person unknown to law enforcement, had been, along with "a guy from Rochester," one of the gunmen in the Loren robbery. *A guy from Rochester?* Trusting the informant, those agents had inferred that Bobby Comfort, whom they knew was now in custody, had to be this person from Rochester, and he and Sammy the Arab must've had a hand in the Pierre.

"Sammy the Arab!" Hammer had come across this nickname when he was first probing the holdup of the buxom Italian film star. And this Sammy, whoever he might be, was Hammer's prime suspect, and now also a target of his colleagues. For the past fifteen months, Hammer had been combing all the corners of the city and the Bureau's database for that obscure man only known as Sammy the Arab. More deflating, the FBI's prized informants, who could usually link a criminal's street handle to a full name, hadn't been helpful either. And just as Hammer, from sheer frustration, was ready to bury the actress's file among the cold cases, a theory lighted in his mind; the phantom Sammy, whom the informant believed him to be a Turk, might've been the choreographer of the Loren ambush and the Pierre stunt as well. "He had to be," Hammer garbled unconsciously. "It could've only been him."

Sammy the Arab, less a surname or a date of birth, wasn't sufficient data to search FBI records for his true identity. And a grimmer fact: had the authorities recovered fingerprints, such a finding wouldn't have been inconsequential; Sammy had never been arrested or processed for mug shots and fingerprinting. No police archive photos, no prints, and no prior record. Where would Agent Hammer begin his hunt for Sammy the Arab?

CHAPTER 44

T he FBI and the NYPD, for logistical reasons, had been coupled
for the Pierre investigation, the kind of case law enforcement
officials longed to be at the center of, though both agencies
despised collaborating with one another. The bickering never
ended. But Hammer stayed on track and checked in with the agents
in charge of the Pierre for fact-sharing and gathering intelligence.

"I should be involved in this case. I can be of help, and I believe
I'm halfway to pinpointing one of the perps, who will, I'm hoping,
lead us to the others," Agent Hammer said with poise.

"By all means, Ed. Sounds like you've laid down the ground
work on the Loren robbery. And who knows, your case and ours
may have common perps," Agent John Masters said, who at times
partnered with Hammer on various investigations.

Hammer briefed Masters on the information he had harvested
about Sammy the Arab, and Masters passed it on to Lieutenant
O'Neil, who voiced a grievance, protesting the FBI's meddling in
the Pierre. Since the beginning of time, the FBI used any means not
to pool resources with the NYPD, which in the early seventies was
awash in scandals and rampant corruption. The Federal Bureau of

Investigation, a clergy of purists who are labeled as "untouchables," at that time deemed it degrading *and* were indignant to work side by side with the prideless, unscrupulous New York City police force, whose taint of dishonesty was breeding within all ranks of the department. The briberies festered at the bottom, beginning with the low-grade patrolmen and trickling up to the top, including the precinct captains. And this wasn't just a runaway rumor. The NYPD was under fire from the Knapp Commission, a committee appointed to conduct an inquisition into condemning allegations of widespread corruption.

In 1972, the Knapp Commission was still ongoing, and the FBI loathed appearing on television news programs and newspaper front pages alongside the incorrigible, publicity-mongering NYPD officials. Nonetheless, Agents Hammer and Masters maintained their course, keeping an open mind that, perhaps, Lieutenant O'Neil and his underlings hadn't been contaminated by the decaying of integrity. Overly preoccupied by his appearances on the Knapp Commission hearings, O'Neil delegated two subordinates, George Bermudez and Edward Fitzgibbons, as assistants to the FBI. Hence, the four-man posse of Agents Matt Hammer and John Masters and Detectives Bermudez and Fitzgibbons was thrown together to flush out Sammy the Arab and whoever else had performed in the Pierre thriller.

Hammer, a lawman whose morals and scruples were as limpid as crystal, construed the fast-talking, know-it-all Detective George Bermudez as a hot-winded charlatan, traits that were obnoxious but harmless. He was stout, and had dusky skin and frizzy hair that was beginning to gray, and spoke in the universally recognizable New York twang. But that was not what had been bothering Hammer. He couldn't quite read Bermudez; was he honest or did he lean on the side of fraud and dishonesty? "John, I hope we didn't get paired off with a couple of bad apples."

"I don't know, Ed. I'd rather reserve judgment. In light of this ongoing Knapp Commission turmoil, the last thing we want to do is start a war between us and a whole bunch of these wild New York

City cops." John Masters was a gentlemanly chap, who whenever in doubt gave precedence to diplomacy over premature assumptions.

"You're right," Hammer said. "Meantime, let's get Bermudez and Fitzgibbons here now—the sooner the better—so we can lay out a map and start looking for our friend Sammy before he blows town—if he hasn't already done so."

That afternoon, Bermudez and Fitzgibbons, in a conference room at the Manhattan FBI office, were facing Hammer and Masters across a lofty, fifteen-foot cherry wood table. In a corner of the twenty-foot-by-twenty-foot room was an American flag atop which an elaborately sculpted, gold-leafed eagle held its perch. Beside it stood a cabinet/refrigerator and a brewing pot, a whiff of stale coffee stemming from it. On a wall hung a black-and-white portrait photo of FBI Director J. Edgar Hoover, whose eyes seemed as though he were presiding at this conference. Following the perfunctory introductions and handshakes, Hammer didn't hesitate to set forth his conditions and said to the two detectives, "For the record, I want to be clear how this operation will be conducted." He paused and looked at Bermudez and Fitzgibbons in a way to underline the meaning of his instructions. "First and foremost, this is the FBI's investigation, and you two are not to make a move without first checking with Agent Masters and I." He glanced at Masters and reverted back to the detectives. "Is that clear, Detective Bermudez and Detective Fitzgibbons?"

"Call me Fitz," said Fitzgibbons.

"Yeah, you can call me George," Bermudez harmonized, a snide smirk budding on his large mouth.

"OKAAAY, Fitz and George," Hammer said condescendingly.

Bermudez was slouched in his chair, an arm dangling on the backrest, his salt-and-pepper hair teased into an Afro. "Do you guys have a plan?"

Masters sorted through a file. "A confidential informant . . ."

Without asking permission, Bermudez took the liberty to reach in his pocket for a cigarette and a plastic lighter. Masters looked as if he'd been violated and swayed his forefinger like a wiper blade. "No, no, no, George. We don't allow smoking in here."

"Oh, I didn't think you'd mind," Bermudez said.

Wrinkling his forehead, Hammer cut in tersely, "When you're on a detail with the FBI, do not assume anything, and don't take anything for granted. Are we clear on that?"

Bermudez and Fitz nodded passively as if they'd been scolded by the third grade teacher.

Masters moved on and said, "We believe that Sammy the Arab has a domicile, probably a roacher, on 45th Street in Hell's Kitchen. And that's where we should begin our footwork."

"What's a domicile?" Bermudez asked in utter bafflement.

Hammer remarked sardonically, "What did they teach you at the police academy, how to extort and take bribes?"

Masters gave Bermudez a look of annoyance. "A *domicile* is a personal residence, an apartment. And as I said, that's where we should start snooping."

"Oh!" Bermudez said. "For a minute I thought a *domicile* was a killer maniac."

Fitzgibbons, more reticent and less of a talker than Bermudez, opened his notepad, jotted a meaningless line of notes, and plowed on, "I think you're right. That should be our first stop. Do you have the building number?"

"Yes, we know precisely where the apartment building is." In the FBI modus operandi, Masters did not mention the complete address purposely to limit the disclosure of the relevant facts.

The agents, Masters driving, were rolling through the Broadway district, advancing westbound on 45th Street, the two detectives a few car lengths behind in an unmarked black Ford LTD. They were weaving to overtake slower traffic and the train of limousines parked in front of the theatres. As the two-car caravan neared Nalo's Hell's Kitchen pad, Hammer spotted someone walking briskly on the south side of the street who resembled Sammy, as he'd been described by the informant. The subject seemed to be wearing a poor-quality wig that could've been a swatch of a black rug. He was short, and strutted unevenly, and had swarthy, Arabic characteristics.

"That's definitely Sammy the Arab, all right!" Matt Hammer said animatedly. "What do you think, John?"

"Where? Who?"

Hammer pointed excitedly to the right side of the street. "That man over there. See him? Pull up to him and stop."

CHAPTER 45

I n haste, Masters steered close to the sidewalk, one wheel practically on it. He braked hard, and the car screeched to a tire-
squealing halt ten feet from where Sammy was walking, the smell
of burned rubber and blue smoke rising from under the car. In the
trailing automobile, Bermudez and Fitzgibbons had watched Master's haphazard maneuver, and Bermudez, who was driving, almost
rear-ended the agents' Ford LTD. He was momentarily stumped, but
his swift reflexes managed to stop less than a yard before crashing
into the FBI vehicle. Hammer and Masters were first to spring open
the doors and rush out toward Sammy. The two detectives quickly
understood why Masters and Hammer had made this unscheduled
stop, and they too joined the charge for their presumed quarry.

All four, Smith & Wesson snub-nose revolvers out in the open,
darted toward Sammy. "Get your hands up," yelled Hammer as
people scampered so as not to be in the way. The erratic driving
and the tire-squealing halt got the attention of the pedestrians who
were clumping on the northern sidewalk of 45th Street.

The perp shot his arms in the air. "What's going on? Jesus, what
did I do?!"

Bermudez and Fitzgibbons gripped Sammy's wrists, constrained, and handcuffed him. The clusters of onlookers were swelling, enjoying this show, which was unfolding on the busy intersection of 45th Street and Eighth Avenue where the original musical *Grease* was previewing at the Martin Beck Theatre.

"What's your name?" Hammer asked the bewildered man, whose eyes had locked into a stunned stare.

"Tony . . . Tony Giamanco."

"What's that, one of your aliases, Sammy? You look Middle Eastern. Are you Turkish?"

"Hell no. I'm Sicilian. Hey what is this? What did I do?"

"We'll ask the questions," Masters said in his FBI mode. "Where you live?"

"Astoria, Queens. Hey, who are you guys?" Giamanco asked.

"We're FBI," Hammer answered, indicating Masters and himself without introducing the NYPD detectives, as if they were merely lowly trainees. "Got any ID?"

"Yeah, in my left back pocket. I wanna know what this bullshit is about? I want a lawyer."

Everyone ignored Giamanco's cries, and Hammer told Fitzgibbons to go for his wallet. Fitz did and handed it to the FBI agent. Rifling through it, he found a driver's license issued to an Anthony J. Giamanco. And the DMV photo was clearly that of this poor bastard whom they'd just handcuffed in public view. Bermudez felt Giamanco's wig and tugged at it. But it wasn't a toupee; he happened to be blessed with dense, bushy hair.

"Shit!" Hammer and Masters realized they had mistaken Giamanco for Sammy the Arab. "Cut him loose," Masters said to Fitzgibbons.

They walked back to the unmarked cars, and the throng of people began thinning out, looking dissatisfied as if they had watched a suspenseful show, and the ending was anticlimactic.

"Gonna call my lawyer as soon as I get home," Mr. Giamanco shouted. "I'm . . . I'm gonna sue the city and all of you. Somebody's gonna pay me for whatchu done."

As Hammer was bending his tall frame to stoop into the automobile, he yelled back to Giamanco, "Tell your attorney the arresting officer was Detective George Bermudez from the midtown 19th Precinct." And he winked, a sneer on his lips.

Not amused, inside the Ford LTD Bermudez muttered, "Son of a bitch, Hammer. You lousy mick."

In the passenger's seat, Fitz put on an expression that said, *You didn't really say that, did you?* After two or three seconds, he reproved, "Watch it. I'm Irish, too, remember, you dumbass."

The two unmarked cars resumed the trip to 295 West 45th Street, Sammy the Arab's hideout. Masters and Bermudez remained at the wheel of their respective autos, and Hammer and Fitzgibbons walked inside the narrow, darkish hallway, an acrid odor of cooking onions in the air. They pinpointed the superintendent's apartment and rang the bell. A dwarf-like, hunchbacked man in his seventies opened the doors to see a pair of badges at face level. The super's brow protruded as though it was an awning over his eyes, and he blinked nervously as he spoke. "How can I help you?"

"I'm FBI Agent Hammer, and we're trying to find a Turkish individual whose first name is Sammy."

The super seemed relieved that these two black suits were not interested in him. "Oh yeah, that's Sammy Johnson up in 3B."

Johnson must've been one of Sammy's aliases, Hammer assumed as the deformed superintendent said, "The elevator is all the way down the hall on your right."

The ride in the small, rickety elevator was bumpy and squeaky, and Hammer was glad to step off it on the third floor. He knocked on apartment 3B, and the voice of a young woman in a Spanish accent said, "Who there?"

"FBI. We want to speak with the man who lives here," Hammer said.

"He no here."

"Please open the door. We have to ask you a few questions."

The door opened slightly, and she peeked her face out. "What you want?"

Fitzgibbons showed her his gold badge. "May we come in?"

She opened the door wider and waved in the two gents. She was thin and had long dark hair. Hammer asked her, "What's your name?" He saw her lips beginning to quiver. "Don't be frightened. It's not you we're looking for. So tell us your name."

"Ana Maria Lourdes Ortega."

That name sounds like that of a partnership. "When do you expect the man who rents this place? And what's his last name?"

She shook her head. "I no have his last name. He my girlfriend boyfriend. He say I can stay here when he no here."

"Who's your girlfriend?"

"Felicia Blanca. She Colombiana like me." Ana Maria Lourdes Ortega said, *She Colombiana like me* with great pride as though as a Colombian she couldn't be more privileged.

"You have a green card?" asked Fitzgibbons.

She looked down and covered her mouth, sobbing and shoulders shuddering. Hammer clenched his teeth and bore into Fitz. "Why did you ask her that? It's none of our business whether she's legal or not. We're not INS officials." He then said to the flustered girl, "Don't worry, we're not here to make trouble for you. Where does your girlfriend live?"

She wiped her eyes and glanced thankfully at Hammer. "Thank you. Uh, my girlfriend live a four blocks away." She uttered her friend's address, and Fitz wrote it into his notepad.

Felicia Blanca lived on 48th Street and Tenth Avenue. Hammer and Masters figured it'd be wise to take along the Spanish-speaking Bermudez, thinking he might be of comfort to Felicia. But the agents' concern was that the newspapers' evening editions had trumpeted Bobby Comfort's arrest in the headlines, and surely Sammy the Arab must've read about it. And why would he linger on in New York City, or for that matter the country? Hammer and Masters did not think he'd lounge in a topless bar waiting for the authorities to throw the net over him. Time was of the essence in tracking down Sammy.

The building where Felicia Blanca resided had no elevator, and Hammer and Bermudez climbed four flights to the fourth floor.

A Colombian woman in her twenties made-up crustily, her thighs fleshy, unbridled breasts sloshing *à la Colombiana*, opened the apartment door. She had on the same skimpy short-shorts and brief tank top she had performed in as a pole dancer. Her mouth instantly grew into a solicitous smile as if Hammer and Bermudez might be potential clients. She twirled the ends of her tinted shoulder-length hair, and in an overly friendly manner asked, "Who are you?" She had a thick Spanish accent and a thin vocabulary, a brown beauty mark on the right side of her neck.

A whiff of burning incense drifted from the studio apartment, and an array of ceramic statues of Catholic saints, portraits of Jesus, and lighted candles were everywhere. Bermudez, bedazzled by the tantalizing pole dancer, said in Spanish, "Are you Felicia Blanca?"

"No. Felicia's my roommate, and she working tonight."

"Who are you?"

"Lulu Munoz."

"Do you know a Sammy? He's Turkish," Bermudez asked, Hammer standing behind him.

"He's Felicia's *amor*."

"What's his last name?"

Lulu drew a blank gape. "I don't know."

"We need to talk with Felicia right away. Can you call her?"

"She no can talk on telephone when she work."

Bermudez translated for Hammer, who said, "Find out where Felicia is working."

This evening, Felicia Blanca was pole-dancing at the Circus Club, a "striptease joint" on Sunrise Highway in Valley Stream, Long Island. Braving the snarling eastbound traffic on the Long Island Expressway, the two pairs of investigators drove there in their automobiles. On entering the Circus Club, a boisterous, smoky "tittie joint," two black supersized bouncers stood vigil near the doorway, and to the FBI agents' flabbergast the male employees who handled the door fees and tended bar were Middle Eastern nationals. This was encouraging to Masters and Hammer. Perhaps Sammy the Arab might've been here, roosting in this hotbed of Arabs. Then

again, presuming that Sammy hadn't read the morning newspapers' headlines about Bobby Comfort's arrest, the evening television news programs were now airing it; and if by chance Sammy had seen any of them, he had surely fled.

NICK SACCO

Since the night of the robbery, I hadn't spoken to Comfort or Nalo. I had no reason to. I didn't even stay in touch with Frankos, Visconti, and Germaine because we all got lost somewhere away from the New York area. I for one had taken a hike and flew to Miami Beach not only to get away from the Pierre heat but to get some sun as well. I stayed at the Fontainebleau and never in my life did I see so many hookers in a hotel. But the real shocker was when the headlines in the Miami Herald *jumped out at me.*

A SUSPECT IN THE MANHATTAN

PIERRE HOTEL ROBBERY APPREHENDED

Naturally, it threw me for a loop, and from down there I couldn't find out anything else. Under no circumstances would we talk about things like this by telephone. The possibility of one of our phones being tapped was always there. And yes, I was shitting a brick, losing sleep that Comfort might rat us all out. But as much as I had been itching to know what was happening, until it all cooled down I sure as hell would not chance going anywhere near New York.

CHAPTER 46

The assistant manager at the Circus Club told Matt Hammer and John Masters that he did know of a regular here by the name of Sammy the Arab, and it was likely he might be here at this very moment. Tonight, the Circus was a full house of approximately 310 debased, horny rowdies, a hoard of chimpanzees in heat.

"Oh yeah," the manager said, snickering in the manner that said, *I know a secret you don't know.* "Sammy comes in and goes. A lot of times he waits 'til that one there dancing right now ends her gig, and he takes her wherever."

"Is her name Felicia Blanca?" Masters asked.

"Yep, that's her," said the obese, pear-shaped manager. "If you wanna talk to Felicia, she's about to end her last gig of the night." He let that hang a while, deciding whether to ask a question that maybe he shouldn't. "By the way, are you cops or something?"

"Something like that," Hammer answered. "Know Sammy's last name?"

"Nope. What kind of business are you guys in anyway?"

"The kind that's none of your business," Masters answered.

Rotating lights, yellow, red, white, blue, and green flounced from one end of the stage to the other, and a pinkish spotlight shone on Felicia. Her gyrations and provocative gestures that left nothing to the imagination were inciting thirty or forty male spectators who were sidling, or rather hugging the edges of the square stage, flinging dollar bills and hollering obscenities at the unabashed performer. Judging by the hypertensive body language of the roused crowd, these men's faces, laced with perspiration, were the picture of savage sexual hunger as they, so overly excited, pounced on the stage floor, tongues pitching at the dancer, whose body was her only asset. And under the hot lights, disco music was beating loudly, and the topless Felicia, *the Chiquita Latina*, thrust parts of her petite but well-endowed build in sync with the song's tempo. She was dancing to an Eddie Kendrick's tune: *Boogie Down . . . Boogie Down*, the catchy beat stirring the adrenaline, stoking the untamed libidos.

Fitzgibbons and Bermudez were at home in this atmosphere. Hammer and Masters, on the other hand, were repulsed. On the whole, FBI agents are academically educated and more polished than the typical NYPD detective. Bermudez had only mustered a GED certificate, though he blamed his lack of focus as a child and scholastic failure on not having known his biological father.

"Here's something interesting, Ed. It's a rarity for two Puerto Rican siblings to have the same father. When into a relationship, the minute the woman gets pregnant the man moves on. This is true. No joke," Masters imparted to Hammer.

Bemused, Hammer pursed his lips. "I didn't know that."

Masters moved in close to where Bermudez and Fitzgibbons were standing. The two seemed enraptured by the stage show. "Instead of getting your dicks hard over the pole dancer, scan the crowd for our target." He stepped back and spoke into Hammer's ear, "It's going to be a long night with these guys. I can't wait to get away from these two and their low-life mentalities."

"I hear you, John. I hear you," Hammer said.

The search for Sammy the Arab at the Circus Club was a futile exercise, but not all was lost. The quartet of lawmen was bringing the barely-of-legal-age Felicia Blanca to her Manhattan apartment for a change of more, relatively speaking, decent clothes—even when off-duty this class of ladies put on display lots of skin—and, who knew—she might lead them to Sammy. Felicia, too, was an illegal immigrant and had vowed to Masters and Hammer she'd help anyway she could. "I no want problem with Immigration."

Throughout the drive to New York City, Hammer asked Felicia, who was a bundle of nerves in the rear seat, a host of questions, beginning with, "What's Sammy's surname?"

"Surname?"

For a moment, Hammer had forgotten Felicia's limited English. "A last name."

"Oh, I no know. When we go out, he use new name."

Hammer could not understand how was it possible for these girls, who knew this Sammy, not to bother to ask for his last name? But for that element the answer was not a complicated one. The likes of Felicia were only interested in what they could siphon from a man addicted to women—dinners in fine restaurants, fur coats and jewelry, nightclub-hopping, and non-repayable loans—so who cared what Sammy's last name was? By the same token, Sammy wasn't interested in love affairs but only dalliances.

"What's your relationship with Sammy?"

She answered tentatively, "Oh, nothing. He take me to good restaurant or night club, you know."

"And what do *you* do for him," Masters asked coyly.

Hammer waved at Masters and said in a hush, "I'd lay off that, John. We don't want this girl to feel we're putting her on the spot." He swung behind him and asked Felicia, "Does Sammy have another place?"

A few moments of silence passed. "I . . . I know he got apartment on Long Island . . . his wife there." Felicia paused. "He got place in the Bronx too, but I there one time. I no remember the street."

"You don't know where in the Bronx?"

Felicia shook her head, fearing her helplessness might push Hammer and Masters to refer her and Lulu to the INS for a free flight back to Colombia.

Hammer discerned Felicia's apprehension and said, "It's all right. Take your time and think, and maybe something will come to mind. For instance, was the apartment near a landmark or something that you remember?"

"I . . . I think it was not far from that big place where you Americanos play with the ball and the bat."

"Yankee Stadium?" Hammer said in a higher octave. This could be the breakthrough to trap Sammy.

"Yes, yes, Jankee Stadiom."

"Yankee Stadium," Hammer repeated to ensure they both meant the same landmark. "Well, good. We'll take you to that area in the Bronx, and you may recognize the street."

"Can my roommate, Lulu, come too?" she asked timidly.

"If it makes you feel better, yes," Hammer answered.

When they entered Felicia Blanca's sparsely furnished studio apartment, Lulu looked perturbed as she saw her roommate in the company of four men. She towed Felicia by the arm into the bathroom. "*¿Porqué usted se volvió aquí con estos americanos? Usted sabe que no tengo gusto de estar alrededor de americanos.*" *Why did you bring these Americans here? You know I don't like to be around Americans.*

"*Tengo que cooperar con ellos, o bien pueden hacernos deportar,*" Felicia said fervently. *I have to cooperate with them, or else they can have us deported.* "*Nos llevarán al Bronx para buscar Sammy apartamento.*" *They'll take us to the Bronx to look for Sammy's apartment.*

"*¡Nosotros! ¿Por qué debo ir?*" complained Lulu. *Us! Why should I go?*

"*Porque quisiera que usted fuera con mí en caso de que suceda algo,*" answered Felicia. *Because I want you to go with me in case something happens.*

The two reappeared from the bathroom, and Lulu was totally against going on a chase for Felicia's boyfriend. She put her palms together in prayer. *"Oh, Dios mio!"* Oh, my God! And she made the sign of the cross.

Hammer and Masters were incredulous. Lulu, a prostitute, calculating and selfish, yet she was fanatically religious. And those saintly statues propped throughout apartment, the home of two lewd topless dancers, seemed . . . well the FBI agents couldn't quite define that mix. But why were they surprised? Ruthlessly violent Mexican drug traffickers are unwavering Catholics as well.

En route to the Bronx, Masters, Hammer, and the two girls were in the FBI car, the Colombian's cheap perfume stinging the agents' sense of smell. Bermudez and Fitzgibbons rode in the Ford LTD, and snowflakes, as if they were thousands of white butterflies, started swirling in the yellowish glow of the automobiles' headlights. At 161st, the two vehicles exited the Major Deegan Expressway, and the 140-foot-high, unmistakable top cornices of Yankee Stadium came into a faint view, the snow blurring that structure.

Felicia recognized one of the streets in proximity to the stadium, and her angst was heightening. She had never been in this predicament, acting as a police informant to arrest a friend, Sammy who had treated her royally, and had recently gifted her with a silver fox three-quarter length coat. And here she was in the rear seat of an FBI car about to seal his doom. *"Pobre Sammy . . . pobre Sammy."* Felicia murmured to herself. *Poor Sammy . . . Poor Sammy.* Even a whore could have a heart.

As they drove on, Hammer swiveled his neck backward and said, "Felicia, anything look familiar?"

"No," she said weakly, resting her head on the cold window, staring pensively. Then a thought struck her. "The street was like hill, and I remember the firemen house."

"You mean a firehouse?"

"Yes, firehouse."

The two-vehicle motorcade had been driving aimlessly, and in the Ford LTD Bermudez and Fitzgibbons had no idea where the FBI agents were taking this reconnaissance, if anywhere at all. The detectives were both chain-smokers, and the interior of the car smelled worse than a chimney. Bermudez saw the lead vehicle stop by the curb, and Hammer jumped out, covering his head with a newspaper, the storm intensifying. He trotted to the Ford LTD, sliding on the light coating of snow, and Fitzgibbons rolled down the window. "What's up?"

"Radio the local precinct and find out where the nearest fire station to Yankee Stadium is," Hammer said.

"Get in the car while we call in," Bermudez said.

Fitz radioed as told, and the fire station in question was four blocks north of Yankee Stadium. They drove to it and past it, but Felicia didn't see any familiar buildings on that street. She was becoming more agitated and increasingly difficult to understand. Lulu spoke even less English, and Masters parked to figure out what to do. Hammer said, "Bermudez should ride with us and be the interpreter."

"Good idea," said Masters.

Again, Hammer trudged back to the second car. "George, ride with us. We can't understand these girls."

Bermudez, happy to oblige, snuggled between the two sizzling Latinas.

They drove here and there, crossing Grand Concourse, then south to Walton Avenue, and right on 161st, halfway circling the stadium. Bermudez and the Colombians prattled on in an avalanche of Spanish, though the conversation was immaterial and bore no fruit. It was 12:45 A.M., and the snowfall had lessened. Hammer and Masters decided to abort the reconnoitering cruise and return to Manhattan. But the twisting and turning left and right, and east and west, had disoriented John Masters, and instead of heading west on 161st for the ramp to the Major Deegan, he swerved north on Anderson Avenue, a steep, hilly block. When they were on the lower end of the street, Felicia cried out, "There, there is!" She was tapping the car window, pointing at a six-story brick apartment building with dimly glowing sconces on either side of the entrance, and the numbers 832 etched at the peak of the archway: 832 Anderson Avenue. "Das it, das it!"

CHAPTER 47

They reversed direction and parked five hundred feet from 832 Anderson Avenue, presumably the address of Sammy the Arab's playpen and love nest.

Hammer said to Masters, "John, stay in the car with Lulu. George and I will take Felicia inside the building. Hopefully she can point out Sammy's apartment." He eyed Bermudez and said, "George, go tell Fitz to wait in the car and keep a lookout for anyone coming and going into the building."

Bermudez did so and jogged back to join Hammer and Felicia as they were entering the building. The snowfall had lessened, and a ceiling of low, pewter clouds had stalled in the stinging cold. Felicia was sniveling, and Bermudez comforted her, *"Calma de la estancia. Todo todo correcto." Stay calm. Everything will be all right.*

Two thirty-watt bulbs on the rusty wall sconces lighted the corridor, and you couldn't see past your nose, a permanent stench of cooking odors reeking. They stepped into the elevator and Felicia, now the one leading, pushed the fourth floor button. "I think is on four floor."

"¿Es usted seguro?" asked Bermudez. *Are you sure?*

"Si."

Sure of herself, she walked right to Sammy's door. "Das it." It was apartment 4E.

Quietly, they soft-stepped into the elevator and left the building. Outdoors, sloshing in the thin layer of snow, Hammer and Bermudez hustled Felicia into the FBI car. "We found Sammy's apartment, John. Meantime, keep her low. We don't want anybody seeing her here," Hammer said.

She crouched in the rear seat and laid her head on Lulu's lap, tears on her light brown cheeks. The improvised role as an FBI informant was overtaking her.

Hammer and Bermudez once again went into the building and located the superintendent's door. Bermudez knocked. A hefty, rugged woman answered, and bleary-eyed, sized up these late night callers. "What would make you wake me up in the middle of the night?" she asked in a German accent, curlers in her salt-and-pepper hair that decades ago might've been blonde.

Hammer showed her his badge. "FBI."

She glanced at it for three or four seconds, unsure of what she was seeing, and an instant later she was fully awake. "Should I be delighted?" she remarked, aloofness in her disposition. "What do you want?"

Hammer caught himself staring at the lady's padded, carbohydrate-fed face, which looked remarkably close to that of a Cabbage Patch Doll. "What's your name?"

"Wanda Rousch. I'm the super's wife. What could you possibly want at this time of night? For me to make you dinner?"

"We certainly didn't come here for schnapps and sauerbraten," Hammer jibed in a dead-pan stare as Bermudez bit his lip to stifle a laugh.

Not appreciating the racial slur, the wisecracking Mrs. Rousch crimped her lips and huffed at the intruders.

Her husband, a shorter, much smaller man, whose white hair sprung in every direction, peeked inquisitively from behind her. "I'm Mr. Rousch. What can I do for you? This is an ungodly hour.

You better have a good reason for waking us up." He, too, spoke in a Teutonic cadence. "C'mon in. I don't want you to wake up the rest of my tenants."

Inside the Rousches' foyer, an enduring smell of fried schnitzels greasing the air, Hammer described Sammy the Arab to the German couple, and the husband said, "Sounds like you're looking for Lenny Jameson. He's in apartment 4E. I don't know why the law wants him, but it's none of my business."

"You're right, it is none of your business," said Matt Hammer. "We're putting you on notice that we may make an arrest here."

The miniature German shrugged as if to say *Do what you want.*

Suddenly, as if something had spooked Mrs. Rousch, she touched the tip of her nose. "Shhhh. I heard the front door in the hallway slam shut." She ran to a window, parted the venetian blinds, and peered out onto the sidewalk. She pointed down at the floor and said in hush, "Mr. Jameson, there he is! Just walked outside, and he's under this window."

Bermudez hastened to the window and spied through the blinds. Though the street lamps did not provide much light, the snow on the ground brightened the night, and he could see a silhouette that sketched Sammy's figure as represented by the FBI informant. "Yeah, that could be him."

In the car, John Masters, too, spotted the same person and said, "You girls get down. Get down below the car windows!"

Fitzgibbons also saw that party. But where he was parked a few hundred feet down the hill and looking through the crust of ice that had frozen on the windshield, his line of sight was compromised. He took a pull of nicotine and fixed his stare on the entryway of 832 Anderson Avenue. In less than ten seconds, he watched Hammer and Bermudez hurrying out onto the sidewalk.

The obscure Lenny Jameson must've heard Hammer and Bermudez's footsteps. *Who's prowling in this neighborhood at one-thirty on a snowy January night?* Without looking behind him, he quickened his pace. He was carrying a black duffel bag under his arm, and fifty feet farther ditched it under a blue panel van. Lenny Jameson changed direction and hurried west toward Jerome Avenue, Hammer trailing him, maintaining an unsuspecting distance, though at 2:00 A.M. that was impossible on this desolate block. Bermudez, nearly falling to his knees on the slippery snow, ran to the van, knelt by the curb, and lugged the duffel bag out from under it. He unzipped the bag and saw what in the dark appeared to be burglar tools, or at least utensils that could've been used to pry a locked door, or a safe deposit box. This was the "probable cause" to take into custody this Lenny Jameson, or whoever he was. Hugging the bag onto his chest and striding up to Hammer, Bermudez whispered, "Look what he threw under that van over there."

Hammer looked inside the duffel bag and rocked his head to say, *I found what I needed.* "This is all we need to arrest this guy and find out who he really is. Let's go."

Pistols in hand, they picked up their trot so to gain on Jameson, who heard the two pairs of running feet sloshing in the fresh snow. He glanced behind him and made a split-second eye contact with whom he instantly presumed to be his pursuers. Hammer, his right arm out stiffly, raised his revolver at him. "FBI. Sammy, stop and slowly take your hands out of your pockets."

Jameson turned to face the chasers and put up his arms. "My name is not Sammy. It's Tony Lavella."

"That's funny," Bermudez said. "The super of your building told us your name is Lenny Jameson."

He held his gun at Jameson, or Lavella, or Sammy, as Hammer swiftly handcuffed and patted him down. "Or at least that's what you told your super."

"I don't know what you're talkin' about. My name is Tony Lavella, and I live in Manhattan. I came here to see a friend," he said, the man's composure even-tempered, without changes in his inhalations, eyes unblinking and gazing calmly. "Are you goin' to arrest me? If so, you got a warrant?"

"We don't need a warrant to arrest you on a public street. But we know for sure your first name is Sammy, and they call you 'Sammy the Arab.' And we're pretty sure you did the Pierre robbery,"

Hammer chanced, watching for changes in the suspect's self-control. None. "He's unarmed," he said to Bermudez.

Tony Lavella preserved his coolness, a self-control that to Hammer seemed almost as if it were an inherent serenity. Bermudez said, "C'mon, Sammy, don't play stupid games. We already got your pal Comfort, and he gave you up."

Lavella blinked for the first time, though he rationalized that, if Bobby Comfort had informed on him, which he didn't believe he'd ever do, these cops would've known his full name rather than guessing who he really was. But they did know he was not Tony Lavella or Lenny Jameson. "I don't know a Comfort."

One of the personal artifacts Hammer had found when he went through his pockets had been a wallet. In it was a Pennsylvania drivers' license in the name of Leon Tate, whose descriptions were: Sex: Male; Height: 5' 4"; Eyes: Black. In addition, Lavella was wearing a black, curly wig, and lifts in his shoes because he seemed slightly taller than 5' 4".

"And what do we have here," Hammer said derisively. "Another alias, and this one is Leon Tate." He gave the driver's license to Bermudez for him to see.

"Well, let's see, you go by Lenny Jameson, Tony Lavella, Leon Tate, and Sammy the Arab. It looks like you change names more often than you change underwear," Bermudez taunted, looking over the license for clues that it might've been a forgery. "So which one are you?"

"If this guy, Comfort, or whoever he is, ratted me out, then you should know who I am. Right?" Lavella said.

This was a solid jab, and Hammer and Bermudez were beginning to realize that this individual, if he was Sammy the Arab, was a tough customer. "Sammy, it's no use trying to hide the facts. As soon as we book and fingerprint you, we'll know who you are, or who you're not."

"I've never been arrested and booked in my life. So if you run my fingerprints, nothing will turn up," Lavella said. He had scored another hard punch.

Hammer and Bermudez were trading glances for a half minute, trying to think of what to do next. Hammer spoke first. "Regardless of who you are, we have probable cause to take you in."

"And what's that?" the intelligent criminal asked.

Bermudez opened the duffle bag and leered at Lavella. "Those are burglary tools in here." He nodded toward the blue van. "We saw you ditch this under that panel truck over there."

"And that's our probable cause," Hammer summarized.

Lavella sighed in acceptance. "Okay, okay, I'm Sammy, and I live here."

"Sammy what?" asked Hammer.

"Sammy Nalo. Let's go upstairs to my apartment and talk there."

Bermudez shackled Nalo's wrists, and Hammer tramped across the street to apprise Masters of the arrest. He opened the door and leaned into the car. "John, we got him. His name is Sammy Nalo," a sense of accomplishment in Hammer's voice.

"Is everything all right?"

"Yeah, yeah. We're going up to his apartment, and . . . and let's see what we find."

"Did he make any statements?"

"Not yet. But he's a cool cat, John. Once we take Mr. Nalo up to his place, we'll start applying pressure. He'll give in." Hammer looked to the rear seat. "How are you ladies doing?"

They didn't answer. Lulu had her arm around Felicia's shoulder, who was sniveling, her eyelids closed.

"Take the girls back home. We don't want our boy Sammy getting a glimpse of his informant," Hammer said to Masters. "Bermudez and I will take Nalo to our office in Fitzgibbons's car."

Hammer rapped the dashboard with his palm as a sign he was ready to do what he had said, and rejoined Bermudez and the handcuffed Nalo. They guided the crafty Turk by the arms, and hustled him inside the tenement. "All right, Sammy, this is the end of the road."

CHAPTER 48

S ammy Nalo's hideaway was unventilated and hot, the radiator pipes banging in a metallic clang. The windows were painted black, and the checkered ceramic tile floor from the turn of the century was speckled with chips and spiderweb cracks, more so in areas that foot traffic had worn. Bermudez handcuffed him to a water pipe that spanned across the room twenty inches below the ceiling, an uncomfortable stance for Nalo.

Hammer pulled a heavy, antiquated suitcase from under a dusty sofa. *This is where the Pierre jewels must be!* "Well, let's open it," Bermudez said in a way that reminded Hammer of a child who couldn't wait to unwrap a birthday gift.

Seeing the NYPD detective drooling at the prospect of luggage loaded with gems and cash, Nalo scoffed and sucked on his teeth. Hammer pressed the latch releases on the corners of the suitcase and opened the brown, leather-bound lid. "Well, well, well!" In it were three one-inch rubber-banded stacks of cash, miscellaneous clothing accessories, five or six rubies, a stiletto knife, three bank safe deposit keys, and an American passport.

He gauged the thickness of the one-hundred-dollar bills and predicted they totaled roughly $12,000. "Where did you get all this dough, Sammy?"

"Last week, I sold my coffee shop I had on East Tremont Avenue here in the Bronx," Nalo answered offhandedly, implying, *See, there's an explanation for everything.*

"Is that so?" Hammer scoffed. He scanned the first page of the passport, one issued by the U.S. Department of State. "Here it says your name is Sorecho Nalo, born in 1932 in Detroit, Michigan."

"Sorecho is my Turkish name."

"And what about these rubies?" Hammer asked, placing one of the gems under the lamp on the side stand of the couch.

"I dabble in buyin' and sellin' diamonds and things like that."

"So you're staking that you had nothing to do with the Pierre robbery."

"No, I didn't."

"What about the Sophia Loren heist fourteen months ago?"

Nalo was a veteran at deflecting this line of questioning. "I'm not sayin' anything else. Either book me or cut me loose. Otherwise, I want a lawyer."

Hammer regretfully knew he hadn't discovered anything to warrant specific charges, and he began to foresee this investigation digressing into a blind alley. At that bleak moment, Bermudez, who had been nosing around in the bedroom, resurfaced, and waving a pocket-size telephone book above his head, said with excitement, "Look at this . . . look at this."

In the phone book, among other names, was that of Bobby Comfort and his Rochester address. "So you *do* know Bobby Comfort, Sammy," Hammer said.

"I don't know a Bobby Comfort per se. If his name is in my phone book that don't mean he's my buddy. He might be someone I did business with, and I just don't remember him. That's all. Don't read too much into it." A plausible scenario. "I'm gettin' very uncomfortable handcuffed to this fuckin' pipe. Either take me downtown and book me, or get the hell out of my apartment."

Hammer tapped Nalo's phone book on the palm of his hand and paced in circles. "George." He called Bermudez by his first name in the manner of a person who views someone else as inferior or inept. "Let's take Nalo to your car. Fitz and I will bring him to the 19th Precinct. You'll stay here and guard this place 'til the morning when O'Neil can get a judge to sign a search warrant."

"Why can't we go through it now? Who's gonna know if we got a warrant or not?"

Hammer furrowed his brow. "*I* will know, and *I* follow procedures." To underscore his seriousness on the matter, he said, "When you work with me, you go by the book. Got it?"

"All right so it's a minor technicality. No need to get uptight," Bermudez said lightly as if searching a perp's residence without a warrant was something he did every day.

"You and all your NYPD jokers do things the way you see fit. But you won't be doing it on my watch. Meantime, stay here and don't let anybody in. And I mean anybody," Hammer ordered.

Nalo was amused by these two contrasting characters, and although he was an incurable outlaw, he had admiration for Hammer's integrity and work ethic.

Fitz, Hammer, and the manacled Nalo were traveling south on the Major Deegan on the way to the 19th Precinct in midtown Manhattan.

It was 4:15 on Sunday morning. Lieutenant O'Neil had learned of the overnight developments and briefed ADA Pope of Nalo's arrest. By the time Hammer delivered Nalo to the 19th Precinct, O'Neil and Pope were there, waiting to savor the catch of the day: Sorecho "Sammy the Arab" Nalo, whom they were confidently anticipating, "he'd spill his guts before the Sunday morning church sermons would be over." Hammer, O'Neil, Fitzgibbons, and Bermudez had been toiling nonstop for the past twenty-two hours—not uncommon for detectives to work shift-to-shift marathons when they're in hot pursuit.

But Hammer was beginning to conclude that inculpating evidence to nail Nalo might be intangible. The FBI agent didn't believe

Sammy Nalo was so careless as to keep anything at his apartment that could land him into the flames, and a search would probably be unproductive. Moreover, he was an old hand at the interrogation game, and Hammer's conclusions were that Nalo could not be tempted into a confession—or even answer basic questions. Exhausted and disillusioned, Hammer called it a day.

In the Bronx, Detective Bermudez, finding himself alone in Nalo's pad, couldn't resist the urge to poke at will. In a drawer were a collection of newspaper clippings from the *New York Daily News*, the *New York Times*, and the *New York Post* about different armed robberies and burglaries that had occurred in Manhattan over the past three and a half years. *These gotta be heists Nalo must've pulled off.*

As he rummaged through the apartment, he came across more newspaper and magazine articles about personages of high society, who, without exception, lived in New York City, many in upscale hotels. One of the stories in *Life* magazine featured Sophia Loren. *Sophia Loren! Is this a coincidence, or what? Nalo must've been casing Loren's hotel suite before he robbed her. And all these other famous people in these magazines. He must've robbed them, too.*

In the bedroom, the detective's findings amounted to a couple of wigs—presumably Nalo's variety of disguises—and toiletries and colognes in a medicine cabinet above the sink in the bathroom. Overall, Bermudez hadn't uncovered anything of consequence. But was he *really* searching for evidence with which to convict Sammy Nalo? Or was the detective on an underhanded quest? While in the bathroom, he had an urge to urinate, and behind the toilet he spotted three oak floor planks that weren't snugly fitted. He kicked those boards with the toe of his shoe, and they weren't permanently nailed in place. Bermudez kneeled, raised the lose slats, and what he saw was unimaginable, his mouth agape, eyes bulging as if they were fixed on a UFO.

CHAPTER 49

L ike I told Agent Hammer and that Puerto Rican detective, I have no idea what you're talkin' about these robberies," Nalo said to Pope and O'Neil. He slurped coffee from a paper cup and rubbed his bloodshot eyes. "You say I robbed Sophia Loren at gun-point? That broad is so gorgeous, a creamy Italian. And those tits o' hers can make any man drunk just by starin' at them." Another sip of coffee. "Shit, if I broke into her suite, she wouldn't have just gotten jabbed with the barrel of my gun. I would've jabbed her with another barrel, too. Know what I mean?" And he laughed at his own joke.

Pope and O'Neil left the interviewing pen. "This Nalo won't be easy to crack," the assistant DA said. "He's not going to buckle. The only shot we have is to put him and Comfort in a lineup and hope that one or two of the victims will make a positive ID." He sliced the air with his hands as if to say, *You have any other ideas?* "We don't have anything else to go on."

O'Neil wasn't resigned, and his expression suggested that ADA Pope should do a bit of magic. Pope shook his head and had on the face of a little boy whose favorite toy broke. "As I said, our only means is if the hostages can finger Nalo or Comfort and, pray they don't falter under cross examination."

Bermudez, on the other hand, couldn't care less whether the Pierre and the Sophia Loren daredevils could be prosecuted. Tonight, he had met his fortune, a once-in-a-lifetime stroke of incredible luck. *I'm rich, I'm rich! Filthy rich!*

A week ago, Nalo had buried in his apartment a velour satchel that contained upward of $1,200,000 in jewels, gems he'd stolen over the past three years. And there, in the bathroom beneath the floor planks behind the toilet, against all odds Bermudez had found that stash. And he had no intention of reporting this blessed discovery. No one would ever know. Would they? And as for Nalo, what could he do, accuse him of stealing his property and file a police report? Of course not. If Nalo attempted such an idiotic move, he'd have to concoct a fairy tale how he came to be in possession of those stones. No, Nalo was not stupid; he wouldn't be so foolish. He'd have to eat his losses and keep quiet about it. All in all, these circumstances were an extraordinary happenstance that couldn't have worked out better had anybody tried to mastermind such a swindle. The stars had aligned for George Bermudez. God bless Agent Hammer for having assigned him to guard the apartment.

Bermudez's adrenaline was pumping through his body head to toe. For years, he had played the lottery without ever missing a week, and finally he hit the jackpot. The detective didn't know the value of the jewels, but knew he had just become a rich man. At last! He had to be careful, though, and not deviate from his lifestyle or habits, at least for a year or so until the Pierre sensation faded away. He had to think about retiring, or remaining on the police force and pretending as if nothing had altered the course of his life. But right now, he had a chore to handle. It was 5:00 A.M.; Bermudez had to stuff the gems in every pocket of his garments. He didn't take four or five stones that were lying inside a pouch in a night stand. Why be greedy? When O'Neil or Hammer found those rubies, Bermudez figured, it'd prove he had been honest for not having taken them.

But at the moment, he had to return the empty satchel to the hole in the bathroom floor and refit the loose planks. He did so and then tore out a good length of toilet paper. He wiped his fingerprints off where he had touched anything in the bathroom. Bermudez couldn't believe he'd just joined the ranks of the millionaires. What a feeling! He pressed his tongue inside his cheek and couldn't stop sniggering. He envisioned the look on Nalo's face when he'd find the empty satchel. Exhilarated, Bermudez sank into the couch and fell asleep in a snoring bliss.

The sun rose; it was Sunday morning, the snow clouds had cleared, and the sky brightened to a blue canvas with glints of sunrays. At eight o'clock, Doug Pope phoned and awoke a judge, asking for a search warrant. "Come to my home in Scarsdale, you know where I live, Doug, don't you?"

"Yes, I do, Your Honor. I've been there before."

"Come here at 10:30, and bring the necessary details so I can prepare the warrant and sign it."

"I'll be there. Thanks for the Sunday morning on-the-spot accommodation, Your Honor."

From the judge's home, Pope phoned Lieutenant O'Neil and told him the warrant had been executed. O'Neil in turn contacted the FBI duo of Matt Hammer and John Masters, who dispatched two search-specialist agents to Nalo's apartment, where Detective Bermudez was still protecting it.

At the Tombs, Bobby Comfort was in the recreation room on one of the six park-bench-like seats, smoking and drinking hot tea. It was loud and unruly from two card games at the tables nearby. On the wall opposite the benches was a pay phone, and one of the prisoners, a tall, skinny African American teenager, a comb stuck in his Afro, was talking, or rather screaming, into it, arguing heatedly with his girlfriend: "Yoh listen to me, bitch nigger. If yoh don't bring me mah you-know-what, when I git outta here I goin' whip yoh black ass 'til it turn purple."

Heightening the chaos, the television was on high volume. More frustrating, the correction officer, who perused the daily newspapers to cut out articles that might've been about a newly processed inmate, hadn't yet done so. That step was taken to afford privacy to those prisoners whose crimes appeared in the print media. And the circulation of today's Sunday paper was delayed.

Comfort, impatient to read or hear an update on the Pierre, would give his testicles to switch the NBC football commentary program that everyone was watching to the news. But he had to overcome a hurdle. The "numbskull sports fanatics," the ones who couldn't get enough of football, and to whom learning to read or write was as unnatural as staying clean is to a pig, couldn't tear themselves from sports shows. But they'd tear anybody's head off who dared to change the channel.

Comfort walked over to "Big Willy," the toughest prisoner, who's the dictator of the cell block and has everyone's respect. Big Willy, one of the blacks who was hypnotized by the foot-ball preview, hadn't noticed Comfort. "Hey man, my name's Bobby." He didn't have to say his last name; it was stenciled on the green jumpsuit. "What's yours?" Comfort put his arm out for a handshake.

Big Willy, a mountain of muscles, his skin as dark as chocolate, didn't answer but looked at Comfort through an intimidating gaze that meant, *Whatever you got on your mind better be to my advantage. Or else, don't waste my time when I'm watching football.*

Comfort turned his palm upward to stress his invitation for a handshake. "So what's your name?"

Big Willy hesitated a second too long, but accepted Comfort's hand, gripping it ever so tightly, a message that told of his strength and status as the ruler of "the joint." "I'm Racine. Whatchu woun from me?"

Comfort pulled out six cigarettes from his pack of Pall Malls. He spread the cancer sticks loosely in his palm. "Racine, how about a few cigs? Here, take 'em."

Racine, whose huge head was bald and had the violet hue of an eggplant, curled one corner of his mouth as if he doubted Comfort's peace pipe was genuine, and that he might've had ulterior motives. "What's all this fuss for?"

"Just a token of our new friendship," Comfort answered with pseudo-sincerity. "Just a token, my man."

Racine didn't take the cigarettes. "Sounds to me like yoh lookin' fer protection. Ain't that right? 'Cause if thas whatchu woun, you come to the right dude."

Comfort nodded at the television, which was mounted on the ceiling. "What I'm looking for right now is for you to let me change the station. Just for five minutes."

Racine broke out into a deep, throaty laugh. "Awl right, awl right. But that'll be eight cigs, man. Eight!"

Comfort slid out two more Pall Malls. "You got it." He placed the cigarettes onto Racine's pink palm and walked toward the TV. He climbed on a chair, and as he touched the tuner knob another black inmate jumped up as though a powerful force had jettisoned him. He thrust his arm in the air and hollered, "Hey white boy, whatchu tank yo doin'?"

Without turning behind to see who had protested, Racine raised a hand high above his head, a signal that he had approved for Comfort to switch stations.

He tuned the TV to Channel 7. A commercial ended, and the light-skinned news anchor Anna Bond, an African American, recited the evening's headlines in a fluid broadcast voice. The second caption was: "Another man is held for the Pierre heist." And Ms. Bond narrated the story. "In the early hours of dawn, in a concerted effort the FBI and the NYPD arrested a second suspect believed to have been one of the masterminds of the Pierre Hotel robbery, and that of the Italian actress Sophia Loren, which was carried out in November of 1970. The suspect who's been apprehended is forty-two-year-old Sorecho 'Sammy the Arab, Nalo, an alleged accomplice of Robert Comfort, who was arrested yesterday."

The appealing newscaster, who trended a soft, brownish hair bob—one as fluffy as that of a white woman—didn't crack a smile, her demeanor serious and decorous. Comfort re-climbed on the

THE PIERRE HOTEL AFFAIR

chair and reverted the TV to the football game. Racine nodded at Comfort. "Whatchu say yoh name be?" He gestured at the television. "Are you the cat she was talkin' about?"

"Yeah." Comfort gave Racine a thumb-up and withdrew to his cell. He sat on the bunk and thought about this latest event. *They got Sammy, but so what?* Mountains would crumble before Nalo would admit to anything or squealed on anyone. But what if the cops had found . . . nah, Sammy wouldn't have hidden in his apartment that necklace he might've snuck into his pocket at the Pierre. Or did he? If so that damn diamond necklace could be the nail that would seal their coffins.

The Sheriff's Department was to transfer Nalo here to the Tombs, awaiting arraignment along with Comfort. This was soothing to Comfort. He'd finally speak with his partner, who'd recap all that had spun awry since Paolino had left his suite at the Royal Manhattan thirty hours ago. In a way, Comfort was pleased that he and Nalo would soon reunite; they'd talk about what had happened and jointly strategize how to deal with the pending charges.

Although it was a sunny afternoon, inside the hallways of Nalo's apartment building it was dark and nippy. O'Neil and Fitzgibbons, armed with the warrant, knocked on Nalo's apartment door, awakening Bermudez. Groggy and not fully conscious, he looked around wild-eyed as if he didn't know where he was, but he quickly punched through the fog. He patted his pockets to feel the stones and smiled, remembering the unthinkable windfall he had landed in overnight. He tightened and straightened the knot of his tie, and walked to the door. "Who is it?"

"It's me, Lieutenant O'Neil."

O'Neil, Fitzgibbons, and the two FBI tech specialists entered the dusty but toasty-warm apartment. "Anything happening, Lieutenant?" Bermudez asked.

"Nothing other than ADA Pope got the search warrant." O'Neil snapped his fingers. "One, two, three. Just like that. What about here, anything going on since last night?"

"Uh, nah. Nothing," Bermudez answered noncommittally.

O'Neil joggled his chin at the agents. "These are lab techs, Agent Samuelson, and Agent Sinclair."

The techs tipped their heads at Bermudez and said nothing, intimating they were there to do a job and nothing else. One of the agents was carrying a tool box. He rested it on a steamer trunk that had been improvised as a table and opened it. They took out a handful of paraphernalia, lab instruments, and began sifting through Nalo's pad. O'Neil didn't interfere, knowing they'd snarl at him, a look that meant, *Stay out of our business.* The professional decorum of the FBI personnel and the blue collar comportment of the NYPD detectives inevitably clashed.

O'Neil paid no mind to the snubbing and said to Bermudez, "Before we got here, you didn't happen to find anything in this rathole, did you?"

A burst of repentance emblazoned Bermudez's face, his ears heating to a red hot. *What's O'Neil really saying? Does he suspect me of foul play? Can he tell that I stuffed a pound of jewels in my pockets? Did Nalo admit he had gems hidden in this joint?* A spell of regret paralyzed Bermudez's mind, and he hoped he didn't look as flustered as he felt. He glanced at Fitzgibbons and contemplated his reaction to O'Neil's inquiry. None. Perhaps, Bermudez hoped, he was overreacting to a harmless question. "Uh . . . no, Lieutenant. Last night, uh, Agent Hammer told me not to do anything 'til you got a warrant. So I just dozed off once in a while." The detective was stammering, and was afraid it'd light the notion he might've been lying. His mouth was suddenly dry, and he stood in a stew of fear and guilt.

"Well, let's turn this place upside down and maybe we'll find that one thing that can connect Nalo to the Pierre job," O'Neil said. He then added dourly, "Otherwise, even if we throw the book at these perps nothing's gonna stick."

"Maybe we should plant something the old fashioned way," Fitzgibbons said jokingly. Or perhaps he wasn't joking.

The FBI agents had heard that and shot scorching rays at Fitz and his equals, who smiled foolishly at one another. And to save themselves, O'Neil and Bermudez invoked a pretentious gaze that inferred, *Fitz was only kiddin' because we, the boys in blue, wouldn't think of such a thing. We're New York's Finest.*

Hours and hours of scouring Nalo's abode resulted in a waste of the taxpayers' money. The FBI lab techs had analyzed the half-dozen or so loose stones that Bermudez so magnanimously had left behind in the drawer of the termite-perforated side stand. But despite the bureau's state-of-the-art testing apparatus, the feds couldn't ascertain from whom or where those gems had been plucked, drastically diluting the strength of the accusations against Comfort and Nalo.

Had these investigative efforts boiled down to a big fat zero whereby O'Neil and his archenemies, Hammer and Masters, might have to release Comfort and Nalo?

CHAPTER 50

T he FBI threw in the towel. Hammer and Masters bowed out;
they hadn't unearthed anything incriminating with which
to support the felony charges Pope was dreaming of lodging
against Comfort and Nalo. At this juncture, it was the decision of
the District Attorney's Office, chiefly ADA Pope, to assess whether
his impeachments against Comfort and Nalo had merit. If his
prosecution were to fail, it'd stir a public outcry, a discontentment
the voters would not forget on the next election for the upcoming
term of the district attorney. Pope's boss, DA Frank Hogan, would
be livid. *Why did you take this case to trial without a stitch of evidence?*
How do I explain this waste of money and time to the press? In short,
it'd trigger a tidal wave of bad publicity.

"Let's arraign Comfort and Nalo for possession of stolen property," Pope put forth to DA Hogan, the intensity of a high-pressure
salesman in his momentum. "We'll recommend to the presiding
judge to set a high cash bail, and I'll postpone the progression of
the trial on the calendar as long as possible. By then, after a few
months in the Tombs, these guys will have lost forty pounds each,
and they'll beg for a plea deal."

Hogan scratched the back of his neck. "This will be as high profile as a case can be. If your strategy doesn't come to pass, and the defendants walk, we'll be smeared in the press from here to Timbuktu."

This discussion was unspooling in Hogan's office, him sitting erect behind his wooden desk, the sleeves of his white shirt rolled up at the elbows, as Pope stood stooped over, palms firm on the desktop. "Mr. Hogan, out of the twenty-three hostages, one or two should be able to pick the perps in a lineup. Wouldn't you think? I mean, Comfort and Nalo were inside the Pierre for nearly three hours."

"So what?"

"Somebody had to have gotten a good look at those two," Pope said, maintaining eye contact to read his superior's thoughts. ADA Doug Pope's career was not on the rise. He, aggressive and enterprising, slaved fifty to sixty hours a week—and sometimes more—and his yearly salary was an embarrassing $11,000. In his childhood, he had defied the odds of many black adolescents, surmounting the negative impact of "the hood," where little Doug's single mother had raised her boy as she groveled in the woes of economic hardship, though they lived in respectable poverty. She saw him through school, rather than permitting her child to derail into the ghetto road to perdition. And at thirty-four years of age, five years into his tenure as an assistant district attorney, the greater part of Pope's prosecutions had been minor narcotic offenses and prostitution. That long-awaited nationally notable trial, the cause célèbre that would propel Counselor Pope to stardom had eluded him. And at last, his boss had given him *the ticket* to take charge of the Pierre robbery, a once-in-a-lifetime opportunity on the wish list of every prosecutor. Pope had to make the most of it. Less than a week since that heist, it had risen to fame not only in the media but in legal circles as well, where criminal lawyers were watching it from the sidelines. And if he succeeded at convicting those two big, deep-water fishes, Comfort and Nalo, Pope would be a coveted prize. He could taste the lucrative offers from prestigious law firms that would surely be on the horizon. And last but not least, it'd be a pleasure to no longer mingle with the petty drug pushers and the five-dollar hookers.

Yes, Pope was desperate to persuade DA Hogan to green-light the prosecution of Comfort and Nalo. "We have nothing to lose, Mr. Hogan."

"What you mean to say is that *you* don't have anything to lose. Nobody knows who you are." The elderly, gray-haired district attorney pecked at his chest. "I'm the one who has a lot to lose. Whatever goes wrong, and it's my neck in the noose."

"You're right, Mr. Hogan. But if we cut loose Comfort and Nalo, everybody will want to know why we arrested them in the first place. And you'd have a mob banging down the door here to ask why we wasted money and time if we didn't have an ironclad case. Worse yet, we'd never find out who else was involved in the Pierre." Pope realized he was hyper, so he paused. He pointed in the general direction of the Tombs and said in a slower, accentuated speech, "As long as we have those two guys in custody, there's a chance they'll name the others."

"Don't bet on it, Doug," disagreed Hogan, who had been the Manhattan district attorney for eighteen years, and had heard it all and seen it all.

Pope sensed he was losing his bid to "win the old man over." He breathed in a gulp of air and felt he was coming across as a Bible peddler. He lowered his voice and put on a relaxed smile. "Look, Mr. Hogan, I can arraign Comfort and Nalo quietly. No press releases, no fanfare. And when they're escorted into the courtroom, I'll see to it that they aren't paraded in handcuffs in front of a bunch of merciless photographers. I'll have the defendants taken upstairs from the Tombs in the judges' elevator and through the private corridors of the complex. *Virtually* no one will know about the arraignment."

"All right, Doug, I'll give in on this one." Hogan upped on his feet and stood in an authoritative stance. "But if this case fizzles out, you can kiss goodbye that promotion to senior ADA."

Kiss goodbye the promotion to senior ADA! Pope felt a stab in his belly. That escalation in status would mean a $3,000 increase in his yearly stipend, and he badly needed it. He had two small children, and his wife had one in the oven. More of an immediacy, the rent on his apartment was due for an increase, and the transmission of the family car had to be replaced. What else could topple over on top of Doug Pope?

Indeed, life was tough for him and his growing family, and the Pierre's high stakes he was combating might defeat him if only he could sway one of the hostages to point out Comfort and Nalo.

The District Attorney's Office sent notification to police headquarters at 1 Police Plaza that Comfort and Nalo would be arraigned at the earliest availability of a court date. The memo cautioned that public statements should be deferred until a grand jury upheld the arraignment and voted to indict the defendants. The underlying message was to respectfully warn the police commissioner not to mislead the press corps and the community into believing the Pierre heist was solved. DA Hogan's objective was to minimize communication with the media so that if the indictments were to be dismissed, the egg on his face might not be as glaring. His reservations stemmed from what is known in legal terms as a Motion to Dismiss. At a preliminary hearing, if the evidence presented by the prosecution is insufficient to support the indictment against the defendant, his lawyer may file a Motion to Dismiss, appealing to a higher court to set aside the pending charges. And this petition, Hogan knew, might likely be granted, unless two or more of the hostages could affirm Comfort and Nalo as the stickup men. After all, so far Pope had no proof to validate those allegations.

But the police commissioner, who jubilant over the upcoming arraignment, didn't pay heed to Hogan's memorandum. On the contrary, he couldn't wait to gather a press conference and tout "the positive progress" of the Pierre case—all eyes and ears across the nation were waiting with bated breath to hear the newest saga of the most notorious hotel in the world. Hastily, the commissioner authorized his deputy, Dan Hodge, to gather a legion of journalists and ballyhoo this wonderful news to the world.

The press briefing was about to begin at police headquarters. On the ground floor was a round, expansive reception hall with a brown polished concrete pavement. Three-foot-high built-in brick planters lining a glass wall served as the bedding for a hodgepodge of indoor shrubbery highlighted by spotlights. On another wall were enlarged, black-and-white photos of ex-commissioners, and pictures, though smaller in size, of fallen NYPD officers.

In his black uniform bearing the gold stripes of his title, Deputy Commissioner Hodge stood at the pulpit. Flanking him were Lieutenant O'Neil, preened and perfumed, and a spokesman for the district attorney, ADA Keith McMillan, both in firm postures, chins slightly upward, staring pompously at the assemblage of hyperactive reporters. Projecting arrogance, as government officials often do at press conferences—a glower on their faces that establishes authority, and that anything they state should be regarded as gospel—O'Neil and McMillan were cocked and primed to tackle the soon-to-come landslide of questions.

Hodge cleared his throat. "Good afternoon, ladies and gentlemen. I'm Deputy Commissioner Dan Hodge. To my right is the district attorney's spokesman, Keith McMillan." He gently placed his hand on O'Neil's elbow. "To my left is Lieutenant Perry O'Neil." Hodge scanned the press corps and pointed at a female reporter who was carrying a recording device and flailing her hand in the air. "You may go first, Miss."

The emaciated, brown-haired woman, her face badly pock-marked—the residual scarring from a past acne condition—asked, "Rumors have been circulating that the Pierre masterminds have been indicted. Does that mean you've closed the investigation?"

"They haven't yet been indicted. But they will," Deputy Commissioner Hodge answered as he looked at O'Neil, waiting to be rescued if he had responded inaccurately. But so far, he was correct. "Uh, no, we haven't closed the investigation. We believe more accomplices will be apprehended, and we also believe, now that the organizers of the robbery are in custody, the others will be easier to locate." Hodge, a silver-haired, robust middle-aged man who spoke in a low tone, exuded optimism to the fullest, a buoyant viewpoint that made Lieutenant O'Neil and Spokesman McMillan cringe. More damaging, his statements were in disregard of DA Hogan's policy to minimize publicizing the case.

But Hodge, ignoring his breach of confidentiality, willingly and happily engaged the media. He indicated another journalist, who asked, "What was the specific evidence that led to the arrest of Mr. Comfort and Mr. Nalo? And have they made any admissions?"

Hodge turned his back to the spectators and flicked a *what's the answer to this?* glance at O'Neil, who, knowing the deputy commissioner was totally stumped, quickly stepped up to the microphone. The mic was set for the shorter Hodge, and the lieutenant had to lean into it.

"Eh, we can't discuss anything about evidentiary matters and admissions the suspects might've made."

O'Neil had saved Hodge from the journalists' lizard tongues. But not exactly because the next question was, "Mr. Hodge said, and I quote, '. . . the organizers of the robbery are in custody . . .' But now, Lieutenant O'Neil, you referred to them as *suspects*. Do you have a solid case against the defendants, or is it circumstantial? And why has the FBI closed the investigation?"

Damn it! How does this pack of hound dogs know the Feds quit? O'Neil's face flared to a warm red, Hodge now practically hiding behind him. The deputy commissioner was owl-eyed, cowering with the humiliation of a man whose penis suddenly softens during intercourse.

The lieutenant covered the mic and whispered in Hodge's ear, "Sir, eh . . . I think we should cut this short."

Hodge swallowed hard and nodded. He readjusted the mic to his height, and palms out at shoulder level, said pathetically, "That's all, folks. We'll keep you posted if there's anything new."

To the reporters' chagrin, O'Neil, Hodge, and McMillan, a shamed trio, their self-indignation pruned, walked off the podium like three dogs who had been clawed and roughed up by alley cats.

"We were told this was going to be a comprehensive conference," shouted an ABC correspondent, waving a notepad high above his head. "I got one more question, please. Have the police recovered the stolen jewelry?"

Competing with the rest of the harried media clique, who were outshouting one another, a *New York Post* writer said loudly, "Uh, I have another question, too. And this is for Mr. McMillan. Sir, is the DA planning to plea-bargain with Mr. Comfort and Mr. Nalo? Or is he confident his prosecution will prevail at trial?"

"Lieutenant O'Neil, I just want to ask, have you located the stolen items?" asked another.

As Hodge and his mouthpieces faded into a long, light-deprived corridor, the torrent of inquiries poured out onto the empty podium, echoing in the cavernous reception hall.

Irate as a constipated bull, DA Hogan walked up to his television and switched off the eight o'clock news, nearly breaking the tuner dial. He called Keith McMillan at his home.

"Hello, McMillan here."

"Whose idea was this sham on the news just minutes ago? And why didn't you inform me of it?"

"The police commissioner instructed Hodge to do the press conference, Mr. Hogan. But it was in poor judgment. I showed up to make sure those morons Hodge and O'Neil didn't get clobbered by the press."

"Those two imbeciles' egos are bigger than their brains. So much for keeping the arraignment quiet." The second Hogan terminated that call, the phone rang, startling him. It was Doug Pope.

"That was a dumb thing Hodge and O'Neil did."

"It was more than dumb, Doug. It was idiotic. By the way, have you arranged to get Comfort and Nalo into a lineup?"

"I did, Mr. Hogan. It's set for the day after tomorrow. The arraignment will be tomorrow morning."

"Good. If you're religious, this is a good time to pray that one of the hostages will come through with a positive ID."

CHAPTER 51

On the evening of January 11, 1972, the sheriffs transported Sammy Nalo to the Tombs. The guards there completed the receiving and registering ritual: supplying the new inmate the jailhouse green jumpsuit, his last name stenciled on it, a blanket, sheets, a towel, soap, and toothpaste and brush. By then, it was too late for dinner at the chow hall, and two correction officers walked Nalo to his cell. He flung the blanket and sheets on his bunk, and lay on it, thinking about on which floor Comfort might be housed. Comfort, too, couldn't sleep; his eagerness to talk to Nalo had been stirring him, and figured that Nalo should already be somewhere inside the Tombs.

The following morning at 7:00 A.M., the time came when, at breakfast, Comfort sighted Nalo's bald white scalp. He was two tables to his right, and Comfort raised an arm. "Sammy."

Nalo pivoted behind him and grinned. He picked up his food tray off the table and went to sit beside to his friend. They shook hands and hugged. "What the fuck has been goin' on, Bobby? What the fuck happened when Paolino met the fence? Did he or you fess up to anythin'?"

"Hell no. I denied, denied, denied. What about you?"

"I didn't tell 'em shit."

They had forgotten about breakfast and debriefed one another. The chow hall, as in all prisons, was loud, with the ceaseless clattering and clanging of eating utensils, and everyone outtalking the other. When finished eating, every inmate had to account for and turn in his knife, fork, and spoon at the door, a measure to curtail the risk that they'd be smuggled out and used as weapons.

Comfort said, "Let's go to the recreation room so we can talk without all these ears trying to listen."

They walked up to the guard who was collecting the utensils and chucked theirs into the three designated canisters, where the knives, forks, and spoons were sorted and later cleaned by inmates on the kitchen detail. In the rec room, the two partners in crime sat in a corner. It was relatively quiet. The rowdies were either still sleeping or eating breakfast, though a prisoner whose tattoos defaced his body head to toe had already switched on the television. And the first card game of the day was underway, which meant the first fist fight of the morning would be erupting shortly. That's prison life.

Nalo affectionately slapped Comfort's bicep. "So how have they been treating you?"

"You know, the usual cop tactics, threatening and pressuring me into confessing. Bluffing me, sayin' they have this and that."

"Yeah, same shit with me," Nalo said. "But I gotta tell you. This was the first time I dealt with the FBI, and they're a whole different breed then those dumb New York cops." But Nalo was unaware that one of "those dumb New York cops," namely Detective George Bermudez, was gloating over the million dollars in jewels he had reaped from his apartment. As they were comparing notes, Nalo became somber. "We gotta assume they got Paolino. That's where all this must've started from. You think he gave us up?"

Comfort shook his head. "Absolutely not. He and I go back a long, long way. I don't have a clue what went down, but I'd bet my balls Dom Paolino would never talk or rat anybody out. Maybe they were tailing Stern, or maybe that guy Roland, who I didn't trust,

turned out to be an informant. Who knows? But you can bet your bottom dollar Dom is not the one who started this whole mess."

"What if they put him under the hot lamp, would he melt?"

"Dom has been in the hot seat before. They couldn't crack him," Comfort said, lighting a cigarette.

Nalo moved in closer and said in a low voice, "Bobby, if you're right, they got nothin' on us. Nothin'!"

"That's right. All we gotta do is stay calm. And even if they put us in a lineup, I doubt anybody can point us out. If they do, our lawyers will easily confuse any eyewitness, and twist things around."

"I think you're right. But right now, I wanna go take a shower. I'll catch you later."

"Before you go," Comfort said, "How did they find you?"

"I got no idea. It might've had to do with the Loren job. This FBI agent, Matt Hammer, might've been onto me for that, and somehow connected me to the Pierre."

"All right, Sammy. I'm going to the commissary to pick up a newspaper. I wanna see if there's anything new about us."

Today's headlines in the papers sure had an outrageous new eye-opener about Sammy Nalo.

CHAPTER 52

O n the second page of the *Daily News*, the headline read:

$750,000 IN GEMS FROM THE PIERRE RECOVERED

Comfort read the article and was stunned, perplexed, and a pang reeled him into a boiling rage. He read it over again, and his disbelief deepened.

The recovered jewels consisted of a single seventy-eight-carat diamond necklace owned by the infamous New York socialite, Aleksandra Petranovic. A restaurateur, Louis Peppo, whose bar and grill was in downtown Detroit at Cadillac Square, had surrendered the choker to the local FBI office. *What an uncanny coincidence for this three-quarter-of-a-million-dollar piece of jewelry to surface nowhere else but in Detroit, Nalo's hometown.* Comfort dissected every sentence of the *Daily News* story, and now knew that this necklace was the piece Nalo had slipped into his pocket in the vault room back at the Pierre. At the time, Comfort had thought his eyes deceived him. He'd never guess his old pal, Sammy, with whom he'd been on top of the glorious peaks, and down through the arid valleys, would steal from him. Despite Comfort's high regard for Nalo, he had cheated him. But this shocker didn't end there.

Days prior to his arrest, Nalo had telephoned Louis Peppo, who was an acquaintance since his childhood years. Under the guise of proposing a business venture, he urged Peppo to fly to New York. He landed at LaGuardia, Nalo met him, and they drove to a hotel. They had dinner, talked about Nalo's proposition, one he had contrived, and at the end of the evening he gave Peppo a sealed, eight-inch-by-twelve-inch package. "Louie, take this to Detroit and keep it safe." Nalo tapped the parcel. "What's in here is very, very dear to me. Somethin' my mother gave me before she died and can't be replaced. It ain't worth much, but it's got a lot of sentimental value to me."

"I understand, Sammy. It'll be safe with me."

Peppo flew back to Detroit and tucked the package in his bedroom closet. Before doing so, he couldn't restrain his curiosity and opened it. He saw a heavy, white velour pouch tied at the end. He unraveled the knot and gulped hard. He had in his hands a gleaming diamond necklace, one so large, "he'd never seen even in the movies." Peppo had no wisdom about diamonds, but he knew this choker must've been worth an arm and a leg. Nevertheless, no notions of foul play crossed Louis Peppo's mind; he and Nalo had been elementary schoolmates, and Peppo trusted and admired him. Maybe, as Nalo had said back in New York, this necklace was his mother's, a family heirloom.

Three days had passed, and as Peppo walked past a newsstand the *Chicago Tribune* headline immobilized him dead in his tracks.

SORECHO 'THE ARAB' NALO ARRESTED IN NEW YORK IN
CONNECTION WITH THE PIERRE HOTEL ROBBERY

Peppo, an honest, bread-and-butter businessman, his record unblemished, was rocked, and his knees began knocking, dreading of being implicated in this nationally ill-famed crime. And fearing the worst, he didn't waste a minute telephoning the Detroit FBI office to cleanse his conscience. But, to ADA Pope's disenchantment,

Peppo, not to suffer legal and physical consequences, declined to sign a sworn deposition as to how the necklace happened to be in his possession.

Nalo stepped off the row of shower stalls, a tattered green towel wrapped around his waist. Comfort, who'd been waiting at the door-less entrance of the stalls, called, "Sammy."

"Are you goin' in to shower?" Nalo asked.

Comfort said nothing but spread the *New York Post* across his chest. He glowered at the betrayer, and Nalo's eyelids blinked faster than a flashing traffic signal, his face reddening as he read the headlines. "What . . . what the hell is this all about?"

"That's what I want you to tell me." Comfort slapped the newspaper on Nalo's bare stomach and jerked his chin at it. "Go ahead, check out the whole story. You're gonna *love it*, Sammy."

Nalo's radar detected bitter mockery. He leaned his shoulder against the wall and warily scanned the article. He read halfway into it and looked at Comfort. "I . . . I don't get it. Where uh . . . where the fuck did this necklace come from?"

Gritting his teeth, Comfort said, "Cut the bullshit, Sammy." With two fingers, he jabbed Nalo's chest. "I *thought* I'd seen you inside the vault shoving that goddamn necklace in your pocket. I just wasn't sure. That's why I didn't have it out with you before."

Nalo lowered his head in shame. "I . . . got so much pressure on me from these bookies that . . . I mean . . . Bobby, I was gonna tell you, and I would've straightened things out with you."

That was a serenade Comfort had heard many a times before. "Yeah, sure, sure. You were gonna tell me, but when? When you came to see me in my coffin to pay your last respects, is that when you were gonna tell me? After I'm dead, that's when you were gonna straighten things out with me?" Raising his voice, he repeated, "After I'm dead, right Sammy? Not while I'm alive. Only after I'm dead."

"You're overreacting, Bobby."

Comfort banged his fist on the wall. "Overreacting! You think I'm overreacting? If anything, I'm underreacting! I should have your throat slit ear to ear in your cell in the middle of the night. That's what I should do."

"Bobby, I'm sorry. I'm really sorry . . . it won't happen . . ."

"What're you think is gonna happen when Al Green finds out that you fucked him and all the other guys? He's gonna say, 'How about that lowlife Sammy? He pocketed the most expensive piece. I bet he and his buddy Comfort must've both been in on it'. See, Green's gonna blame me, too. And the satchel with millions in jewelry we gave him to hold for us, guess what? You can forget about it. Green's gonna say, 'Fuck those two pieces of shit. I'm gonna stick it up their asses'. And you and I will never see him or our jewels ever again. And all because you took something for yourself."

"Bobby, look . . ."

Disgusted, Comfort threw his burning cigarette butt on the cement floor, snuffed it under his shoe, and heavy-stepped to the rec room.

NICK SACCO

Bobby Comfort was right. I was still in Miami, but I had found out through one of Furnari's connections that when Al Green and Ali-Ben read about the necklace, they flew off to Europe. And if Germaine and Visconti would've gotten their hands on Nalo, they might've boiled him in oil. Furnari and I didn't care; who were we to bitch? We had hoarded more of the Pierre loot than we ever expected, not to mention the $4,500,000 in stones we got back from the Rochester gangster, Piccarreto. We split that with Visconti and Germaine. But Frankos, who was counting on getting his end from the batch that Green and Ali-Ben were supposedly safekeeping, must've been pissed as hell. And if I ever feared a man, I'd have to say it was the Greek. Frankos could rip your heart out before you felt the pain.

CHAPTER 53

Vexed by his partner's duplicity, Comfort couldn't close an eye throughout the night. Nalo though, instinctively unscrupulous, didn't lose a minute of sleep. At 4:00 A.M., correction officers woke him and Comfort, and told the two inmates to prepare for court. They'd be arraigned that morning at 9:30. "You gotta be ready in a hour, Comfort. Let's go," said the six-foot-three, three-hundred-pound black correction officer. His tonality had the standard rudeness of a prison guard, the self-empowered attitude that said, *I don't care who you are. In here, you're under my thumb.*

"Learn to be polite and know how to treat people. And maybe you'll amount to more than a three-dollar-an-hour babysitter for convicts," Comfort said.

"Like I said, you got a hour, and not a minute mouh. Ready or not, Imma comin' to git you." The correction officer's hint at his mean streak didn't faze Comfort.

More ballsy, he had to have the final volley in this exchange and said, "By the way, learn to speak English. Lucky for you, the state takes care of unskilled jerks like you."

Comfort stayed in the shower for less than forty-five seconds, hurrying out, chattering teeth. Hot water at the Tombs was a scarcity, and often in the middle of January the floor in the shower stalls iced. "Brrrrr! This place ought to be shut down. The conditions in here are deplorable," Comfort complained to a prisoner of Argentinean origin as he stepped off the stall.

"*Deplorable!* What's that mean?" asked the Argentinean in a dumbfounded stare.

"Never mind."

As Doug Pope had orchestrated it, the delivery of Comfort and Nalo to the courthouse part of the complex was guarded but uneventful. No photographers, no reporters, and no pests of any kind. They were ushered into the courtroom in shackles, clanging along in green jumpsuits and plastic sandals. They were led to sit at the defense table, and now all the players were in their respective chairs. Judge Andrew Tyler, a tawny-skinned African American, a crop of frizzy gray hair whitening his scalp, was on the bench. ADA Pope represented the People of the State of New York, and Leon Greenspan, a real estate lawyer, stood for defendants Comfort and Nalo. When it came to practicing law, Counselor Greenspan was more comfortable with land deeds than ill deeds. But Comfort intentionally retained a non–criminal attorney so that in the event of a trial and conviction, he could invoke the *ineffectual rendering of counsel* as a basis for an appeal. Three days ago, Greenspan had conferred with Comfort in the attorney conference pen at the Tombs, though they hadn't formulated any particular strategy. But following the arraignment, Comfort, who was far better versed in criminal law than Counselor Greenspan, was contemplating filing DA Hogan's anticipated worst nightmare, a Motion to Dismiss.

"Defendants please rise," Judge Tyler ordered.

Standing beside Greenspan, Comfort and Nalo faced His Honor, who glanced curiously at the defendants as if to ask, *Have we met before in some social setting?*

The court reporter nodded at Greenspan to go on record as the defense attorney. He acknowledged her smilingly and said, "My name is Leon Greenspan, and I'm filing a notice of appearance on behalf of the defendants."

"Duly noted," the judge said.

ADA Pope, in a shiny, brownish suit that changed shades as the light reflected off it from different angles, rattled off a litany of felony charges, chiefly Possession of Stolen Property.

Judge Tyler removed his glasses. "Anything else, Mr. Pope?"

"No, Your Honor."

"Defendants, how you plead?" the judge asked in a slight black American accent, which he made an effort at minimizing.

Greenspan, a conservative lawyer, his hairline ebbing, wore black-rimmed glasses, and a plain but creased gray suit. "Not guilty on all counts, Your Honor," he responded in a stentorian voice that was not representative of his physique. Greenspan's spine was curved, and his neck leaned forward, the skin on it loose and droopy.

Pope stood. "The People recommend no bail."

"And why is that?" Judge Tyler asked in a vein that said, *You'd better have a damn good reason, son.*

"The defendants are presumed to have stolen five to fifteen million dollars in gems and cash. And in possession of such valuable assets, they are a flight risk. They could flee the country and have the means to vanish and live the rest of their lives anonymously. Not to mention that one of the defendants, Mr. Comfort, has a criminal record dating back to his adolescence." Pope, too, spoke in an almost imperceptible Southern accent.

Judge Tyler replaced the glasses on his nose and perused a stack of documents. He skimmed over that material, and the courtroom vaporized into a stillness of silence save for His Honor's shuffling and leafing of papers.

Comfort covered his mouth and whispered to Greenspan, "Tell the judge the DA doesn't have any proof that we stole anything. His allegations are nothing but pure conjecture."

Greenspan upped off his chair and cleared his throat to get the judge's attention. "Your Honor, my clients have been committed without reasonable probable cause." He outstretched his arm to the right, in Pope's direction. "At this hearing, so far, the esteemed Mr. Pope has failed to proffer any evidence, material or circumstantial, in support of his contentions. And that's all they are, *his* contentions."

Judge Tyler didn't as much as lift an eye off his stack of paperwork, turning pages as if he were hearing nothing. Thirty seconds into this, he finally acknowledged Greenspan's rebuttal to Pope's no bail recommendation. His Honor looked at the elderly defense counsel, though a second or two too long, as if waiting for him to expound why the defendants should be granted bail. When Greenspan said nothing else, Judge Tyler pronounced, "At this time, bail is denied." He swept the courtroom with an unyielding glare. "I'll set a pretrial hearing for Tuesday, January 18, at 9:30." He then asked Greenspan, "Counselor, you plan to file any motions before the pretrial hearing?"

"Yes, it is likely I'll be filing a motion," Greenspan affirmed.

"Court is adjourned." Tyler rapped his gavel, and two bailiffs, who had been standing directly behind Comfort and Nalo as if they were serial killers, guided the prisoners through a rear door twenty feet from the judge's bench.

Greenspan winked at his clients, "I'll be visiting you tomorrow. We'll chat then." And the hobbling commotion of people rising and gathering belongings shattered the complacency in the courtroom.

Two more deputy sheriffs moved in front of the defendants as they walked through the head-spinning maze of corridors down into the Tombs. Comfort and Nalo, still uninformed about what Paolino and Stern might've spilled to O'Neil's minions, were stressed and wired, anxious for tomorrow's consultation with Greenspan. Was the counselor of the opinion that Pope's charges were unsubstantiated and warranted filing a Motion to Dismiss? Bobby Comfort thought so, but his point of view was subjective.

As the next dawn glowed to a purple-gray, again the gigantic black correction officer woke Comfort and Nalo. "What now?"

Comfort said in a sleepy voice, his eyes squinting in the bright, yellow beam of the guard's flashlight.

"Git up and git ready. You're goin' in a lineup."

"A lineup! My lawyer is supposed to be notified, and I know he wasn't."

"Das none o' mah damn business, Comfort. Mah job's to git you up and goin'. Das awl. The rest's yoh problem."

The guard then went to Nalo's cell and banged on the steel bars. "Git ready, you're goin' to a lineup."

"What the fuck is this?" he said to the correction officer. "My lawyer don't know nothin' about a lineup." *Wonder if the DA is tryin' to pull some shit.*

CHAPTER 54

The New York State Court Center at Foley Square in lower Manhattan is in itself a landmark. The limestone-veneered front elevation of the courthouse is an architectural wonder, an impressive façade. The design comprises a 110-foot triangular arch atop a colonnade of columns five feet in diameter, projecting the aura of authority, power, and strength of American justice. On the ledge of the arch are three statues, symbols of judicial impartiality, fairness, and equality for all. Behind that magnificent arcade, inside that stately edifice on the seventh floor was the lineup facility, a stark room that did not correspond to the nobleness of the building's exterior. The walls were a drab gray, and the peeling paint was marred with cartoonish drawings and graffiti. The subjects of the lineup sat on a wooden bench as they waited for the viewing process to begin.

Comfort, Nalo, Stern, and Paolino, all in handcuffs and each displaying a numbered tag pinned on the front of their prison garb—which covered the suspects' stenciled names—sat side by side on the bench, three uniformed police officers hovering in vigilance. None of the prisoners' lawyers were present, and that might be an advantage; later if convicted, this could be another basis for an appeal.

This was the first time Comfort and Nalo had seen Paolino since this ordeal had begun. But talking was not permitted, though they communicated sneakily, eye signaling and mouthing words. And Paolino's message was clear: he had said "nothing about nothing" to any of the investigators. Now that Paolino had lived up to Comfort's unwavering confidence in him, the consternations of any possible evidence that could've been in the hands of O'Neil or the FBI were no longer wrenching Comfort and Nalo. And they huffed sighs of relief. But one liability was still outstanding; the chance that one or more of the Pierre hostages might've recalled Comfort and Nalo's faces. At the moment, however, why fret over a setback that hasn't yet presented itself? If it did, Comfort would meet it head on. This was his axiom in life, but not Nalo's. He avoided confronting and tangling with a dilemma; no, he'd run from a crisis and hope against hope it'd somehow pass over and land elsewhere.

"Okay, we're gonna get the show goin' in a few minutes," joked a cop who coordinated the lineup. "If anyone of you ever dreamed of doin' a tap dance on a Broadway stage, well ours here may not be a Broadway stage, but it's a start for you actors." The clownish policeman laughed mischievously as if he believed he was blessed with comedic talents. "Soon, you'll be under the spotlights. And remember to smile."

"Fuckin' jerk," Nalo mumbled in disdain.

The cop had heard him and locked his gaze on him as if daring him to repeat it.

"What's your problem?" Nalo asked rebelliously.

Comfort elbowed his codefendant in the ribs. "Sammy, knock it off." He flicked his eyes at the cop and said to Nalo, "If he wants to be an asshole, it's a free country."

His ego shredded in the presence of his colleagues, the comic police officer blushed. "Both of you shut the fuck up." Bitterness in his voice, he pointed at Comfort and Nalo. "I don't wanna hear another word from you two."

Nalo stared coldly at him without blinking.

Just then, Pope trudged clumsily into the room breathing heavily, cheeks moistened from perspiration, and melting snow under his galoshes. His 1964 Plymouth Belvedere wouldn't start on this twenty-eight-degree morning, and knowing he'd be delayed he had phoned in with instructions not to begin the lineup without him.

"Mornin', Mr. Pope," said the caustic cop.

"Sorry I'm late. Everybody here?" Pope shed his overcoat, an army-green, full-length fake Burberry, and draped it on the backrest of a chair.

"Yeah, here are the stars of the show," the police officer said, indicating the four sitting on the bench. "The witnesses are in the waiting room."

"I guess we're ready to go." Pope blew his nose and coughed, the symptoms of a festering cold, and went into the reception hall to prepare the witnesses.

One of the walls in the lineup room served as the "exhibit stage." It was brightly lighted and the markings of a height chart were painted on it. There, when called, the accused would be in full view. On the opposite wall, was a three-foot-by-two-foot one-way window, through which the witnesses in the viewing room could look at the suspects in question, though they couldn't see them.

One by one, Pope called the willing though reluctant eyewitnesses from the waiting room. The hostages whom Pope had persuaded to participate were only eight. The first six hadn't recognized Comfort, Nalo, Paolino, or Stern. The seventh, Elijah Weathersby, the black elevator operator, was regretting having agreed to cooperate, and was reneging on even looking at the alleged perpetrators. He lowered his head, eyes glued to the floor. "I ain't messin' with them boys. They be Mahfeea people. I know they are, and you know it, too. I be gittin' killed."

"No, no, no, Elijah," Pope said as if he were speaking in kindness from *brother to brother*, reversing his educated vernacular to the Black English that Weathersby could relate to. The assistant DA tenderly rested his hand on the elevator operator's shoulder. "They be nothin' but street punks, bro. They ain't no Mahfeea. Believe you me, Elijah."

Weathersby's eyelids opened to the maximum, and the whites of his eyes enlarged in disbelief, seeming even whiter in contrast to his dark brown skin. "They ain't no Mahfeea?!" He sucked on his teeth to stress that nothing could be further from the truth. "If yoh beeleeve dat, yoh a fooh. No street punks are gonna try to pull off that kinda job." Weathersby pecked his temple. "Unless they be crazy. They's professionals, and professionals got the backin' of the Mahfeea. I know dat!"

"I can promise you that no matter what, I got yoh back, Elijah," Pope said as though he had the wherewithal to provide Weathersby round-the-clock protection.

"And another tang," Weathersby added, "Why should I help the powleece? You know damn well theys always against us blacks."

"Yoh right, Elijah, but in this case everyone o' them thugs are whites." Pope moved in closer to Weathersby as if he were foregoing all formalities. "Here's your shot at gittin' back at Whitey. See?"

"I doun know . . . I doun know, Mr. Pope." The witness shook his head ever so slowly to mean, *I ain't buyin' it.*

"Awl righ, forget everythin' else. Don't you wanna help a brother?" Pope had played his last card, the Black card.

Weathersby, head bowed, droplets of sweat glistening on his scalp, didn't speak.

Again, Pope placed his hand on the *brother's* shoulder and came in to him eye-to-eye in an overture for solidarity. "I don't get no bonuses if I win a trial, but I move up the ladder. And the higher I go, the more I can help us black folks. Know what I sayin'?"

Weathersby, arms dangling by the waist, entwined his fingers of one hand in with those of the other. He stared at his shoes, mulling those last sentences the assistant DA had spoken, and Pope felt he had softened him. "Elijah, why don't you have a look at these criminals. C'mon, do it fer me."

"Awl righ." Weathersby waggled a forefinger at Pope. "But nothin' better happen to me." As if he were taking his final steps to the gallows, he walked slowly toward the one-way window, and said in a whisper, "They can't see me, righ?"

"No, they can't see you," Pope said, nodding in assurance.

In the lineup were Comfort, Nalo, Paolino, Stern, and two detectives posing as suspects. Weathersby, his inflated, balloon-like face now inches from the viewing window, peered through it. Fifteen seconds clicked on, he stepped back from the glass, and turned to Pope. "Number five and number six," he said in a hushed voice.

The number five tag was pinned on Stern, and Comfort wore the number six. Weathersby had been fifty percent correct, Stern hadn't been one of the stickup men. But for Comfort, this was a bloodcurdling moment. The reality of a conviction and a long prison stretch would take him from his wife and daughter, and he couldn't conceive how he'd cope with that unthinkable outcome. The pragmatic gene in him, though, alleviated his acidy stomach. At times, Comfort mused, a lawyer can challenge an eyewitness's testimony and dilute it to merely an unconvincing conjecture, especially if the person is an unwilling witness in the first place. And on cross-examination, if harried by a defense attorney a hostile witness becomes unsure and hazy, more often contradicting himself or herself. And Comfort, an informal scholar of jurisprudence, was well aware that such incidents were an ordinary occurrence.

A ray of hope shone as he thought about Millie and Nicole.

Pope summoned another Pierre employee from the waiting room, the overweight Louis Rabon, who wheezed as he talked. Rabon's occupation, a bellman, was not only his job title but also the shape of the man's body, the silhouette of a church bell. And as Rabon laughed he bellowed loudly. Speaking about his encounter with Nalo at the Pierre, he said to Pope, "See, I never had a look at him. He come up on me from behind and said, 'Don't move a muscle, and put your hands up. And don't even think about gettin' a look at me'. So I didn't make a move."

"Mr. Rabon," Pope said, "I want you to concentrate on the one with the number four tag." The fourth man in the lineup was Nalo. "Was he the gunman you're talking about?"

"I . . . I don't know, sir. Like I said, I never got a look at him." Rabon answered in a sorrowful lilt as if he wanted nothing more than to be helpful. "But . . . but, if I hear his voice, I'll recognize it right away. Can you let him say what he said to me that night?"

Pope knew that intercepting one's voice is a gray method of identification. A defense lawyer could argue that it isn't uncommon for two or more people to have the identical tonality, more so if they are of the same ethnicity. Every nationality has a prevailing *phonation*, and a phonetician can detect an individual's background by the phonetic sound his or her vocal cords strike. Therefore, identifying someone by his or her voice isn't legally conclusive.

Pope's strategy, though, was that if Rabon could distinguish Nalo's speech, however inadmissible that would be, it might tempt Nalo to confess. But that was wishful thinking on the part of the assistant DA Nalo couldn't be bluffed and seldom panicked; he was the epitome of coolness; so much so that he seemed to have the enthusiasm of a hippopotamus. And although his knowledge in law was limited, he had acute reasoning aptitude, and understood that in a courtroom voice identification testimonies would be struck off the record. But Pope was only slightly acquainted with Sammy "the Arab" Nalo, and thought that by applying pressure on him he might fold. Pope picked up the intercom handset and said into it, "Lieutenant O'Neil, have suspect number four say, 'Don't move a muscle, and put your hands up.'"

Nalo refused to speak, and at the same time he was in a heated argument with O'Neil, who was making him wear one of the wigs that had been confiscated from his Bronx apartment. Nalo, recalcitrant, snatched the poodle-like curly wig from the lieutenant, and threw it on the floor. "I ain't puttin' on no wig, and I ain't sayin' shit. I know my goddamn rights," Nalo said, white, foamy spittle bubbling on the corners of his mouth.

The much taller O'Neil bent into Nalo's face and prodded a finger too close to his nose. "You listen to me and listen good, you Turk. If you keep on being an uncooperative punk . . ."

"I ain't no punk, you shanty mick."

O'Neil grabbed a handful of Nalo's jumpsuit below his neck and growled, "Keep on doing what you're doing, and here's what's gonna happen." He paused, thumbing at the one-way window. "The DA on the other side of that glass has been watching your antics. And I can tell you that no way in hell he's ever gonna give you a plea deal. That's the first thing."

Nalo cut him off and said, "I ain't lookin' for any plea deals. I'll go to trial if I have to." He jutted his chin at the others in the lineup. "You ain't got nothin' on any of us. Why the fuck would I cop a plea?"

O'Neil motioned in the direction of the viewing room. "Those witnesses out there already picked out your buddy, Mr. Comfort. And you're next. But that's not all. One thing is for sure: you're not gettin' bail, and you'll rot in the Tombs 'til you come up for trial. And guess what, you Arab worm, the DA will pull strings to put off the goddamn trial for the next eighteen months." The lieutenant leaned into Nalo's right ear and uttered in a hush for no one else to hear, "Who knows, maybe I got someone down in the Tombs who'll cut your jugular vein and let you bleed to death. All it'd take is a book of stamps and a dime of pot. And you know that." O'Neil paused for this to sink. "Now are you gonna put on that black rug and speak what I want you to say loud and clear?"

Comfort nodded dimly at Nalo, urging him to give in. And the Turk bent his head forward, allowing the lieutenant to affix the wig onto his dome. "So what is it you want me to say?"

"Now we're getting somewhere, Mr. Nalo. Just say, 'Don't move a muscle, and put your hands up.' That's all."

In a vain attempt at masking his voice, Nalo garbled out that sentence.

"Yeah, that's him," Rabon said, a tinge of remorse biting him.

"Are you sure?" asked Pope, a tingling sensation lightening his burdens.

"Yeah, I'm sure."

Elijah Weathersby and Louis Rabon had deflated Comfort and Nalo's upbeat moods.

CHAPTER 55

T he results of the lineup amounted to a dismal obstacle for
Comfort and Nalo; two of the victims had singled them out.
This eliminated the possibility of filing a Motion to Dismiss.
And as matters now stood, Weathersby and Rabon would testify
to the effect that Comfort and Nalo were two of the stickup men
of that unforgettable night of January 2, 1972. But Counselor Leon
Greenspan, across the table from his clients in the lawyers' conference pen at the Tombs, wasn't too pessimistic. "Don't lose any
sleep over it. Look, anytime an eyewitness identifies you it's not
necessarily a slam dunk for the prosecution."

Comfort, unshaven, his hair oily, glanced at Nalo, who didn't
have to worry about oily hair. "Tell me about it."

"In light of what happened in that bullshit lineup, what's next,
Leon?" Nalo asked, eyes wandering about the room as if he were
scanning it for signs of eavesdropping, an inborn paranoia of his.

"Well, the Motion to Dismiss is out the window." Greenspan,
palms facing up, veered down his lips, and shrugged. "I'll just
have to wash away those two witnesses on cross-examination."
Greenspan said it so casually as if discrediting someone on the
stand was as easy as cracking an egg.

"Whatever you're gonna do, do it fast. Locked up in this place you might as well be in a grave," Comfort said, discouragement in his mood. "Leon, you know how bad the conditions are in this joint. I mean, even in here—and this is supposed to be the attorneys' conference room—it's cold as a bastard, and it smells like a bunch of skunks are under the table."

"What are you really saying, Bobby?" Greenspan asked, cocking his head and arching an eyebrow.

"What I'm saying is, if you can work out some kind of a plea. We just wanna get the hell out of this hellhole."

The lawyer closed his eyes and nodded negatively. "That won't happen." He swilled his coffee, and to warm his hands cradled the cup. "Unless you're willing to give up the stolen goods."

"Fuck no," Nalo said.

"I don't wanna give up anything," Comfort concurred, waving around him. "Just that this place is like no other jail I've ever been in."

"You'll both have to weather it," Greenspan said as though he were talking about a minor inconvenience.

"Easy for you to say. Tonight, you're going home to a nice warm house, a nice meal, a soft bed. And tomorrow morning you'll stay under a nice hot shower for as long as you want, and you'll have a nice breakfast," Comfort said. He flicked his finger from Nalo to himself. "When Sammy and I leave this so-called conference room, this . . . this shit hole, we'll be going to the chow hall to eat some shit they call food. After that, we'll be locked into our freezing cells that we each share with a sick criminal—which means we always gotta sleep with an eye open—and we'll lay on a bunk as hard as a slab of stone. In the morning, if our bunkies haven't slit our throats in the middle of the night, we have to piss and shit in front of somebody else, and when we go into the cold showers, we gotta hope that some big-dicked nigger doesn't stick it up our asses."

"You made your point, Bobby," Greenspan said, gathering the paperwork before him and placing it in his leather briefcase. "I'll file a motion for a bail reduction hearing. I'll also open the lines of communication with ADA Pope and see if he's disposed to talk about a plea bargain." He turned his palms up and ventured, "He may or may not."

Among the items O'Neil and FBI Agent Hammer had collected at Nalo's Bronx apartment were three keys, but not ordinary ones. They were flat and longish, and each was stamped with a three-digit number. O'Neil guessed these were safe deposit box keys. He drove to one of the branches of the Manufacturers Hanover Trust bank on the corner of 56th Street and Third Avenue in Manhattan. He knew the manager, Mr. Wells, a diminutive man with neatly parted black hair and a disproportionally small head. Mr. Wells was suited in a navy blue jacket complemented by a yellow bow tie. He spoke in an artificial British accent that gave him connotations of eminence and an unspoken membership in an academic fraternity.

"Good afternoon, Mr. Wells," O'Neil said in his cop-like demeanor.

Mr. Wells's desk, though displaying a gallery of framed photos of his blonde, Waspy wife and four blond children, a handsome gold-plated pen set in the center of it, and stacks of papers everywhere, every object was in perfect order. He stood as if he were a soldier saluting a higher-ranking officer, and thrust forward his hand. "How are you, Lieutenant?" Mr. Wells's nature was invariably cheery, and his smile seemed to be a permanent fixture. "How can I help you?"

O'Neil opened his fist and dumped the three odd keys onto Mr. Wells' glass desktop. The banker seemed puzzled, and the lieutenant asked, "Would you say these keys are to safe deposit boxes?"

Mr. Wells looked at one of the keys. "Yes, they are. But they're not to our deposit boxes." Then he looked at a second key. "They're not all identical. There's a wide variant of these types of keys. See, every bank uses an alternate variation, and these three belong to three different banks."

A *variant* . . . an *alternate!* O'Neil didn't have a clue what Mr. Wells was saying. The banker saw that he had thrown the lieutenant off kilter. "In other words, Mr. O'Neil, all three of these are safe deposit keys, but they're slightly different because not all banks use the same exact ones."

"Can you tell me what banks they're for?"

Still inspecting the keys, Mr. Wells answered, "I'm afraid not, Lieutenant. There are fifty to seventy banks in the New York metropolitan area, plus thirty to forty thrift associations, and these keys could belong to any one of those financial institutions." He adjusted his bow tie. "Sorry, I wish I could be of more help."

O'Neil, working under the theory that the safe deposit boxes matching those keys were chock full of jewels and cash from the Pierre, telephoned Pope, who seconded that presumption. The conundrum was how to locate the banks where Nalo's safe deposit boxes were. The assistant district attorney, ingenious and ambitious, thought of an approach to this puzzle. "Lieutenant," Pope said, "I'd say Comfort and Nalo aren't havin' a good time down in the Tombs."

"That's an understatement," O'Neil said, chuckling vindictively.

Pope leered at the lieutenant, an impish grin that said, *I have the solution.* "I'm gonna call Leon Greenspan and offer him a proposition that I'd bet he won't reject."

CHAPTER 56

"Leon, Assistant DA Pope is on the phone for you," announced Greenspan's secretary as she peered in through the partly open door to his office.

"Thanks, Roseanne." The counselor then said into the phone receiver, "Hello, Mr. Pope."

"Please call me Doug. The purpose of my call is this: I have a proposal for your clients."

"A lawyer who doesn't listen to offers is a deaf lawyer."

They laughed in good humor, and Pope said, "In Nalo's residence, we had found three keys to bank safe deposit boxes. But we don't know the banks they're in. So here's the deal: If your clients tell me where those deposit boxes are, I'll consent to a reasonable bail. The Tombs is not exactly a five-star hotel, and I would think Comfort and Nalo may want to check out of there. I'm sure they can use a seven-course meal at the Rainbow Room and a good night's sleep."

"Interesting. I'll confer with Mr. Nalo and Mr. Comfort and call you in a few days or sooner." Indeed, Greenspan's clients couldn't wait to check out of the Tombs Hotel & Resort Casino. In a minute wasn't too soon.

Comfort and Nalo accepted, in principle, Pope's offer. Two days later, the assistant DA had the sheriffs deliver the defendants to his office. Greenspan also was there. "Let's all have a seat and relax," the assistant DA said, pointing at a few scattered chairs. His three guests each placed one nearer to Pope's wooden desk, and they all sat, four sheriffs in Gestapo-like uniforms standing by in the cramped office.

The talks began, and the first question Pope posed to Comfort and Nalo was, "What's in the boxes?"

Greenspan gestured to his clients not to answer. Instead, he said, "Doug, they will not divulge the content of the safe deposit boxes."

"When was the last time they visited those boxes?" Pope asked.

Again, Greenspan interceded. "I will not allow my clients to answer that question either." Greenspan removed his glasses and regarded Pope. "Doug, I was led to believe all you require of my clients," he nodded with his chin at the two inmates in jumpsuits, "is the whereabouts of the boxes. They will not make any more representations on this matter."

Greenspan, Comfort, and Nalo were seated in a half-horseshoe formation, Pope in his tattered swivel chair across the desk. He described the amount of bail and related conditions, and a list of stipulations that had to be discussed. Several hours into talks that escalated frequently to disputes, all parties compromised and forged an agreement. One proviso was that the defendants would not be released until O'Neil would find and impound the safe deposit boxes. Of course, Comfort and Nalo had to accede to surrendering any and all materials in the boxes. And they did. But why their sudden change of course? The inhospitable, dire-straits environment in the Tombs was the catalyst that would bring prisoners, however tough, to their knees, and relent to the system. Sacrificing illegally acquired assets and pleading guilty so to be sent to a state prison, which comparatively was a heaven, would be an inmate's desperate, and at times, sole option.

Bail would be set at $90,000, pending the approval of Judge Andrew Tyler, the other black component of this case. Mulling it over for three days, and not totally in accord, His Honor sanctioned the terms of the bail: the disclosure of the location of the safe deposit boxes, *and* the forfeiture of the content, in return for the $90,000 cash bail.

O'Neil and Pope were thrilled, rubbing palms in joy at the prospect of opening deposit boxes overflowing with jewels and cash. Comfort and Nalo, too, were uplifted, though a risky trial still hung on their necks. *If only Elijah Weathersby and Louis Rabon would disappear.*

Assistant DA Pope, chirpier than usual, flounced about his office, a bounce in his step; it was time to rejoice. Comfort and Nalo had coughed up the names and locations of the banks where the safe deposit boxes were. "Those boxes will be the proof to win a conviction, or most likely, clip those two thieves' smugness, and maybe they'll gladly take a plea bargain," Pope ruminated to himself. "They'll be too happy to plead guilty. And maybe, facing a twenty-year sentence, they'll give up their cronies in exchange for mercy." This was the break he'd been hankering for since his first day as a prosecutor. Oh, he could just see the headlines:

MANHATTAN DA ANNOUNCES GUILTY PLEAS
FROM THE PIERRE BANDITS

Indeed, he could taste success, and without further ado, he cleared O'Neil to round up those indispensable boxes. "Because of their value, I want you to take along two detectives and one of your sergeants."

"Oh, I plan to. I want plenty of people around when I open the boxes," O'Neil said, nodding in a manner that meant, *You can't find a more capable person to handle this.*

The first stop for the lieutenant and his entourage of minions was the Franklin National Bank on Canal Street near the Williamsburg Bridge. They emptied the black, unmarked Plymouth, the unloading of the hefty four plainclothesmen decompressing the car's springs, and it rose six inches. They marched into the bank, displaying badges as if this were a raid by the Federal Reserve Board. An unfazed but sprightly secretary took O'Neil's business card and said, "I'll let the vice president know you're here." She waved at a carpeted seating area. "Gentlemen, please have a seat."

O'Neil and his boys in polyester suits and garish ties, sitting on the edges of the bank's plush, leather chairs, looked as edgy as a drove of orangutans at a wine tasting event. They waited and glanced impatiently at one another as if the vice president of this branch had nothing else to do but to cater to Lieutenant O'Neil and his underlings.

The protocol and paperwork for the impounding of the boxes was handled in the assistant manager's office. The banker led the foursome to a lower level, where the safe deposit vault was nestled. He told the guard there to open the locked steel-barred gate. The security officer, a white-haired retired policeman, his pink scalp glowing, quickly warmed to his comrades. He arced his arm in a grand sweep as though he were inviting the four cops into a palace. "Come right in. Come right in. You know, I was on the job. Retired now. How long you guys been on?"

No one replied, intimating this was not a social call, the guard seeming resentful. Trailing the vice president, the detectives entered, unsure what to make of this windowless, subterranean setting, rows of ceiling-to-floor safe deposit boxes on every wall.

The banker upheld his decorum and limited the conversation to official business minus idle talk. He instructed the custodian of the vault, "Assist these police officers to access box 331, to which they have a key."

O'Neil handed the key to the guard, who squinted to read number 331 stamped on it. "This one is in the last row over there. I'll show you."

To unlock the boxes' small flap doors, two keys were needed, the bank's master and the one in possession of the box holders. On pinpointing box 331, the guard used the two keys, and unlocked the encased brass flap door. He pulled out the box, which was eight inches wide by twenty inches long, gave it to O'Neil, and nodded at three privacy booths across the floor. "Go in one of those cubicles to do what you gotta do."

O'Neil said to his cronies, "Let's all squeeze in the middle one."

"Are we gonna fit in that little closet?" asked Detective Fitzgibbons.

"We'll have to."

The four policemen took off their coats so to be less bulky and huddled inside the brightly lighted booth. Inside there, O'Neil laid the safe deposit box on a built-in wall desktop and winked at the others, who were all toe to toe. This was the big moment, the defining point of the case against Bobby Comfort and Sammy Nalo. The heartbeats of the burly detectives were accelerating; what they were about to uncover had the earmarks of a milestone in their careers. And who knew? Promotions might've been a definite possibility. "Man, this box is pretty heavy," Lieutenant O'Neil said. "That's a good sign." He opened the lid, and everyone's eyes widened in stupefaction. "Son of a bitch!" two of the cops exclaimed almost in a chorus.

"Fuck!" O'Neil blurted.

CHAPTER 57

Lieutenant O'Neil was bewildered. "This box is full of pennies!"

"I can't believe this," said Fitzgibbons, staring at the hundreds of pennies. "They must've stuffed the jewels and cash in the other two boxes."

"Those boxes are supposed to be at the National Westminster Bank on 57th Street and Third Avenue. Let's go there. No sense in wasting any more time here."

O'Neil repeated the same protocol of obtaining clearance from the National Westminster branch manager to open the safe deposit boxes. But to O'Neil's dismay, in those, too, were nothing but pennies. Not a jewel, not a dollar . . . absolutely nothing. The lieutenant was breathless.

Pennies!

O'Neil placed a hand on the nape of his neck and lay still seething, gnashing his teeth, the jaw bones tightening beneath the skin, "Those varmints fucked us royally. ROYALLY!"

On hearing he'd been blindsided by Comfort and Nalo, Assistant DA Doug Pope was fit to be tied. "Those two con artists swindled me, and I didn't see it coming," Pope mumbled to himself over and over. If in those boxes had been even one piece of the Pierre jewels, this legal action would've been clinched. But now all he had were his two star witnesses, Weathersby and Rabon—and bright stars they weren't. And Pope damn well knew that on cross-examination, the defense lawyers could chop them to pieces faster than a blender minces vegetables.

But not all was lost. He'd been pondering another strategy. He'd subpoena Louis Peppo, the Detroit man who had alerted the FBI about Nalo's necklace. Serving and enforcing a subpoena in a different state is a complex and lengthy route. But through legal arm-twisting, Pope thought, Peppo might cave in and testify against his thieving pal. Meanwhile, District Attorney Frank Hogan was trying to persuade, or rather pester, the FBI to avail at the trial the informant who had pretended to be Harry Towson—the liaison to the mysterious Roland. But despite Pope and Hogan's efforts, they were shut down on all fronts. Peppo flatly refused to testify, and undercover Agent Jack Goodwin objected to the district attorney's request to produce his informant. "The FBI doesn't *ever* reveal the anonymity of our paid informants, mainly for their safety. For that reason, I won't permit him to testify. And that's that," Goodwin said heatedly to Hogan.

At this stage, Pope and Hogan's prosecution of the Pierre *bandoleros* was more anemic than an anorexic. And how was this for an anomaly: Pope devised every legal trick to postpone the trial, feebly hoping new witnesses or evidence might come to light. Normally, the defense is the procrastinator, wishing for circumstances to change in its favor.

Three days after the safe deposit box fiasco, Sammy Nalo's mother posted bail, and the Tombs became a bad memory. At last, he was breathing untainted air. To him, this liberty was as though he'd been released from a lion's den. It had been Nalo's first stint in a jail, and the first time is always a sobering experience. And when you add to it the Tombs factor, well, it was indescribable. Comfort decided not to post bail at this point; it would've surely prompted the authorities to probe who had supplied the cash. He was relying on an expeditious preliminary hearing that would eventuate to the dismissal of the charges. But desperate to build stronger evidence, should the defense neutralize Weathersby and Rabon, Pope did everything in his power to delay the proceedings. Fortunately, Comfort stayed clear of the perils and was managing in the Tombs. He befriended the convicts who "ran the cell block," and bought them off with the customary prison commodities, stamps and cigarettes.

But what about his wife Millie in Rochester? How was she surviving? Comfort was having a nostalgic seizure, though comforted by the financial cushion he'd provided her, a hundred thousand dollars. At least she needed not fret how to keep a warm roof over her and Nicole. But Millie missed Bobby dearly, and her face and that of his lovable child rolled across his mind as if it were a self-rewinding slide projector.

As for Nalo, he had haunting evils to harness. The bookmaker to whom he owed his losses hadn't forgiven the debt, and the moment he'd learn Nalo was out in the streets, he might wish he were back in the Tombs. But Nalo was also fretful about his Bronx apartment; after the search, was it in shambles? And he couldn't stop thinking about the satchel of jewels he'd buried under the sink in his bathroom. Did the FBI or the NYPD find it? If so, it would solidify the charges against him.

Nalo walked gingerly into the apartment, switched on the lights, and scurried to the bathroom. He crouched by the sink, and saw that the lose planks beneath which he'd hidden the satchel were intact. He breathed a sigh of relief and removed the wooden slats. He plunged his hand into the hole and felt nothing. Nalo's heartbeat suddenly pounding, he lowered his head above the hole to look inside it. "Ough!" He pounced on the floor harder than an enraged ape. "Those motherfuckin', thieving, bastard scumbag cops. They robbed me." Indeed, they did, namely Detective George Bermudez. And Nalo couldn't do a damn thing about it. And maybe this was for the best; had Bermudez not pirated Nalo's jewels, assistant DA Pope would've had an ironclad prosecution.

The second set back, or so it seemed, came to light when Nalo, through an intermediary, sent messages to Al Green. No response. It was becoming more and more apparent that he, and possibly, Ali-Ben, had absconded with the bulk of the Pierre gems. Comfort, who hadn't yet posted bail, was oblivious to these calamities that were simmering Nalo into a stew.

CHAPTER 58

A t last, in early June of 1972, Pope's legal contrivances to repeatedly adjourn the preliminary hearing ran aground. The proceedings were now on the New York State Supreme Court calendar for June 5.

The function of a preliminary hearing is for the presiding judge to weigh statements and evidence proffered by the prosecution, so to determine if there are grounds for the charges or indictment lodged against the defendant. If the judge deems the prosecutor's allegations justifiable, he orders the accused to stand trial. If the indictment is *defective*—baseless—he may dismiss it or reduce the charges to lower class felonies. Both sides can introduce witnesses who may be examined and cross-examined. The jury is not present, and spectators are not in attendance.

In the matter of *The People of the State of New York vs. Robert Comfort and Sorecho Nalo*, the preliminary hearing was underway. The courtroom had an overall worn appearance and a stench of staleness. The brownish wood wainscoting lining the walls was dull and graying from decades of dust. And the tan marbled floor was scuffed and had lost the luster it once must've shone. An alabaster

chandelier, six feet in diameter, with ornate brass stems spanned grandly in the center of the ceiling, and two smaller replicas hung over the judge's bench.

At the prosecution table was Assistant DA Doug Pope, and Assistant DA Keith McMillan. Tapping nervously on a manila folder, Pope, in a dowdy gray flannel suit that draped him too loosely, an elbow planted on the tabletop, stared at the door fifteen feet to the right of the judge's bench. Behind that door, the prisoners, whom the deputy sheriffs herded up from the bowels of the Tombs, waited in rows of cells to be called in the courtroom.

At the defense table was Sammy Nalo, Counselors Leon Greenspan, and James La Rossa, who had substituted him in representing Nalo. It would've been a conflict of interest for Greenspan to simultaneously represent Nalo. La Rossa's sartorial taste was the portrait of luxuriant male fashion. In a light-gray worsted wool suit—Italian made, of course, that fit him as if the tailor had used his body as a template—he seemed as though he were an advertisement in a glossy magazine. But for his modish garments, costly Italian shoes, year-round tanned face, and pompadour-styled jet-black hair, he was often taken for a gangster. The inflection of La Rossa's speech, too, simulated that of a Mafia mobster, though his movements were deliberate and slow. He walked slowly, turned slowly, sat slowly, and stood slowly.

In defined dissimilarity, Greenspan always wore the same shabby gray suit and white wrinkled shirt.

A bailiff knocked on the door to the holding cells, and it opened. Two marshals preceded the manacled Comfort, ankle chains clanging, and another tailed him, all in a short procession to the defense table.

"So this is your partner, the illustrious Bobby Comfort," defense attorney James La Rossa said to Nalo in a hush.

"I don't know about illustrious, whatever that means," Nalo jested.

The Honorable Judge Tyler stepped through another door to the side of the bench, his black robe billowing.

"All rise," crowed a bailiff.

The attendees stood, and the tall Judge Tyler, whose fat, dark brown face did not relate to his otherwise medium build, said in a baritone voice, "Be seated." He barely raised his eyes to look at the bailiff and instructed him, "Proceed."

The stenographer, seated in front of the bench, nodded to mean she was ready, and the bailiff bellowed, "This is docket number 72-00101433: *The People vs. Robert Comfort and Sorecho Nalo.*" And he handed the judge a packet of papers.

Tyler read those documents, and half a minute passed. He coughed and spat into a white handkerchief. He said, "Mr. Pope, you may begin."

Following the perfunctory statements by Assistant DA Pope and the defense lawyers, he, Pope, sent McMillan to fetch one of Comfort's arresting officers, Will Bannon. He had been in a room across the hall with the prosecution's roster of witnesses, all waiting to be beckoned to the stand. Other than when testifying, witnesses aren't permitted in a courtroom in session. At the end of Greenspan's blistering of Bannon, Pope called Lieutenant O'Neil to recount the specifics of Comfort's arrest at the Royal Manhattan. The lieutenant's testimony amounted to a jargon of police parlance less any substance. Next, Detective George Bermudez took the stand. Seemingly competing, but not quite, with the exquisitely accoutered La Rossa, he was sharply dressed in a pale blue suit accented by a violet tie. His nappy, graying hair contrasted against the blue jacket.

On cross-examination, these witnesses hadn't fared well; their testimonies only verified they had played a role in taking into custody Comfort and Nalo, and nothing else. More disarming, and even comedic, when La Rossa probed Bermudez, his justification for apprehending Nalo was as pointless as last week's newspaper. The adroit-tongued lawyer had asked Bermudez, "What made you decide to arrest Mr. Nalo?"

Bermudez touched the knot of his tie as if it needed to be centered. "Well, he was carrying a bag that had a large crowbar, a sledge hammer, and some other things."

La Rossa placed his elbow on the top edge of the witness stand and leaned on it. "What kind of *things*?"

"Uh, you know . . . tools, burglary tools."

"No, I don't know. What exactly are *burglary tools*?"

"Uh . . . things like . . . pliers, eh, chisels."

"You call common hand-tools . . . pliers, chisels, and hammers, *burglary tools*?"

The detective, usually an overall sly expression in his eyes, was suddenly stammering.

Judge Tyler saw fit to intercede. "Detective Bermudez, what else impelled you to arrest Mr. Nalo?"

Bermudez looked up at the judge. "Eh . . . excuse me, Your Honor, what do you mean by impelled?"

Irritation was stamped on Tyler's face. "I'm not here to teach you English. I'll rephrase the question. What caused you to apprehend Mr. Nalo."

"Oh, I see. I also found a passport in his apartment."

La Rossa said deprecatingly, "Detective, I have a passport at my home. And in my garage I may have the same type of tools you discovered in Mr. Nalo's bag." He stalled, and his eyes shot toward the ceiling for a moment of drama. "Well, now you got me thinking. Does that mean I should be in fear that you may arrest me as well?"

Laughs and guffaws drowned the courtroom, including the usually serious-faced Pope. Tyler rapped his gavel. "Order please."

And La Rossa terminated his cross-examination.

The morning grew to a sultry day, and the courtroom warmed to a sticky temperature, sweat staining the judge's crisp white collar, and those of everyone else. His Honor decided to spare himself and his court the muggy heat. He pounded his gavel with extra force as though he were forging a fiery-red horseshoe, and fanned his face. "This hearing is adjourned until tomorrow, June 6."

The next day, the proceedings reconvened. The same cast of characters took their respective places, and once again Comfort burrowed from the door to the holding pens, shackled ankles and feet swishing on the floor, Nalo winking at him from the defense table.

As everybody settled in, Doug Pope declared he'd be placing on the stand Louis Rabon and Elijah Weathersby, his only ammunition for the trial. Assistant DA McMillan came through the swinging doors of the courtroom with Louis Rabon, his black, slicked-back hair shining as if he had used a can of axle grease to plaster it. Rabon went into the witness box, and a bailiff swore him in. Pope navigated him through the obligatory questions and then asked, "Mr. Rabon, do you see in this courtroom any of the gunmen who held you at gunpoint in the course of the robbery?"

Unhesitant, Rabon pointed at the defense table. "The third one from the left . . . uh, the bald cat."

"Mr. Rabon, please explain to the court what do you mean by the 'cat.'"

"The bald dude over there," Rabon clarified. In the fifties through the seventies, *cat* was a term referring, particularly by Puerto Ricans, to an unfamiliar person.

"Let the record reflect the witness indicated Sorecho Nalo, also known as Sammy the Arab," Pope boomed as if he had won the battle, striding to his chair in a swagger of triumph.

Nalo dropped his head as though he was losing faith, and his lawyer tapped his arm. "Everything will be fine, Sammy."

La Rossa sauntered to the witness stand as though he were strolling through a museum. "Good morning, Mr. Rabon," he said smilingly. "Sir, when you picked out Mr. Nalo in the lineup, was he bald or not?"

"He didn looh bald to me. He had a whole head o' hair." Rabon was born in Puerto Rico but raised in the United States, and his enunciation rang in a Black-American accent.

"Did anyone tell you Mr. Nalo is now bald?"

"Eh . . . uh . . . whatchu mean?"

The obese bellman seemed flustered and La Rossa increased the heat. "The question is simple. Did anyone tell you Mr. Nalo is now bald?"

Rabon, a drop of sweat dribbling on the side of his face, looked to Pope in a way to ask for help. Pope's head sunk, and he was about to crawl under the table.

La Rossa persisted, "Mr. Rabon."

"Uh, yeah. Somebody told me he's bald now," Rabon answered in a meek, inaudible voice, unlike his cockiness on direct examination.

"*Who* told you, sir?"

Rabon stole another desperate glance at Pope, praying he'd give him a sign of an inkling. Nothing. The assistant DA was studying the floor in shame, knowing that at this very moment the judge was probably thinking the worst of him.

"Answer the question, Mr. Rabon," Tyler admonished.

"Mr. Pope told me," said Rabon, garbling his words.

The Honorable Judge Tyler ripped off his glasses, crinkled the eyelids, and shot a scowl at Pope.

"I have no further questions for the witness, Your Honor." La Rossa had scored a win on this first round, and the grimness on Nalo's face perked up.

NICK SACCO

When they put Comfort, Nalo, Paolino, and Stern in the lineup, O'Neil also put in three detectives as decoys, two of which Rabon had seen earlier in the waiting room. The third one, even a child could've picked him out as a stand-in. They were clean shaven, groomed, and had on nice, clean clothes. On the other hand, O'Neil's men had given the four accused shabby, poor-fitting clothes to change into from the green jumpsuits they'd been wearing. Given all this, the lineup had been a sham, and it wasn't hard for Rabon to guess who the criminals were and who were not.

CHAPTER 59

J udge Tyler dismissed Rabon, and Weathersby replaced him. Would he be Pope's savior? The assistant DA's pleas to Weathersby, *"Don't you wanna help a brother?"* had been taunting him day and night. He did want to help a brother. If blacks, Weathersby professed, unified and favored fellow blacks, rather than undermining one another, African Americans would prosper as a populace, and gain fair treatment and equality. "Das how them Jews done it," Weathersby ruminated. "But what about them Mahfeea guys?" Wrestling with his inner self, he paced in the waiting room, hands wringing in despair. "I doun know . . . I doun know about this."

The prosecution and the defense predicted the hearing might lag on for another week. Millie, terribly missing her husband, saw this as an opportunity to see him, and for him to update her on how matters stood. She drove from Rochester to the New York metropolitan area and lodged with Comfort's sister, Rose, for the duration of the hearing. In a conservative, olive-green dress that covered her knees, she was the emblematic dutiful housewife. Millie's ruby lipstick highlighted her pearl-alabaster skin, and lent sleekness to the fluffy, black hair that framed it. A silk scarf enfolding her tall neck, and brown, low-heel shoes, Mrs. Comfort's angelic countenance could only project positively on the African American judge, who eyed her more often than he should have. Was he attracted to the *white sistah*?

Mrs. Comfort sat behind a glass partition, and before the hearing would begin she'd chat with her Bobby, reheating passion for one another. They'd press their palms on the partition, longing for physical contact. "It's all gonna work out, baby. It's gonna work out. You'll see," Comfort said, sensing she didn't believe it.

That morning, Pope called Weathersby to the stand, but the result was not what the prosecution had expected. Weathersby's testimony was ambivalent and convoluted, not at all how Pope and he had scripted it. The witness said he had recognized Nalo, Comfort, and Stern in the lineup, when in fact he had sorted out only Comfort. Knowing that, Judge Tyler understood the damage of Weathersby's ambiguity, an irreparable discrepancy. Was Weathersby now having second thoughts and intentionally contradicting himself?

Pope was on the ropes from this blow, and cut short his examination. Motioning off-handedly at the witness box, he said dejectedly, "He's all yours, Counselors."

Pope was scribbling away in his yellow pad, and Greenspan quick-stepped to the witness box. "Mr. Weathersby, why here in the courtroom you just accused those two additional defendants and did not do so in the lineup?"

"Well . . . 'cause . . . 'cause then I wasn't really sure."

Greenspan fired back acridly, "And what makes you so sure now?" Greenspan, in the stance of a pirouette, spun on his feet 180 degrees, and pointed at the defendants. "Did they come to you in a dream?" He nodded at Weathersby as though he wasn't anticipating an answer. "Or did you see a fortune teller?"

Everyone laughed, save for Pope, who was chewing nervously on the cap of his pen. His humor had melted as the chances of winning a conviction were becoming bleaker than bleak.

"No, das not what happened," Weathersby answered weakly. "Just that back there at the lineup, well, I wasn't sure."

"And now you're *absolutely* sure. Is that right?" Greenspan asked scornfully.

"Well . . . I'm pretty sure."

"You're *pretty sure*! But you're not *positively* sure, Mr. Weathersby. Are you?"

The witness, eyes downcast, glanced at *Brother Pope* as Greenspan, walking back to the defense table, said, "No further questions, Your Honor."

Pope was still scribbling in his pad so to avert eye contact with the judge.

The defense lawyers filed motions to disqualify Rabon and Weathersby's testimonies on the basis they were inconsistent and nebulous. In so far as the affidavits of the arresting officers, these too should be tossed out, Leon Greenspan and La Rossa contended. Other than ascertaining that they were the ones who had arrested the defendants, the cops' accounts were irrelevant in establishing Comfort and Nalo's culpability. In his Opposition Brief, Pope's arguments to dismiss the motions were meritless for the sole reason that the validity of Greenspan and La Rossa's motions was irrefutable.

The proceedings were adjourned, and at an attorney-client conference Leon Greenspan prophesized, "The way I see it, the judge *has* to grant our motions to suppress." He chewed on his lower lip and shook his head. "I read Pope's Opposition Brief, and I can tell you it's worthless."

La Rossa said, "I read it, too. And Leon's right. I believe Judge Tyler is duty-bound to disregard Weathersby and Rabon's testimonies."

If that were to happen, then Pope's case might dissolve quicker than ice in boiling water. And then, what else was there for the assistant DA to hurl at Comfort and Nalo? Not much of any substance. Agent Jack Goodwin had forbidden his informant to appear in court. Louis Peppo steadfastly declined to come forward against Nalo. Paolino, who had pleaded guilty to a misdemeanor, withstood O'Neil's pressuring him to implicate anyone. And Bert Stern, who had also pleaded guilty to a minor offense, was an innocent bystander and truly knew nothing about Comfort and Nalo's past. And Greenspan and La Rossa were euphoric that an acquittal was definite.

It had been twenty-four hours since the defense lawyers filed the Motions to Suppress, and Judge Tyler was ready to render a preview of his ruling. But anticipating that his analysis of the evidence before him would be met with hostility and objections, he invited all parties back to his courtroom. "Gentlemen, I carefully considered your motions and Mr. Pope's Opposition Brief. I must say, both sides put forth compelling arguments."

Both sides put forth compelling arguments!? This doesn't sound good, Greenspan and La Rossa felt. What is this judge talking about? Pope's opposing arguments were senseless.

His Honor proceeded, "Whenever the arguments from all sides are on an even par, I'm inclined to leave matters as they are. And although I haven't yet decided on the Petitioners' motions, I'm leaning toward denying them. Anyhow, tomorrow morning, I want you attorneys to begin selecting a jury."

The defense lawyers gasped and winced, as did the defendants, and Pope, laughing on the inside, couldn't hide a beaming smile.

Greenspan sprang to his feet. "Your Honor, according to law you can't begin jury selection until you rule on the pretrial hearing."

"Well, I am in the interest of expediting things," the judge said.

This judge is out of his mind, Nalo so badly wanted to say as loud as he could.

NICK SACCO

In spite of Pope's muddy response to the Motion to Suppress, nobody could understand why Judge Tyler was on the fence. I felt bad for those guys, but at the same time we were shitting a brick, thinking they might turn on me and everybody else. I was paying attention to what was going on from far away. And although I had come back from Florida, I stayed clear of the 19th Hole, and every other joint I used to hang out in—just in case Comfort or Nalo pointed the cops in my direction. I didn't have to worry about Dom Paolino or Bert Stern because they didn't even know me or the other guys.

CHAPTER 60

Unbeknownst to the defense lawyers, Judge Tyler initiated a covert phone call to Assistant DA Pope to discuss the pending Motion to Suppress, an irregularity that is unethical and even illegal. An honorable judge does not communicate with either side unless all parties partake in the conference or phone conversation.

Pope was sipping tea, and picked up the handset on the third ring. "Hello, ADA Pope."

"Doug, Judge Tyler here."

On hearing Tyler's voice the assistant DA tensed. *Why is he calling me?* "Good morning, Your Honor. Is anyone else on the phone with us?"

"No. Just you and me."

Just you and me!? "Oh!"

"Doug, my calendar is overloaded, and I'm tryin' to clear some cases out of the way. As I see it, your case against Comfort and Nalo is weak . . . very weak."

"I beg to differ, but I disagree. I have . . ."

"Look son, you can disagree all you want, but I still say you got very little to present to a jury. In fact, I'm in favor to granting counsels' Motion to Suppress. If I do, which I most likely will, your case goes out the window, and those two scoundrels will walk. You understand, Doug? I strongly recommend for you to work out a plea bargain with defense counselors."

Pope couldn't believe this judge was violating ethics. In essence, he was saying, either offer a plea that would be accepted, or he'd grant the Motions to Suppress. But why? Was his court docket *really* overbooked? Or maybe he didn't want to spend his entire summer in a hot courtroom. Or did he have ulterior motives? But what?

The next covert step Judge Tyler made was a telephone conference with Greenspan and La Rossa. "Gentlemen, this won't take long."

"Is Mr. Pope on the line with us?" La Rossa asked.

"No, he's not."

Greenspan and La Rossa were astonished. They were silent for two to three seconds, and La Rossa spoke first. "What is the nature of your contacting us, Judge?"

"Counselors, my calendar is overloaded, and I'm trying to lighten it. Reconsidering your Motion to Suppress, I will most probably deny it. So I suggest . . ."

"Deny it!" barked Greenspan. "The prosecution has absolutely nothing on our clients other than a scarcity of facts and an abundance of speculation. And two questionable eyewitnesses who equivocated on cross-examination. What you're telling us is ludicrous."

"Now, now let's not get hot under the collar," His Honor said.

"Let's not get hot under the collar?!" La Rossa cut in. "Mr. Pope's Opposition Answer is fraught with nonsensical issues and gibberish he used just to fill the pages. Aside from the witnesses' conflicting statements, the lineup was flawed, and you know it. It was rigged to make it easier for Weathersby and Rabon to discount the decoys."

"My *strong* suggestion to you both is to work out a plea agreement with Mr. Pope. He has a much more substantial case than you think. And if I deny your motions, you have no defense. Plus, I don't have to remind you that your clients are no angels, and have a reputation for these types of armed robberies." Judge Tyler concluded. "Take my advice, Counselors. Good luck."

Good luck?!

"Something doesn't ring right," La Rossa later said to Greenspan. "I've known judges who communicated with one side while excluding the adversary. But only on rare, rare occasions. And even then, it was under extraordinary circumstances. Judge Tyler must have something up his sleeve."

Neither side knew that His Honor had been in touch with the other, and that he dispensed to them conflicting opinions. Why would Tyler insinuate to the prosecution and the defense, in separate conversations, that their respective opponent had the upper hand, and recommend to plea bargain because of the *high* probability of losing at trial?

What could Judge Tyler be brewing?

NICK SACCO

I told Christie Furnari that two hostages from the Pierre had picked out Comfort and Nalo in a lineup. Furnari knew damn well this might've led to bigger problems for him and the rest of us. Comfort and Nalo were stand-up guys, but stand-up guys or no stand-up guys, when facing thirty years in the joint, who knew how they might've reacted. They could've given up all of us to save themselves. Something had to be done about this, and fast.

CHAPTER 61

The third week of July 1972, Bobby Comfort's sister, Rose, visited him at the Tombs. The visiting room was crowded and noisy to a level that one had to shout to the person three feet away. A locker room-like odor sullied the air, and its source was those inmates who bird-bathed to avoid the shower stalls, where danger lurked.

Rose, a petite brunette who wore short, layered hair and had pencil-thin lips, was uneasy in these environs. Tattooed, scar-faced undesirables whose visitors' comportment often suggested they, too, belonged in the Tombs, were a disconcerting scene.

"So how are you, Bobby?" Rose asked apprehensively, scanning the room uncertainly. She and her brother were close in age, and tendered a special feeling of affection to one another ever since they had been in a playpen together.

He blew out a cloud of smoke toward the ceiling and heaved a sigh. "You know, Rose, I gotta make the best of a situation." He nodded at the sea of green jumpsuits. "This is not a nice place. You can never let your guard down."

Rose grimaced, tears welling. "How can I help, Bobby?" If she could only kiss him.

"I can get out o' here if I post bail. Ninety grand. I have it, but if I use my money, they're gonna look up my asshole with an X-ray machine."

Rose didn't need to be asked twice, and said, "I can use my house as collateral. My husband won't mind. He knows you're good for it." She glanced to the left and to the right, aghast by what she was seeing. "They all look like bad people. I . . . I just want you out of here."

"In here, everybody's innocent, and everybody has a story. Me, I did what I did, and I'll survive. Anyway, thanks, Sis. I'll have my lawyer call you. His name is Leon Greenspan."

The bondsman was Al Newman, a thin, Jewish accountant with an aquiline nose that at first sight you'd mistake for a bird's beak. Within minutes of meeting someone, he'd drop hints of his Semitic heritage, and in every sentence he slipped in a Yiddish term. Newman catered exclusively to underworld figures. He was Christie Furnari's contact, who had recommended, rather dictated, for him to be flexible in negotiating with Rose, and not ask for a high home-equity-to-bond ratio.

Newman waved away any doubts. "Oh, sure, sure, Christie. If it's important to you for Bobby Comfort to make bail, I'll take care of things with his sister."

Indeed, Comfort's freedom and well-being was of paramount importance to Furnari. He wouldn't chance that Comfort, distressed over the awful conditions at the Tombs, and his uncertain fate, might join the rat pack of stoolies and inform on the FBI's much wanted prize, the Lucchese consigliere. "Thanks in advance, Al," Furnari said.

The bald, medium height bondsman patted Furnari's biceps as men do when a hug is too intimate. "Don't mention it, Christie. For you, anything."

Furnari sent a courier to Leon Greenspan to arrange for a place and time to meet. When they saw one another in person, the consigliere gave Greenspan the business card of "the right man," whom Greenspan was to introduce to Comfort's sister. Furnari said, "Leon, this guy, Al Newman, will have Bobby Comfort out before the sun goes down."

The house was deeded jointly to Rose and her husband, and by subway they went to Newman's office on White Street across from the Tombs. The bondsman's office was the size of a walk-in closet, and his desk didn't measure much larger than a milk crate. Rose gave the deed to Newman, and he prepared a packet of documents, which she and her husband signed. The next morning, July 22, 1972, a sunny day, Bobby Comfort was free to leave the sweltering, damp jailhouse, and walked outdoors into the fresh air, taking in the stroller-crowded Foley Square.

Comfort didn't waste a minute to go and see Millie, who was still staying at Rose's house. It had been a passionate reunion, one that reinforced Millie's faith in her beloved husband. And Nicole, on seeing Daddy reentering her life, was emblazoned with that sense of security when a child knows the mother and father are a happy union.

Comfort had pressing loose ends to rein in. But Christie Furnari asked to see him to talk about "his future." The Lucchese consigliere told Comfort that what he was about to say was strictly *only* for his ears. And Comfort avowed solemnly that he would keep it a secret. Their conversation, a touchy but acute topic, lasted twenty minutes.

"Christie I appreciate what you're doing, and you can count on me to take it to my grave. As far as the amount it's gonna take for you to do this, you have my word that you'll get it back as soon as everything is straightened out."

"I know I will. By all accounts, you're a stand-up guy."

They shook hands, and Furnari hugged Comfort. "Remember, Bobby," Furnari whispered into his ear, "No one is to know about this. Not even that worm Sammy. Understand?"

NICK SACCO

At this point, I didn't know exactly what Furnari was up to, and neither did the other guys, Frankos, Germaine, and Visconti. Al Green and Ali-Ben hadn't been seen since they took off with Comfort and Nalo's jewels, so they were out of the loop and didn't care. I had an idea what Furnari was trying to do, but I wasn't sure. I knew at some point he'd fill me in.

CHAPTER 62

Comfort's other priority was for him and Nalo to coordinate the retrieval of the multi-million-dollar satchel from Green and Ali-Ben. "What are you talking about, Sammy?" Comfort asked in an agitated voice, a flood of warm blood rushing up to his temples.

"Yeah, for real," Nalo answered, nodding as one does to impress that he has no time to banter. "I haven't heard from either Green or Ali-Ben."

Comfort stomped his feet, and with fisted hands stiffened his arms at the waist. "Fuck! I knew it, and this is all because of the goddamn necklace you snatched. You and your fuckin' greed, Sammy. There's no doubt they think I also knew about it, and they figured, fuck them, if they can steal from us, we'll teach those two con artists a lesson."

Nalo was speechless, but not repentant, and Comfort asked, "What else went wrong?"

"That stash I had in my Bronx apartment . . . well it's gone. One of the cops must've taken it when they searched the joint."

"Good thing," Comfort said somewhat blissfully. "Good thing, otherwise we'd be in a worse pickle."

"Green and Ali-Ben will turn up. I don't think it's all lost." Nalo said. "You'll see."

Comfort chucked his cigarette butt to the side with a snap of the wrist in a show of repugnance. He spat on the ground. "Don't bet on it. You got a better chance at winning the lottery."

"I gotta get my hands on some cash. This bookie that's chasing me is gonna squeeze me."

Comfort lit another cigarette. "What're you want me to do? You steal from me, and then you come for help. I already got myself locked up for coming to your rescue." Comfort sucked on his teeth. "This time, you're on your own, Sammy. As soon as the hearing is over, or if we're gonna have a trial, when that's done, I'm going back to Rochester with Millie. The farther away from you, the better it'll be."

The staggering jolt of millions of dollars in jewels missing hadn't yet sunk in, and Greenspan called Comfort to his office. He listened to his lawyer retelling Judge Tyler's urgings to negotiate a plea agreement. "Here's the beauty, Bobby. The judge is leaning on the district attorney to cut a deal."

A well thought-out plea bargain might be the tool to remedy a bag of problems, chiefly the Pierre monkey, and a long string of past sins: the Sophia Loren lark, and other robberies Comfort and Nalo had organized. One such heist had occurred in February of 1970 at a Sutton Place penthouse, and another at the Regency Hotel nine weeks prior. These were unsolved crimes, and because they'd been executed in a similar modus operandi, the common denominators were Bobby Comfort and Sammy Nalo. The authorities would put two and two together, and soon scrape at their heels. Knowing this, Judge Tyler's insistence for Pope to plea bargain couldn't have been timelier.

"We have one glitch," Greenspan said grimly. "Pope won't agree to no less than fifteen years."

"Fifteen years! No way . . . no way." Comfort pushed himself away from Greenspan's desk. He bent over, elbows on his knees, and supported his forehead with both hands. He sulked for ten to fifteen seconds and raised his head. "Look, Leon, Pope doesn't have much to win at trial. I'm going to stand my ground. I want no more than a four-year sentence and the judge's recommendation for early parole. *And* I want acquittal for all known and unknown crimes so I can clear my slate clean."

Greenspan threw his hands up to mean, *You're asking too much.* "Bobby, that's a big, big gap between what Pope wants and what you want. But we'll try it."

On July 21, 1972, the pretrial hearing resumed. "Good morning, gentlemen," Judge Tyler said. "As I've already recommended, I'm asking you to have a conference and sketch out a plea deal that will be acceptable to all parties, and ultimately me." His gaze swept the courtroom, and he glanced at the clock on the wall to his right. "It's now 9:45. We'll reconvene here at 12:30 to report to me on your progress. I'll adjourn until then."

In one of the conference rooms at the courthouse, Assistant DA Pope, his sidekick ADA McMillan, La Rossa, Nalo, Greenspan, and Comfort grouped around an oblong table. For this occasion, the flamboyant La Rossa was modeling a navy blue, double-breasted suit, and Comfort and Nalo were bedecked in custom-fit suits, a gray-blue Versace for Comfort, and a black Bill Blass for Nalo. This was the first time Pope had seen Comfort not in a green jailhouse jumpsuit.

"What are you proposing Mr. Pope?" Greenspan began, unfolding his palms.

"I gave this a great deal of thought. And in light of the facts, I'm willing to settle for a fifteen-year sentence, and a one-million-dollar fine for each defendant."

"In light of what facts?" Nalo said bitingly. La Rossa clasped his client's wrist to reel him in.

But Comfort added logs to the fire. "Yeah, what facts? You don't have any facts. I won't take a day more than four years, and I'm not paying any fines."

Pope shut a manila folder he had in front of him and stood, buttoning the middle button of his gray tweed jacket. "We're too far apart. I *may* reconsider the fine, but I won't agree to anything less than fifteen years."

And the conference ended.

Pope and McMillan strutted through the door, and those who were left in the room traded glances of disillusionment.

CHAPTER 63

They reassembled in Judge Tyler's courtroom. His eyes roved from the prosecution's table to the defense's, striving to read if Pope and the defendants' lawyers had forged a settlement. "Do we have a tentative agreement?"

The four attorneys, Pope, McMillan, Greenspan, and La Rossa rose, and Pope said, "No, Your Honor."

Tyler peered from above his glasses, a pair of thick spectacles that magnified the judge's brown eyes to the size of acorns. "In my chambers, please." He stepped down off the bench, and tramped into his chambers, everybody trailing him in a single file as though they were hiking boy scouts following the scoutmaster.

This so-called chamber, which was nothing more than an office, had a sweet aroma of pipe tobacco. And sure enough, the judge pulled out his pipe from a desk drawer, and lighted it, puffing on it three or four times, smoke spiraling up to the ceiling. He took the pipe out of his mouth and gestured with it. "Hope this doesn't bother anybody." Whether anyone minded, the judge wasn't about to snuff out his pipe. The feuding parties shuffled chairs in front of His Honor's desk, one so huge that a single-prop plane could've landed on it. Judge Tyler again leered over the top of his bifocals.

"Tell me, why haven't you haven't come to an understanding?"

"Your Honor, I will only consent to a minimum of fifteen years," Pope stated. "They want four years, and that's not going to happen. Even if I were to agree to that, District Attorney Hogan would not approve it."

"And from our perspective," Greenspan said resoundingly, "we can't move forward to working out the details unless my client and Mr. La Rossa's are sentenced not a minute over four years. And that is not negotiable."

"Mr. Pope," Judge Tyler said in a voice lower than normal. In his chambers, he always called Pope by his first name, Doug. Referring to him as "Mr. Pope" was the byproduct of the judge's irritation for the assistant DA's unreasonable stipulations. "I can't understand why you're so inflexible."

Although Pope's obstinate objection to reduce Comfort and Nalo's sentencing was unwavering, the Honorable Tyler would not concede to such a harsh stance. The hearing disbanded, and that afternoon the judge, whose moral compass needed recalibration, bypassed Pope and opened a dialogue with his boss, Manhattan District Attorney Frank Hogan. Pope, Tyler knew, had to abide by the terms of any plea agreements his superior would consent to. And His Honor telephoned Hogan. "Sir, I called to request a concession from you."

Hogan guessed what this was all about. "What can I do for you, Your Honor?"

"I don't know how much you know about me," Tyler said.

Hogan thought, *What I do know, judging by your reputation, is that I wouldn't put anything past you.* Instead, he replied diplomatically, "Frankly, Your Honor, I'm uninformed in respect to your tenure on the bench."

"Well, I'll tell you. When I'm in my black robe, I'm fair-minded— and anyone who's appeared before me will attest to that. I uphold another principle: I never forget an accommodation and never forget a discourtesy. In simple terms, I'm the sort of judge who subscribes to the motto that if you wash my hands, I'll wash yours. And our world, the legal profession, is a small carousel of judges, lawyers, prosecutors, and law enforcement agents that spins in a tight circle. And one never knows when he or she will find themselves confronting somebody whom they've slighted."

"I see," Hogan said. "And in this instance, how can I *accommodate* you, Your Honor?"

"Oh, it's a minor favor I'm asking. My docket is terribly overloaded. To add insult to injury, I'm arthritic, and this summer the high temperatures cursing us New Yorkers has me in agony. I need to spend time at my vacation home in Vermont. And I want to clear my calendar as much as possible by disposing those cases where the prosecutors' charges are anemic—and even frivolous. If I can accomplish that, it may afford me to take time and get away from the humid heat we've been enduring here. One such case that should be disposed of is *The State vs. Robert Comfort and Sorecho Nalo.*"

"Ohhh, yes," Hogan said in a chord that suggested, *I knew this was coming.* "And how can I indulge you?"

"I'm asking you not to oppose a four-year sentence for guilty pleas from the defendants. Your deputy, Doug Pope, is adamant and won't consent to anything less than fifteen years, which I find utterly ridiculous, considering the indictments are baseless." And this is where Judge Tyler administered a bitter dose of reality by placing Hogan on notice that, "In fact, I'm inclined to grant the defendants' Motion to Suppress."

If I'm reading Tyler right he's telling me that If I don't play ball with him, he'll rule against me. "I see, Your Honor. Before deciding, may I have the opportunity to confer with Mr. Pope?"

"Why of course, Mr. Hogan. You're a respected district attorney, and I trust you'll act accordingly. *And* anticipating your cooperation, I thank you in advance. I'll be much obliged to you and your office."

◆

NICK SACCO

Christie Furnari phoned and asked me to round up Al Visconti, Bobby Germaine, and Frankos the Greek, and drive those guys to a pool hall he owned in Brooklyn on 73rd Street and 20th Avenue. Furnari, as he normally would, didn't say much over the phone other than him wanting to talk to all of us about something urgent. In the rear of the pool hall at the end of an alley was a narrow outdoor cement stairway leading to the basement of the joint. It was out of plain sight, and it suited Furnari just for that reason. He and I go back since I was fifteen, and as long as I can remember that's where he held sit-downs and meetings with people who didn't want to be in the public eye, him included.

The Lucchese consigliere, unlike John Gotti, the addicted attention-getter, was private, discreet, and secretive. He didn't talk much, and didn't ask too many questions. And he didn't want you to ask too many questions. He never drove luxury cars, or dressed in fancy clothes. And you'd think Furnari was a working-class stiff and nothing more. I don't recall ever seeing him with gold rings, or expensive watches, or Havana cigars. An average man.

We climbed down the stairway, one so steep it made you dizzy, and I knocked on the black steel door. Furnari welcomed us in the basement of the pool hall, and music from the big band era of the forties was playing, his favorite. In the center of the cement floor was an octagon-shaped card table and eight chairs. We sat around it, and he said to us, "I took out insurance on Bobby Comfort and that Turk Nalo. Just to make sure they don't get the idea of rattin' us out." He raised a palm and cocked his head. "I'm not sayin' they would. Especially Bobby. But when somebody is up against the wall and lookin' at thirty years in the joint, you never know how he'll take it."

I had an idea what Furnari was talking about. "What did you do, Christie?" Germaine asked.

Furnari smiled. "I paid off the judge." He nodded in confirmation. "I funneled two hundred and fifty grand to him to make sure Comfort and Nalo don't do more than four years in the slammer."

None of us were surprised; Furnari's tentacles were long and mighty. "A couple o' days ago," he went on, "I spoke with Bobby and told him I was gonna get to the judge. He sure was glad to hear I'm able to do that. He said he'd pay me back when things are straightened out, and I have no reason to doubt him. He's a man of his word." Furnari pointed at all of us. "But if things don't go right, or somethin' happens to Bobby or Nalo—God forbid they should get killed—you guys gotta give me back your share of the two hundred and fifty grand. Got that?"

I said, "Oh, yeah. I don't have a problem with that." And neither did Germaine, Visconti, and the Greek. And even though we knew that Comfort and Nalo wouldn't buckle if new charges for their past felonies started falling on top of them, nevertheless we felt a lot better knowing the fix was in. Money, the evil of all and the solution to all.

The only problem that was getting in the way for Judge Tyler to seal the deal was the goddamn prosecutor, Pope. "Number one on his agenda was to make a name for himself," Furnari said. The assistant DA wouldn't budge from wanting to put away Comfort and Nalo for fifteen years. And it wasn't anything personal. It was business, but that's how the system works. The average American believes anything the government says and everything they read in the papers. They think that judges, prosecutors, and cops place justice above any situation. Wrong! It's all about self-serving motives at anybody's cost.

Frankos the Greek hadn't said a hell of a lot. And that wasn't unusual; for the most part, the Greek never talked much. But here I saw a certain look on his face and knew what he was thinking. He turned to Furnari and said, "Maybe I should whack this mouleenian, *Pope."*

Furnari crimped his lips and nodded at the Greek. "That may not be a bad idea."

CHAPTER 64

Three days had passed, and District Attorney Hogan had not yet replied to Judge Tyler's overture. The judge was incensed at Hogan's irresponsibility for timeliness and asked his law clerk, Gertrude Higgins, to phone him. Ms. Higgins, a spinster in her fifties, rimmed glasses on her thin, hook nose, graying, straw hair in a bun, spoke with the Manhattan DA's secretary, and imparted his message to Tyler, which was, "Mr. Hogan will call you tomorrow."

His Honor was displeased and felt Hogan's indecision was an ominous sign.

Judge Tyler was coercing Hogan, and the district attorney was not the average politician who easily bent to strong winds. But sometimes it's wise to yield to a gale. Hogan conferred with Doug Pope and rehashed the salient facts by raising these points: "Doug, besides Weathersby and Rabon, we don't have anyone else to corroborate their stories. Worse yet, Tyler told me, in so many words, that if we don't assent to the four-year sentence he'll suppress the testimonies of those two witnesses. Then we'll have less than nothing to introduce at trial."

Pope was shaking his head in discord. "I'm confident I can push Comfort and Nalo into taking longer sentences than four years."

Hogan, too, was shaking his head but more vigorously. "I totally disagree. These are astute veterans at their game and are not easily dissuaded."

"With all due respect, Mr. Hogan, I couldn't live with myself if those two thieves get away by spending so little time in jail. It's unfair to those who committed far lesser crimes and are imprisoned for a lot longer."

What Pope couldn't live with was missing out on the nationwide publicity that would spark at press conferences as he'd tout how he had so cleverly outwitted the foxes of jewel thieves, and wiped two treacherous felons off the streets for a long time. He'd stand gallantly in front of cameras and microphones and claim boldly, "That pair of robbers will no longer pose a threat to the thousands of hotel guests in Manhattan." Indeed, Doug Pope, the rising legal eagle, would be stepping foot on the golden ladder to stardom.

But what if . . . what if Hogan were to override Pope and cave in to the scant four years? The sentencing would have to be executed discreetly without sounding off before an orchestra of press corps. Such a quiet, dull ceremony would dampen the effect of Pope's goal. And the elite sector of jurisprudence, that league of high-powered lawyers with year-round tanned faces; yes, those impeccably attired barristers, who dwell in mansions and flaunt trophy wives a third their ages, and own stables of luxury cars, would never know of Doug Pope. This was miserably depressing to him; and he couldn't bear the thought that he'd never again be in the epicenter of an exceptionally high profile case. This was why Pope had to ensure that Comfort and Nalo, the two most-sought jewel thieves in the whole USA, would not escape the punishment they deserved, so he could trumpet his victory from the highest mountain and become a shining star.

Yes, Pope's indomitable ambitions were in top gear; how could he be bridled? Perhaps Frankos's blunt impulse to assassinate the tenacious assistant DA might be the solution.

CHAPTER 65

S peaking of Frankos the Greek, he had stumbled upon a major discrepancy, the total worth of the Pierre haul, and he was keen on speaking with Nick Sacco about it. They met at Café Mille Luci in Brooklyn.

Frankos and Sacco were at a table in the marble-veneered dining room, an expansive hall reminiscent of ancient Roman bacchanalian décor. The Cat, in a mauve silk jacket and violet-blue custom-made shirt, said, "How've you been, Greek?"

Frankos waved a hand in a negative signal. "As if it's not bad enough that I haven't gotten my full cut, I gotta worry that someone may rat us out." Frankos leaned into the table, his black, bushy mustache twitching. "But listen to this, Nick. Bobby Comfort gave a huge chunk of his take to Rene the Painter up in Rochester to fence for him. A couple of days later, Bobby asked Rene when he can get paid, and Rene told him to take a walk." Frankos chuckled as if Comfort's misfortune was the most hilarious story he'd ever heard. "Rene's boys roughed him up a bit, and Bobby figured he's better off cutting his losses and keeping his mouth shut about it."

Sacco saw an opportunity in this. "How much of those jewels did Bobby lose to Rene?"

"From what Bobby told me, although he wasn't too committal," Frankos fluttered his hand as if he were estimating, "I'd say about four million. And to think that he and that little prick Sammy told us the whole score was only about two million. And here, another four million turns up in Rochester. Never mind the necklace that surfaced in Detroit." Frankos lay back in the chair and rested his arm on the table. "How about those fuckers? They've done us wrong."

"Are you sure about Rene swindling Comfort?"

Frankos waved at a waiter as he answered, "I'm absolutely sure. I ran into Bobby at Dangerfield's, the new comedy club on 61st and First Avenue. I went to see George Carlin there, you know, the comedian. Bobby happened to be there at the bar, and he gave me the whole rundown."

"Umm, very interesting . . . very interesting!" Sacco said.

That afternoon, he was with Furnari and told him about Frankos's findings. "So they beat us out of a few million, eh?" Furnari said in a not too surprised tone.

"It could even be more."

Furnari pondered this revelation. "Nick, get a hold of Germaine and Visconti. Tomorrow morning we're all goin' up to Rochester. We're gonna pay a visit to Rene," Furnari said roguishly, winking at Sacco. "We'll leave here early at six o'clock, and we'll be back by tomorrow night, hopefully with a few million bucks in diamonds."

CHAPTER 66

T he powder-blue Lincoln Mark III, purring at an 85-mph cushion-ride, was in cruise control mode on Interstate 90 for Rochester, New York, seventy miles to the west. The occupants, Christie Furnari, Al Visconti, Bobby Germaine, and Nick Sacco at the wheel, were drowsy from the long, monotonous drive. It was 10:20 A.M., and judging from the low, dark-gray clouds, and the humid air inside the car—despite the air-conditioning on full blast—a thunderstorm might've been imminent.

"We're comin' up to a rest area," Sacco said. "Youse wanna stop and get some coffee?"

Germaine, in the rear of the smoke-hazed Lincoln, tapped Furnari on the shoulder to wake him. For the past forty-five minutes of the six-hour trip, the Lucchese consigliere had been asleep in the front passenger blue leather seat, his balding head resting on the window. "Christie, we're stopping for coffee and to take a leak."

"Uh . . . oh, yeah. I . . . I do have to take a piss," Furnari said as he wakened. "Nick, how far we have to go?"

"Another hour."

"I wanna get there before Rene wakes up. This way we'll catch him when his brain is still fried from last night's whoring. The bastard sleeps 'til twelve o'clock."

As Sacco already knew, and Bobby Comfort had feared, in retribution for Nalo's underhandedness in so far as the notorious necklace, Ali-Ben and Al Green had in fact fled to Europe, touring that continent, throwing money around as if they were two Saudi princes.

As Furnari and his posse were en route to "shake down" Rene the Painter, Green and Ali-Ben landed at Leonardo da Vinci Airport in Rome. They had flown from Amsterdam, Holland, where black and Arabic men are the ladies' preference. And evidently, the same applied to Italian airline personnel. On the two hour and forty minute Alitalia flight, the female attendants had been quite flirtatious with Ali-Ben. It is known that those stewardesses, too, host a fondness for Arabian chaps. It must be the middle easterners' male musk.

Ali-Ben and Green, sporting European chic apparel, had coupled with two women they'd solicited at the red light district of Amsterdam. Katja and Georgina, a pair of fleshy loosie-goosies, had been through the woods in the past, tantalizing and outsmarting the wolves in there.

Walking through the airport terminal, the Dutch ladies, wrapped in skintight décolleté dresses that were less than three inches below their crotches, smothered Green and Ali-Ben, slithering like snakes all over the bemused Americans. As the four lovers waited for the carousel to spit out the luggage, they embraced, and kissed, and grinded, cackling and giggling, behaving as though they were ready to climax right then and there. They retrieved the suitcases—Louis Vuittons, of course—and began the exhausting walk to the terminal exit where the taxis queued for their fares. The horny couples crammed into the subcompact taxicab, a Fiat 124, and Al Green said to the driver, "Grand Hotel Plaza on Via Del Corso." He pronounced that, *Grean Hote Plasa on Vya Dee Curso.*

The driver, darkly tanned with a black pencil-thin mustache and eyes an inch apart, did not speak English, and made a face that said, *What planet are you from?* He asked, waving his arm, *"Ma cosa dici? Mannaggi, questi Americani sono tutti scemi."* *What are you saying? Damn, these Americans are all morons.*

Green asked in his black lingo, "Anybody know what he be tellin' me? I don't speak no Aitalian."

Georgina had a faint knowledge of the romantic language and translated for the driver in a slightly more intelligible pronunciation, though he didn't understand her completely.

Her tongue loosened, and she and the cabbie connected. Hand-gesturing, he said, *"Ah! finalmente ho capito. Grazie signorina."* *Ah! Finally, I understand. Thank you, Miss.* *"Ma lei da dove viene?"* *But where are you from?*

Georgina groveled to answer in Italian. She looked at the ceiling of the cab as if the translation was written there. She rehearsed the response by whispering it to herself, and in a staccato, a broken sentence, answered, *"Uh . . . io, eh . . . sono, uh . . . dal'Olanda."* *I'm from Holland.* Georgina's stuttered and butchered words amused the cabbie, and he swung back and winked at her.

The taxi rolled away from the curb, and drove south on Via Mario de Bernardi, a tree-lined road graced by a magnificent vista leading to the end of the airport service road. Within three kilometers, the Fiat turned east for the entrance ramp to Strada 80-Este, a three-lane highway. The lovebirds in the backseat couldn't wait to fondle and tongue-kiss and plunged right into it, the driver, seemingly envious, stole glances in the rearview mirror.

It was a warm but dry sunny afternoon, and the foursome, so entangled into themselves throughout the ride, couldn't be bothered to take in the perfect Roman weather. The twenty-kilometer distance to Via Del Corso, where the extravagant five-star Grand Hotel Plaza charmed that famous street, consumed forty minutes, mainly due to high-volume traffic. The hotel is nestled in a small square, a quaint setting three blocks east of Fiume Tevere, the Tiber River, a sinuous tributary that slices Rome in half. A mile to the west is Vatican City, and from the top floors of the Grand Hotel Plaza one can ingest the breathtaking view of la Cupola di San Pietro, St. Peter's Basilica.

But breathing in that splendid panorama and basking in the posh suites of this famed hotel was not what the two Dutch whores had in mind.

In the USA, it was 11:30 A.M. in a downpour of rain, lightning fracturing the skies. In the Corn Hill section of downtown Rochester, the blue Lincoln exited I-90 and turned south on Eagle Street, where "Rene the Painter" Piccarreto lived, a third of a mile west of the Genesee River. This waterway, as does the Tiber River in Rome, carves Rochester in two. Piccarreto's residence was a two-family home; he, his wife, and three children occupied the second floor apartment, and his mistress, conveniently, resided on the ground level.

Sacco parked the car across the street. He and the others walked over to the front door of the brick home, a smell of industrial pollution in the air. No one answered the bell until three or four minutes of ringing. As Furnari had figured, Piccarreto was still asleep, and woke to the persistence of the ringer. Bleary-eyed, he poked his full head of black hair through a window and hollered in a croaky voice, "Who the fuck is it so early in the . . ." On seeing Furnari, thoughts of why he and three hoods were at his doorstep quickened his pulse. "Oh, it's you, Christie. What . . . eh, what do I owe this visit to?" Piccarreto's delight to see the Lucchese consigliere didn't sound too convincing.

"Let us in, Rene, before we break down the door," Furnari said quite convincingly.

If it hadn't dawned on the portly Rochester made man why Furnari had been on a 360-mile odyssey to see him, now he had a good hunch. It must've been something to do with the jewels he had swiped from Bobby Comfort, Piccarreto feared. "Give me a minute to put on clothes." As he withdrew from the window, he banged his head on the frame of the glass.

"Come in, come in." He led his guests to an overcrowded den of gaudy furniture that was covered with clear plastic, an Italian-American custom. "Sit, sit anywhere you like. Can I get you guys coffee?" Piccarreto's wife had brewed a pot of Colombian coffee, and the aroma drifted throughout the apartment, a radio murmuring in another room.

"No," Furnari answered. On cue from him, his entourage didn't sit. "I'll make it short and sweet, Rene. I want the swag you took from Bobby Comfort." Furnari jabbed Piccarreto's hairy chest, his three backups standing stoutly behind him. "Most of those jewels were supposed to have come to me and my friends here. Understand?"

"I don't know none o' this, Christie."

"You didn't!" Furnari said dryly. "You knew that Comfort's score went down in my backyard, and you should've checked with me first. Keep this in mind, Rene; I don't forgive disrespect."

Piccarreto clasped the back of his trunk-like neck in thought. "I got a fence who wants the whole package."

Sacco interjected, "Fences don't pay much. We can do a lot better. I got jewelers in the Diamond District that I consign my swag to, and they give me seventy percent of retail. That's a hell of a lot more than what any fence will ever pay."

"Rene," Furnari said, "where are the goods right now?"

Piccarreto hesitated a bit too long, and Furnari said forcefully, "Where are the goods, Rene?"

"Eh . . . in a bank safe deposit box."

"Let's go get them."

"Well . . . I need to . . ."

"I said, let's go get my property," Furnari ordered through tightened teeth.

CHAPTER 67

A bellhop unloaded the luggage from the Fiat taxi and stacked it on a cart. Ali-Ben and Al Green paid the driver, and walking arm in arm with Katja and Georgina, ambled into the Grand Plaza Hotel, an edifice that has been a fixture on Via Del Corso for a century and a half. The frontage of this marvelous structure is of sculpted, rectangular stones that veneers the exterior walls of the first floor. A balcony protrudes above the entrance foyer, a portico consisting of three double doors recessed under multiple ribbed grand archways, and the center doorway opens into the lobby. The length of the building, up to the height of the first story, is accentuated with tall arched windows, which are the showcases of the hotel's boutique shops. As a whole the architecture is reminiscent of the Renaissance period.

The lobby, grander than grand, rivals the Pierre's in opulence, reminding Green and Ali-Ben of that audacious adventure of a few months past. The main staircase is a mass of white granite, and brass tie-rod retainers snuggle a red carpet into the lower corners of the risers. And most dramatic, a life-size white marble statue of a lurching lion straddles the forward end of the wrought iron railing.

The four tourists sidled up to the reception desk, and registering vamped into a comedy act. Communicating with the check-in clerk was soon reduced to sign language. The fewer than few Italians in Italy who do speak English aren't easily understood. They speak English in a melodic cadence and enunciate it as if they are reading Italian verse. But thanks to Georgina, they managed to finalize the check-in and scuttled to their suites for a tumble in the sack.

The lovemaking was raw with indescribable fetishes. Green was through in eight minutes as he ejaculated, and Ali-Ben boiled over in even less time. They were a prostitute's ideal Johns: one-two-three, and her job was finished. The boys, tired and satisfied, needed sleep, but the girls, full of energy, were wired to shop on Via Del Corso, a boulevard populated with upscale shops and boutiques.

In a Dutch accent, Katja said to Ali-Ben, "Baby, you rest because me and Georgina are going shopping." She rubbed her man's chest, kneaded his testicles, and said in a slow, enticing hush, "Are you going to give your girl spending money?"

He nodded at his pants crumpled on the floor at the foot of the bed. "Hand me my trousers." He peeled out a thousand dollars (ten thousand at present value), and she took the wad. "Bye, baby." Happily, Katja danced away, waving with her fingers. "See you later."

In the adjacent suite, Georgina succeeded in the same feat, sucking cash from a John. And the two girls were off to a wild spending spree, setting Via Del Corso on fire with their provocative clothes, or lack thereof.

In Rochester, Furnari & Company were in a bank, waiting for Piccarreto to emerge from the safe deposit vault, presumably with three or four million dollars in gems and gold. Fifteen minutes passed, and Furnari said to Sacco, "Nick, Rene has been in there too long. Go see what he's doin'."

As Sacco started walking to the vault room, Piccarreto came into sight, a metal lunch pail under his arm. He gave the container to Furnari. "It's all in there, Christie."

"All of it, Rene?" the consigliere asked diffidently.

"Yeah, yeah. It's all there," Piccarreto said gloomily as though he had lost his right arm.

"I hope so. I don't wanna have to come back here again."

On returning to New York City, Sacco sorted through the precious contents of the lunch pail. He calculated the gold and stones at $4,200,000. "Not a bad haul," the Cat said laughingly.

Furnari's instructions to him were to parse out those jewels in equal amounts to himself, Germaine, Visconti, and Sacco. "I'll take care of it, Christie." But the Cat gave a portion of his end to Frankos.

Comfort was unaware Furnari had recovered his goods from Piccarreto, but that was neither here nor there. More pressing issues were plaguing him. A plea deal was still not consummated, and he phoned Greenspan in search for answers.

"Bobby, just three hours ago I told you I haven't heard anything yet from Pope. I can't keep calling him. What do you want me to do, put a gun to his head?"

"That may not be a bad idea."

"Look Bobby, things have to fall into place, and sometimes it takes much longer. But I'll get La Rossa on the phone, and we'll call Tyler's law clerk. Maybe she has some news. All right?"

Greenspan and La Rossa, on a teleconference with Judge Tyler's law secretary, Gertrude Higgins, inquired if District Attorney Hogan's office had decided on the proposed four-year plea deal.

"Thus far, Mr. Hogan hasn't confirmed it nor denied it," she said apathetically. Ms. Higgins was a social iceberg who seemed to loathe anyone else but herself. She was so flat-chested that if she turned sideways you couldn't see her.

"A week has come and gone, and we have an obligation to our clients to expedite this issue," La Rossa said.

"If you gentlemen wish, I can have Judge Tyler phone you later this afternoon. That's the best I can offer."

Two hours had lapsed, and Judge Tyler did return the two defense attorneys, call. "I'm just as perplexed as you are. I don't have an answer as to why DA Hogan is avoiding me. I'll speak with him tomorrow morning, and hopefully I can pry him a bit."

Greenspan, though he didn't mind it, couldn't begin to guess why Tyler was so obliging, as if he had an incentive to push for leniency. Greenspan couldn't have thought that Furnari had channeled a $250,000 bribe to His Honor. La Rossa, though, was not in oblivion; he had been the conduit to Tyler, and it was he who delivered the cash to the judge. But postponing the outcome of the case was a torture for Nalo and Comfort; and it wasn't any less unbearable for Millie, who was carrying the grief of a widow. They'd been on pins and needles for the past three weeks, and a settlement had been intangible, if not unattainable.

CHAPTER 68

JULY 14, 1972

Al Green and Ali-Ben were acclimating to living in Rome in a regal hotel at three hundred dollars per night ($2,500 at present value). As far as the blonde-haired Katja and the Afro-sporting Georgina, they were becoming stale and wilted to their dates, and by the weekend Green and Ali-Ben would fly to Amsterdam and trade in "the worn out bitches for two fresh whores." They were ignorant to the fact that flying to Holland to shop for sex was unnecessary. Rome had its own red-light district, and it wasn't far from the Grand Hotel Plaza. A fifteen-minute taxi ride, barring traffic, and you'd be in proximity to the Hotel Pulitzer on Via Guglielmo Marconi, a wide concourse boasting a row of mature elm trees on its center island. This boulevard was a runway of prostitutes of all kinds: heterosexuals, homosexuals, lesbians, transvestites, and bisexuals. This mélange of debauchery attracted a potpourri of effeminate males, bizarre freaks, and even eunuchs. And irrespective of one's preference and persuasion, on Via Guglielmo Marconi he or she could satiate all sorts of sexual appetites. It was the Fulton Fish Market of prostitution.

Between now and the weekend Green and Ali-Ben would be taking pleasure in their last licks of the buxom Katja and the luscious Georgina. At the moment, as the sun sank, they roved here and there, sightseeing for a preview of Rome's nightlife. The Romans were out wandering about, many lapping ice cream cones, and others munching on paper bags of peanuts, all chatting at the same time with laughter after every sentence. Green, Ali-Ben, and the girls strolled on Via Veneto, promenading in and through boutiques. They paused in front of an art gallery, which they didn't care to visit, and walked farther toward the shoe stores. On display in the brilliantly lit window of one shop, named Rossana Sul Veneto, was a pair of tan lizard-skin boots. The price tag read 400 lira, or $2,300. Katja, excited as a second-grader, arms flailing and wiggling her hips, pounded Ali-Ben's chest and jumped up and down. "Look at those boots, Ali." She wrapped her arm around his and asked in a girlish voice, "Will you buy those beautiful boots for me?"

Ali-Ben couldn't resist; Katja's eyes could morph from those of a street-smart slut to the look of an angelic, adolescent virgin.

"Shit, they're so expensive that not even the lizards can afford them. But I'll make you happy," Ali-Ben said.

They all went inside the boutique, and Katja tried on the boots, looking in the mirror this way and that way. She said they fit fine, and the shop owner boxed the dazzling footwear. Ali-Ben counted out a sheaf of liras and paid him. Georgina was not to be outdone. Browsing in another corner of the shop, she spotted a Gucci leather handbag that cost Al Green 730 lira, or $3,800. But money was no object; the $11,000,000 in jewelry they had swiped from Comfort and Nalo, even at this spending rate, could last a lifetime.

Dusk had fallen, but Via Veneto was bright from the street lamps and the light spilling out from the beautifully propped store windows. Contrary to popular belief, clothes-shopping marathons are laborious for women, more so when spending someone else's money, and by now Katja and Georgina had an irrepressible hunger. Green hailed a cab and they were off to Corso Vittorio Emanuele II, the Park Avenue of Rome. There, two blocks east of the Teatro Valle was a highly recommended restaurant, Don Carlo, an eatery that specialized in exotic recipes. And that depends on what one considers exotic. The maître d`, outfitted in a white, long-tail tuxedo, sat the party of four at a round table in the center of the softly lit dining room. The new customers—an African American with garish gold chains on his neck and wrists, a swarthy, bearded Arab, and two women, whose comportment and clothing advertised their wares—were conspicuous and intrusive to the other diners.

Luciano Pavarotti's powerful, melodramatic voice—a tenor that vibrated everyone's intestines—emanated from the ceiling speakers, singing an aria from Puccini's opera, *La Bohème*.

> *Che gelida manina*
> *se la lasci riscaldar.*
> *Cercar che giova?*

The menu, exorbitantly priced, naturally was in Italian, and Georgina once again did the interpreting. One of the specialties at Don Carlo was the braised horse flank in ragu sauce. The thought of eating horse meat upset Green and Ali-Ben's stomachs, though it shouldn't have disturbed the Turk. He, a native of Turkey, was accustomed to feasting on goat meat, lambs' heads, raccoons, rabbits, and donkeys, but maybe his palate must've been Americanized.

"Fuck this fancy shit," Green groused, flinging his napkin. "I ain't havin' no horse meat, and all this crap. Let's go to a place where we can get some barbecue ribs and fried chicken. And maybe a couple o' bags of French fries."

Ali-Ben chortled. "What's wrong with you? Ribs and fried chicken! Where're you think you are, down south in Alabama on your grandfather's pig farm?"

He laughed boisterously, the girls cackling, though they hadn't understood Ali-Ben's spoof. And Don Carlo's patrons, disrupted by the outbursts, pitched snide looks at the unruly vacationers.

Katja and Georgina had a taste for Belgian waffles and cheese blintzes, a favorite of the Dutch, but those delicacies did not exist in Italy. Italians, staunch braggarts of the local cuisine, are stubbornly unreceptive to sampling other countries' foods.

The dinner cost another thousand dollars, and of course, for Ali-Ben and Al Green, two rich American music promoters, as they'd represented themselves, the carousing would not be over without snorting lines of cocaine, drinking, and dancing at Bacchus, a world-famed, snobbish nightclub on the eastern end of Corso Vittorio Emanuele II. It was not too far from Don Carlo, and the quartet of revelers tramped and skipped merrily to Bacchus as the girls, to the appall of the night strollers, kissed sloppily and groped their gentlemen's genitals.

The nightclub's bouncers were discriminately selective in admitting the eager applicants at the door. And one look at Ali-Ben and his entourage was all it took for the doormen to wave him and his lewd company away. Green stepped forward and did his own waving, but with a US one-hundred-dollar bill, the world's universal currency. The bouncer swallowed the green bill into his palm, and motioned the two couples into Bacchus's lounge. A fifteen-foot marble statue of Julius Caesar in a toga and sandals, sword in hand, loomed in the middle of the four-sided bar.

Sly Stone's hit song "I Wanna Take You Higher" was blaring from the loud speakers, and you couldn't hear yourself talk. The dance floor was large and twenty meters square. Above it rotated a slow-spinning glass ball four feet in diameter, strobe lights illuminating it, shooting colored rays of flashes careening in every direction, impairing one's vision. That was part of the discotheque trend of this period.

Ali-Ben and Katja inched to the dance floor, and began swaying more and more to Sly Stone's beat, "getting into the groove." A slick Italian man, who cut the personification of a Roman Casanova, was dancing alone, pantomiming a lewd advance at Katja; not that the lascivious gesture offended her, but it bruised Ali-Ben's masculinity. Amid the ear-piercing rock music, he and the intruder hissed and cursed at one another, the bickering soon ensuing to a shoving match. The mob of dancers gaped incoherently, and three or four bouncers dove in. A gun materialized, and *PAH, PAH, PAH,* three shots rang out, resonating above the music, and Casanova was mortally wounded. Someone pointing at Ali-Ben and Green hollered, *"Sono stati quei due, il negro Americano, e l'Arabo che va con lui." Those two did it, the American negro and the Arab with him.* Which wasn't true.

Under the blinding strobe lights, Ali-Ben or Al Green hadn't seen who had produced and fired the pistol, but they knew that if they didn't disappear pronto, the authorities would've implicated them in the shooting. They took the Dutch girls by the hand and scuttled for Bacchus's exit.

Out on Via Vittorio Emanuele II, they piled into a taxi, Ali-Ben and Green panting faster than a dog in heat. "The Grand Hotel Plaza," Green instructed the driver.

As the cab pulled away from the curb, Georgina muttered somberly to the boys, "Somebody in the club said you two did it."

Green and Ali-Ben stared at her, a gaze of incredulity on their faces.

"I don't know what happened in there, but we gotta get off the streets and get outta Rome tomorrow morning," Green said to no one in particular.

But they didn't have flight reservations, and this was the middle of July, the height of the travel season. Ali-Ben, a Muslim, prayed to his Allah to avail two tickets for the next Alitalia flight to New York—or anywhere in the USA. And Green, who didn't believe in a god, started praying now. He wiped his forehead and murmured, "Oh, dear Jesus, git me outta this mess, my man."

CHAPTER 69

W e're in high season," said the Alitalia ticket agent in barely understandable English. "If you no have reservations two weeks in advance it is impossible to find empty seats. All flights are one hundred percent full." She placed the edge of a hand on her neck in emphasis.

"So what do we do?" Green asked, befuddled and panicky, Ali-Ben standing next to him hunched over the counter.

The fashionable ticket agent, in a navy blue jacket, white crepe blouse, and a red scarf tied around her neck, shrugged indifferently. "Boh."

Green and Ali-Ben were clueless as to what she had said; *boh* is Italian slang expressing, *Who knows? It's not my problem.*

They had to leave Italy, and fast. Actually, they had to flee Europe, period. The Italian authorities would transmit to Interpol the two Americans' status as persons of interest, and an expanding dragnet throughout the continent would be at the fugitives' heels within the lifespan of a bee.

Normally, the pretty ticket agent, her face a rainbow of colors—cherry-red lipstick, black mascara, and rouge on the cheeks—would've aroused the sex buffs, Green and Ali-Ben, but this was not the time for that. She seemed fascinated by these dark-skinned travelers. "I see if we have seats on flight out of Malpensa Airport in Milano."

Green and Ali-Ben sucked in their breath as her fingers flew across the computer keyboard. "Yes, you can get on flight this afternoon at 1:35. You can board a domestic flight from here to Milano at 10:55." She looked at her wristwatch. "You have time to make it if you hurry."

Green shook his head in confusion. "Wait, wait. Run that by me again."

"You have forty-five minutes to catch next domestic flight to Milano, and at 1:35 you can take international flight to New York Kennedy Airport." She smiled and pushed out the inside of her jaws with the tongue, a subliminal signal of attraction.

"Awl right! Les do it."

The brunette ticket agent typed into her keyboard and generated boarding passes, Green and Ali-Ben's crisis seemingly over. Green leaned into the counter, imbibing the lady's perfume, and asked, "Uh . . . you ever come to New York?"

She lifted her eyes from the computer screen and blinked her long lashes. "Why you want to know?"

"Well, maybe I can show you aroun' Manhattan," Green said, a wide grin opening on his lips.

The young lady tilted her head as though she were apologetic. "Sorry, Signor Green. Is against company policy for Alitalia employees to socialize with passengers." Again, she pressed the tongue inside her jaws, cheeks heaving as if she were rolling a penis in her mouth.

He wrote his name and phone number on an old boarding pass and passed it to her. "If you feel like breakin' the rules, call me. It be worth it."

Earlier that morning, Green and his brother-in-law Ali-Ben had hustled the Dutch floozies onto a KLM aircraft bound for Amsterdam. And in three hours, the two Americans would be on a Boeing 747 in flight to the good ol' USA. But that might be like jumping from the frying pan and into the fire.

Meantime, arrivederci Roma.

NEW YORK, MID-JULY, 1972

District Attorney Hogan and his deputy, Doug Pope, were lunching at a luncheonette in Foley Square. They were in a relatively private booth surrounded by the working-class customers who were employed at the court complex a short distance away. The hissing of frying bacon in the background and the salivating smell that came from it pricked Pope's craving for eggs and pork bellies. Hogan didn't have much of an appetite and dug into the crux of things. "Doug, the pressure from Judge Tyler regarding the Comfort-Nalo case is mounting. He's about to grant the Motion to Suppress. And I can't for the life of me imagine why he's indulging Comfort and Nalo's lawyers."

"Nah, nah. We gotta stick to our guns," Pope said.

"We gotta stick to our guns? Our guns have blank bullets," Hogan countered. He flipped his palms upward. "This judge has backed us into a corner. We have no choice but to capitulate and negotiate the four-year term with Greenspan and La Rossa."

Pope tapped his chest. "Are you telling me to concede to those two hoodlums' stipulations?"

Hogan wagged his index finger. "No, I'm not telling you. I'm ordering you to do that."

"Bobby," Greenspan said over the phone, "tomorrow we've been called to Judge Tyler's chambers."

"What about?"

"If I were to guess, Mr. Hogan has folded and will go along with the four years we asked."

Comfort, Nalo, and the attorneys were late arriving in Judge Tyler's chambers. They pulled up chairs and sat across from Pope and McMillan. His Honor was behind his desk, busy blowing into the damn pipe, his cheeks expanding and retracting as he sucked in air to vent the unlit tobacco. Forty-five seconds of this, and everybody' eyes were rolling. *Here he goes again with that stinking pipe.* A sudden coughing fit sent the judge into spasms as he rapped his chest, those before him looking on helplessly. "Want a glass of water, Your Honor?" Pope asked.

The hacking persisted a while longer, and Judge Tyler's eyes were tearing. The hacking stabilized, and he cleared his nose. "Excuse me, gentlemen. Excuse me. So where were we?"

"Well, we reached an understanding with defense counselors," Pope said in a manner inferring that if he had his druthers he wouldn't have agreed to it.

His Honor had a quizzical look as though he were baffled, and La Rossa stepped in, "Judge, myself and . . ." pointing at Comfort's lawyer, "Counselor Greenspan, and the District Attorney's Office did draft a plea agreement for your approval."

"When you say you drafted a plea agreement with the District Attorney's Office, are you telling me that Mr. Pope had no input?"

Pope spoke up on his behalf and said, "I'm acting on the orders of Mr. Hogan. But I per se would never have . . ."

Tyler cut him off. "It's irrelevant, Doug. If District Attorney Hogan sanctioned the arrangement that's all there is to it." He nodded at Greenspan and La Rossa but omitted Pope. "So let's hear this deal, Counselors."

Comfort and Nalo, the former decked out in a light-brown suit—the creases of the pants as sharp as a knife—and the latter in a tan sport jacket and a crimson shirt, were ecstatic at the judge's restraining of Pope.

La Rossa opened his briefcase and withdrew a typed sheet of paper, a synopsis of the plea bargain he, Greenspan, and Hogan had forged through Pope as an intermediary.

"Your Honor, these are the stipulations we came to terms with, so far," La Rossa said in the gust of a victor.

CHAPTER 70

Alitalia flight 7602 from Milan Malpensa International Airport to New York JFK was about to touch down on runway 22L. As the Boeing 747 neared the apron of the runway, decelerating to 130 knots, its nose tilted upward at a thirty degree angle, the landing wheels screeched, skidding for more than four hundred feet, blue smoke from the burning tires engulfing the belly of the fuselage. Once the mammoth aircraft was anchored to the passenger terminal, Al Green and Ali-Ben made way through the crowded cabin and disembarked.

At a customs checkpoint, an agent cleared the two, and they tramped to the baggage area on the lower level of the international terminal. "Nothin' like breathin' da air in the good ol' USA," Green said, sighing blissfully.

"You ain't kiddin'. I feel like kissin' the ground," Ali-Ben said.

But here in America Green and Ali-Ben would have to hide from Frankos the Greek—and whomever else.

Summer vacations, miscellaneous recesses, and routine delays prolonged the plea negotiations. The defense lawyers had to consult their clients whenever a stumbling block arose, and Pope had to confer with Hogan at every step of the bargaining sessions. And because of the volleying back and forth, summer had waned, and the early fall season was homing in.

In Judge Tyler's tobacco-scented chambers, La Rossa was specifying, for His Honor's benefit, the provisions of the plea deal. Tyler asked, "Mr. La Rossa, may I have a copy of those stipulations?"

"Certainly." La Rossa slid the three-page agreement across the judge's desk.

For three or four minutes Tyler perused the documents and read the content aloud. He began, "The defendants shall be confined for an indeterminate sentence of two to four years in a state penitentiary. Judge Andrew Tyler's recommendation for release at the earliest parole eligibility will be attached to the court's commitment decree." He removed his glasses. "So far, it looks good." He replaced the spectacles and coughed. "Excuse me. I'll proceed. Defendants shall receive unconditional immunity for any known and unknown crimes they may have committed, abetted, conspired, or implicated in." The judge looked at his audience and nodded. "I'm also in accord with that."

"Your Honor," Pope interrupted, "I'd like to note for the record that I totally object to the acquittal of any unknown crimes."

This time, Tyler almost tore the glasses off his nose, and waved the papers in front of him. "Mr. Pope, has your superior, the Honorable Manhattan District Attorney Frank Hogan, consented to these conditions?"

Pope didn't answer as quickly as the judge wished him to.

"Mr. Pope, did he or did he not?" Tyler asked heatedly.

"Yes, he did."

"Then your objections are immaterial."

Immunity for past robberies was of paramount importance to Comfort; those burglaries were currently under investigation, and though he and Nalo had not yet been targeted, they knew the curtain would soon be falling.

The last stipulation was that any federal and state taxes Comfort and Nalo might've owed would be forgiven.

Judge Tyler blessed the deal and set sentencing for December 14, 1972.

CHAPTER 71

S ammy Nalo was not definite about accepting the plea deal. The positive side was that he remained free on bail until the sentencing date of December 14, allowing him to mull over the four-year prison term.

On a Wednesday night in September of 1972, Nalo was relaxing drinking a glass of ouzo at his partly-owned club, Port Said, lusting over a belly dancer. Perspiration glimmering her skin, she had spotted Sammy in the audience, and through explicit body expressions subtly dedicated her performance to him. Incited by the dancer's carnal temptations, Nalo was slipping into a daze when he heard a familiar voice, "Sammy."

He stiffened into awareness, and rotated his upper torso to look at the caller. It was a trusted friend, Bill Comas, with whom Nalo had traded secrets in years past. He invited Comas to have a cocktail and fantasize about the belly dancer. Nalo and his mustachioed guest talked meaninglessly in broad terms. They did reminisce about a jewelry store they had burglarized in Queens before Nalo graduated to his current specialty, robbing Manhattan's upper-crust hotels. But in telling Comas the stories of his recent bravados, Nalo did not broach the Pierre or the Sophia Loren adventures. But he did confide to Bill Comas that in the course of the search of his Bronx apartment the cops stole more than a million dollars in diamonds.

"It had to have been those pieces-of-shit cops. Who else could've done it?" Nalo said. "Those bastards!"

The dancer gravitated toward Nalo's table, the spotlight following her, bringing Comas and Nalo out from the shadows. The tempo of the musical instruments increased to a crescendo and then ended abruptly, as did the dancer's sensual whirls. An interlude of silence stalled the euphoria, and the spectators everywhere in the room could hear Nalo and Comas's secretive chat.

Comas, round-faced and stout, who spoke with a lisp, lowered his voice and inched closer to Nalo. "Lemme understand something. How're you know the cops stole your diamonds? I mean, what if somebody who knows you broke into your apartment, went through the joint, and found them?"

"You mean somebody like you?" Nalo said, his olive-black eyes fixed at Comas.

Comas, unsettled, leaned back as if to distance himself from Nalo, and raised his hands, palms outward. "Hey, hey, wait a minute, Sammy. I don't even know where your apartment is. I mean . . ."

In a motionless stare, Nalo said, "It ain't hard to find out where I live."

"Now . . . now hold your horses, Sammy. You and I go back a long . . ."

"I've known the best of friends fuck each other, and then they go and get drunk together."

Comas, his face reddening, couldn't believe Nalo was blaming him for his stolen gems. "Sammy, I ain't like that, and you know it."

From one second to the other, the fury on Nalo's face changed to a smirk, and he ruptured into a laugh. "Just kiddin', just kiddin', pal."

Comas yelled, "You prick. You goddamn Turk." Comas, too, laughed, revealing the gap of a cracked tooth. "But like I was sayin', how're you know the cops did it?"

"First off, my apartment was not broken into. No sign o' that. Secondly, only a couple of bitches have been at my pad, and they wouldn't try anything like that. So if it's not the cops that took my shit, it must've been the FBI. One or the other."

Yes, *one or the other*. But a trap was being set in place. Nalo could not have envisioned that Comas was Agent Hammer's paid informant. Hammer, still tracking the Loren case, and convinced that Nalo had been the engineer of that robbery, told Comas to rekindle his friendship with him for the express purpose of eliciting incriminating information.

"If the cops or the FBI found the diamonds, they would've turned them in. Right?" Comas said.

"Yeah, maybe an honest cop. But how many honest cops are left in this city?"

"And you doubt that it might've been someone else?" Comas asked.

"It's not that I doubt it might've been somebody else. I know it wasn't anyone else but the cops or the FBI."

That was what Bill Comas needed to hear.

CHAPTER 72

Bill Comas, his thin nose snorting due to a cold, was in a phone booth on the corner of 92nd Street and Second Avenue. "Hello, Mr. Hammer. Bill here."

"Everything all right?"

"Oh, yeah."

"You need to see me, Bill?" asked Agent Hammer.

"Yeah, as soon as possible."

"All right, Bill. I'll see you at Elaine's in twenty minutes."

Elaine's, a restaurant on the southwest corner of 88th Street and Second Avenue in Manhattan's Upper East Side, fancied an eclectic cuisine. Over decades, it had become a lair of writers. The restaurant adopted celebrity authors, and not-so-famous ones. It was also a sanctuary for self-proclaimed writers, and those starving, unpublished souls who ate there at the generosity and expense of the overweight proprietress, Elaine Kaufman. Elaine's featured a bar, a dining room, and a secluded alcove reserved for household-name authors and personages of notoriety. A cabal of *Daily News* reporters, a raucous clan who fancied themselves as writers, fritted away time at this New York attraction, mingling with the bona fide authors.

Hammer locked the door to his office and undressed, shedding his suit. He dressed in dungarees and a plaid, short-sleeve shirt. To complete his disguise, he donned an orange-and-blue Mets baseball cap and sneakers. The FBI assumes immeasurable caution not to uncloak an informant's cover. If a targeted suspect learns that he, the informant, is cooperating with a law enforcement official, such exposure could lead to deadly consequences.

Comas's attempt at flying incognito was lame: dark wraparound sunglasses, a brown beret, and a green polo shirt, the collar up, enclosing his bony neck. He and Hammer were at a table in the semiprivate corner of Elaine's main dining room. The daily midday customers filled the large part of the seating capacity. At the bar, the drinkers indulging in a liquid lunch stood three deep, vying for the bartender's attention. The special of the day was Long Island caught sole fillet in a lemon butter sauce garnished with anchovies, an aromatic recipe that lured in the regulars.

"What's going on, Bill?"

"You're not gonna believe this, Mr. Hammer," Comas said, eyes darting.

Hammer adjusted into the chair and clasped his hands as if poised for a long-winded story. "I can't wait to hear it."

"Last night I was with Sammy the Arab."

"Oh!" Hammer exclaimed, surprise in his tone, eyebrows rising.

"Yeah," Comas nodded. "He told me that a couple o' days before you and Detective Bermudez arrested him, he had hidden in his apartment—he didn't tell me exactly where—about a million bucks in jewelry."

Hammer curved down his lips. "Really!"

"Oh, yeah. When Sammy made bail and went to his pad, guess what?" Comas sipped water and whispered, "His stash was gone. Gone!" He spread his arms. "Gone, just like that."

Hammer gnashed his teeth and banged on the table top, the water decanter and glasses shaking. He raised a hand as a sign something had just dawned on him, but he didn't want to share it with Comas. *Bermudez. That no-good bastard! He had to have been the* one who took those jewels. *He was the only one left alone to guard Nalo's apartment. That crooked punk!* He nodded as the whole picture was sharpening to a clear focus.

"Sammy said one of the cops or maybe one of you guys from the FBI might've done it," the informant added, not meaning to place Hammer on the defensive.

"Nalo is fifty percent right," Hammer said with the assertion of someone who had nothing to hide. "It *certainly* wasn't me or anyone else from the FBI for the simple reason that we were never alone in the apartment. Someone from the NYPD was always present." He sat straighter and regarded Comas with a cop look. "Bill, did Nalo say anything about the Loren or the Pierre robberies?"

Comas readjusted his buttocks onto the brown, wicker chair. "Uh . . . no, not at all."

"Stay on top of him, Bill, and keep in touch."

NICK SACCO

Christie Furnari found out that Bermudez had clipped Sammy's swag and told me about it. But nobody was crying for Sammy. Hadn't he taken that humongous diamond necklace for himself? And who knew what else he pocketed? We figured if he screwed us, then who gave a shit what happened to him. He was lucky that Frankos the Greek hadn't killed him.

Meanwhile, Agent Hammer had reported Bermudez to his superiors at the NYPD. Naturally, when they put Bermudez under the hot lamp he said he didn't touch a thing in Nalo's apartment. And he swore on a stack of Bibles that he didn't know anything about Sammy's supposedly stolen jewels. "Hell, Nalo didn't lose whatever he claims he lost. He made it all up," Bermudez told his precinct captain.

But the examiners who were looking into this reminded Bermudez that Nalo hadn't complained to the cops. Sammy mentioned it to someone who happened to be an informant, so he had no motive to make up such a lie. The examiners needed Sammy to file a complaint; without that they couldn't officially accuse and charge Bermudez. But how could Sammy admit those jewels had been taken from him? If he were to say, "Yes, during the search someone swiped a lot of valuables from my apartment," then he'd have to explain how he had gotten his hands on a million bucks of gems and gold.

"Did you steal those lost items from the Pierre or from Sophia Loren?" Lieutenant O'Neil had asked Nalo.

Nalo's answer was, "I never had any jewelry, or gold, or silver, or anythin' like that in my apartment, or anywhere else. And I never stole anythin' from anyone. So if you're tryin' to tell me that somebody stole a million bucks in jewels from me, that's a lotta horse shit."

The NYPD closed the investigation, and Bermudez, wisely, went into an early retirement, and moved to Florida, thinking that would be the end of the story.

CHAPTER 73

DECEMBER 14, 1972

Bobby Comfort, Sammy Nalo, and the lawyers Greenspan and La Rossa appeared for sentencing before Judge Tyler. Pope was also present. As prearranged, Comfort and Nalo pleaded guilty to possession of stolen property. His Honor guided Comfort through the customary allocution, a series of questions a judge asks a defendant prior to accepting a guilty plea: 1) Did you authorize your lawyer to change your not guilty plea to a guilty plea?; 2) Did anyone coerce you to change your plea?; 3) Did anybody promise you any form of compensation or special treatment in exchange for your guilty plea?; 4) Are you currently of sound mind?; and 5) Are you satisfied with your lawyers' rendering of counsel?

Upon finishing Comfort's allocution, Judge Tyler subjected Nalo to that same custom. His Honor then asked Assistant DA Pope if the defendants' guilty pleas were satisfactory to him as the representative of the People of the State of New York.

"Yes, the People are in accord with the guilty pleas to a Class E Felony, possession of stolen property," Pope answered against his own will.

"Very well. I hereby sentence Robert Comfort and Sorecho Nalo to a determinate sentence of seven years confinement in a state penitentiary as deemed by the Department of Corrections. You are so ordered to begin serving your sentences on January 2, 1973."

Seven years! All parties had agreed to a four-year sentence. What was going on?

As Pope's sullenness vanished and a cheery smile bloomed on his lips, Greenspan and La Rossa objected vehemently. La Rossa, his cheeks now red, barked, "That was not our understanding. You and the district attorney consented to a maximum of four years."

Greenspan was about to voice the same grievance, but Comfort whispered in his ear. The lawyer nodded and remained quiet.

"Mr. Greenspan, you were about to speak your piece?" Judge Tyler said.

"I concur with Mr. La Rossa. What you are doing is unacceptable. We had an agreement." Greenspan hurled a sheaf of papers onto the tabletop. "My client will withdraw his guilty plea."

"Mine as well," La Rossa echoed affirmatively.

"This is not a kindergarten game. I will not permit the defendants to withdraw the guilty pleas," Tyler decreed. "Since our last conference, I reviewed Mr. Comfort and Mr. Nalo's backgrounds, criminal histories, and propensities, and the crimes they *presumably* committed are far graver than I had known. For that reason, I support the district attorney's original wishes to imprison the defendants for longer than four years."

"Your Honor," Greenspan said, "The judicial precepts of the United States of America uphold a defendant's innocence until he or she is proven guilty. Judge, you, on the contrary, are presuming these two gentlemen are guilty. And you're in breach of the plea bargain that was set forth *and* agreed upon by everyone concerned, *you* included."

But Tyler wasn't listening; he banged his gavel and said, "Court adjourned."

NICK SACCO

That was all an act, and the only one who had not been in on it was Pope. Judge Tyler intentionally did not honor the deal he had cut with Comfort and Nalo's lawyers. And that was a smart move. The judge damn well knew that on appeal the seven years would be reduced to the four years that had been worked out. But for now, handing out a harsher punishment gave legitimacy to the sentencing; who'd ever believe a judge had taken a $250,000 payoff and then reneged on a plea deal?

Brilliant!

Free on bond for another three weeks, Bobby and Millie Comfort drove home to Rochester. They wanted nothing more than to be together every day, every hour, every minute before he had to surrender to the New York State Department of Corrections on January 2, 1973. This was the beginning of a second honeymoon. Millie laid little Nicole in her bed, and the moment she fell into a deep sleep, mom and dad were tumbling in the master bedroom. Bobby and Millie's orgasms quelled, and they sat smoking in bed. Millie kissed him on the nape of his neck, and in a resolute manner said, "I want you to promise me something right now."

Bobby emptied out his throat of smoke and watched it disappear into the air. "Anything, sweetie. Anything."

"Anything?" she repeated, a smirk on her perfectly shaped mouth. "Well, for one thing, when you come back from prison you better have stopped smoking." A sudden seriousness vamped on her face. "And I want you to promise me you'll never do another job ever again, and that you'll stop hanging out with that Sammy." Millie caressed Bobby's chest and rested her head on it. "I made up my mind. I can't live like this anymore. Not knowing when the other shoe is going to drop. Not knowing when a cop will come knocking down our door. Not knowing when you'll be gone."

Bobby felt a drop on his chest, one of his wife's tears. He pulled Millie tighter into him, his nostrils whiffing the fragrance in her hair. "Oh, c'mon now, stop crying."

Millie's shoulders began shivering. "No, I mean it. It's not fair. Not fair to me and Nicole. If . . . if you can't make that promise, you won't find us when you get out."

He inhaled another drag and stared at the ceiling, his arm around Millie's rib cage, a hand on her breast. "I don't think I'll be doing any more jobs. As far as Sammy . . . well, we've been friends for . . ."

She wiggled from his embrace. "I don't care how long you and that snake have been friends. I want you to stay away from him. Sammy's bad medicine. Period."

"If that'll make you happy, then that's what I'll do." But did Comfort really mean it?

Speaking of Sammy, his propensities and ideals were altogether different than Comfort's. Not many days before he'd begin his incarceration and still gambled incessantly, forever obligated to bookmakers and loansharks—debts that often led to fatal near-misses. But in these final weeks of his liberty, Nalo frequented Middle Eastern restaurants, though never in the company of his wife, a retired prostitute and active pole dancer. Nalo, a cryptic being, had two lives, one of which he kept secret. Apart from his gambling addiction, he had another vice, one far more destructive: women. He was addicted to anyone in a skirt, and fanned a penchant for Moroccan and Egyptian belly dancers, quenching his libidinous appetite at the Arabic-themed Sirocco on 29th Street and Madison Avenue in Manhattan. And there, Nalo practiced his perverted rituals.

One evening, diamonds and emeralds in his pockets, Nalo was eyeing the top-billed performer of the night, Nabila. On ending her frenzied number, she walked off the parquet dance floor and passed close to Nalo's table, her ankle-length, yellow, veiled skirt brushing past his leg. Obsessed by Nabila, and tingled by her skirt, Nalo outstretched his arm, grasped the dancer's hand, and dropped a three-quarter-carat diamond in her palm, a baiting ploy he had tempted on countless women. "Hi Nabila. I'm Sammy." He grinned and winked at the caramel-toned belly dancer.

"I got many more of those." Nalo was seducing Nabila—no, mesmerizing her. He patted the seat of the chair next to his. "Sit and have a drink with me."

"Okay, but just one," she said in what sounded to be an Indian accent, her voice tinny. "I don't drink with men I don't know." An outright lie.

Sure, tell me another one. "Nabila! What a pretty name. And you're such a pretty girl. Can I get to know you?"

"What makes you think I wanna get to know *you*?"

Nalo raised his forefinger as if to say *I got something to show you,* and said, "Give me your hand." She did. "Close your big, beautiful eyes." And she obeyed. He dug into his jacket pocket for a half-carat ruby, and rubbed it in her hand. "You can look now."

Nabila's mouth fell open in total surprise. "Oh, Allah! Is this for me? It's . . . it's beautiful, but I can't keep this . . . I don't even know your name."

Nalo folded his arms. "Of course you can keep it. It's my gift to you, and only because you're so beautiful and talented. And I don't want you to think I want anything from you. So you still don't wanna get to know me?"

"I'm . . . I'm not sure. And look, I have to get ready for my last dance set tonight at one o'clock."

He slid the sleeve of his jacket, uncovering the gold-banded Piaget, which was partly obscured by his hairy wrist. "It's 11:30. I gotta go take care o' somethin'. What time will you be finished?"

"One-thirty."

"I'll be back then and take you to my place, Port Said." Nalo had set the hook, and was reeling her in. "I'll talk to my partner, and from time to time he may book you there. By the way, my name is Sammy."

Nabila knew of Port Said. She was thunderstruck.

Nalo, so rapt in conquering Nabila, his female fix of the evening, did not notice that the shifty eyes of three Middle Eastern hoodlums, arcane undesirables who were habitués of Club Sirocco, had been watching him. He paid his check, and inebriated by Nabila drifted toward the door of the club, a floating bounce in his step. It was a blustery winter night, and Nalo started walking north on Madison Avenue to where his Volvo was parked. The swishing of three or four pairs of boots was not too far behind him. He quickened his pace, but the cagey footsteps gained on him before he could unlock the door of his car.

CHAPTER 74

Nalo fumbled in his trouser pockets for the key to the Volvo, but couldn't find it. In what seemed an eternity, at last his finger-tips touched the key ring. He yanked it out, and hands shaking, struggled to wiggle the door key inside the lock. "Oh shit!" He lost his grip on the key ring, and it landed somewhere under the car.

A hundred feet into the darkness a voice called him, "Sammy."

In four to five seconds, Nalo felt the aggressive weight, arms, and hands of three muggers, gruff Arab goons who had stalked him when he left Sirocco. They scrapped and tussled, and the hoods immobilized the outnumbered Nalo. Quick, harried movements were all he remembered as they battered him. Baseball bats were the thugs' preferred weapons, and dizzy and unsteady, Nalo collapsed to the ground. One of the attackers frisked his pockets and stripped him of the gems he had on his person, the others looking on in a pouncing stance. The ruffians ran off, and Nalo lay on his back in the gutter of the sidewalk, drowning in his own blood, looking listlessly at the star-speckled sky.

Ali-Ben and Al Green were living large, and though carousing in Amsterdam and Rome had been a splendid excursion, nowhere else, they felt, could replace New York, the Big Apple. But they had to stay clear of the old haunts and not be under the nose of anyone who had a score to settle. New York City was populated by eight million people; what were the odds of running into someone they'd double-crossed? Ali-Ben, a foreigner, had never heard of Murphy's Law, but Green was familiar with that widely accepted adage: *If something can go wrong, it will, and usually at the worst time.*

They tuned their radar to the longest range on the alert for anyone who might've been on the hunt for them. The person of most concern was Donald "the Greek" Frankos—and for good reason. Comfort and Nalo's calculations in dividing the Pierre boon, Frankos knew, had been a flimflam. The total they shared with him was a paltry $70,000. And to add insult to injury, Nalo, or maybe he and Comfort jointly, had cheated everybody else of other items, the $780,000 diamond necklace, for example. And more infuriating, word reached Frankos that Green and Ali-Ben had run off with the bulk of the Pierre swag. The Greek had been shortchanged, and he was dead set on correcting that indiscretion.

Unlike Comfort and Nalo, and even Sacco, Frankos was not a passive, forgiving burglar. No, he was a cold-blooded contract killer, and the world wasn't vast enough for those two fraudsters to run from him. But where would he begin scouring for Green and Ali-Ben? One of Frankos's spies had told him they were somewhere in Europe, painting it red, spending lavishly, in part, his rightful stake.

It had been a week since Sammy Nalo's beating outside Sirocco, and he was convalescing, his bruises and lacerations healing from the bludgeoning of the baseball bats. He had a few lasting bumps on his head, and considering the brutality of the assault he cheated death.

Nalo sent an envoy to Frankos. He wanted to clear the air with the Greek, rather than to constantly look over his shoulder. And perhaps Frankos might become his ally in salvaging the satchel from Al Green and Ali-Ben—if only they could be found.

Nalo, still sore and limping, hobbled into the Ibis Club, where Frankos was waiting for him. They sat at a banquette table and ignored the belly dancers; these trying days had been taxing, and Nalo had no appetite for women. The only agenda on his mind was to amend any misunderstandings with Frankos. The Greek, too, seemingly restless, didn't waste a minute tackling a bitter subject.

"Sammy, you and Bobby Comfort fucked me on my cut. You guys said the take from the Pierre was about a million, and the papers said it was more like eleven million, and only you and Comfort know what it *really* was. So what do I gotta do to get what's due me?" He pointed as if he were holding a gun and taking aim at Nalo. "And we gotta straighten out the money from that necklace you took for yourself."

The music was loud and tinny, and they had to speak at high volume, which made Nalo jumpy. He was feigning that all was well so those within earshot wouldn't hear Frankos menacing the indomitable Sammy the Arab. That would dilute his reputation as a no nonsense heavyweight.

Nalo squirmed in his chair. "I don't have the necklace. It wound up in the hands of the FBI."

"That's not my problem. If you hadn't taken it for yourself, it wouldn't be in the hands of the FBI. Would it?" The Greek's face was contorted with wrath, his upper lip curled into a snarl. "Like I said, it's not my problem, Sammy." He jabbed the air with his index finger, as though he had the urge to stab Nalo if only he had a knife. He eyed the eating utensils on the tablecloth, a fork and a knife. One of those might do, he thought. But another time for that. "It's your fault you lost the necklace. So I want my cut for it. Understand?"

Nalo, dried saliva on the corners of his lips, guzzled a half glass of water. "Look, Greek, Bobby and I took the fall all by ourselves without takin' down you or any of the other guys. In a few days, we're goin' into the joint for four goddamn years. But we kept quiet and didn't push you into the hot coals. And now you're breaking my balls for a bigger cut!"

"You're damn right you kept quiet, otherwise you wouldn't be goin' into the joint; you'd be goin' to your grave. Understand what I'm talkin' about, Sammy? You better straighten me out before you turn yourself in. Got it?" The Greek chucked a ten-dollar bill on the table and stormed away.

Sammy slouched into his chair and released a breath of air he'd been holding for the past fifteen minutes.

Frankos was on a rampage, and Nalo believed him when he had said that should he cross the Greek he'd be in a grave. That was no idle threat; it was due notice that Frankos would duly follow through. Nalo had to appease him. But who could he ask to intervene in subduing the Greek's vengeance? No one. He had bought his own coffin; when the newspapers had published the articles about the FBI recovering the necklace, everybody was livid.

And it was a miracle Nalo's heart was still beating. What was he to do? Even if Nalo ducked the Greek until he had to begin his prison bid, that wouldn't be a solution. For a pittance, Frankos could just as readily have him killed in prison.

Forlorn, Nalo drove to his Bronx apartment. As he lay sleepless in bed thinking what might be his best course of action, the telephone shrilled. It was 2:10 A.M., who could it be at this hour? Pondering whether to answer the call, he reluctantly did. "Hello, who's this?"

The caller spoke for fifteen seconds, and Nalo, hanging on to every word, sat up in bed. "You saw who? Where?" He was listening into the phone without breathing. "You're sure it was him?"

CHAPTER 75

Nalo couldn't sleep for the rest of the night; he was too wired from the news that had soothed him three hours earlier. Immediately, if not sooner, he had to speak to Comfort, who was in Rochester, relishing his second honeymoon. Not having had Millie's affection for nine months, and loving her more than ever, in moments of intimacy Comfort experienced the sensation as if she and he were fusing into one being bound by one spirit and one heart.

At 8:00 that morning, Nalo phoned Comfort, and they followed the usual routine: Comfort would go to a pay phone and call Nalo at a phone booth on 116th Street and Broadway across the street from Columbia University.

"Sammy, it's me, Bobby. What's up?"

"You won't believe this."

"So tell me, maybe I will. What's going on?"

"Bobby, I got a call from someone I know, 'One-Ear' Willie. He saw Al Green and Ali-Ben. These guys are in town, man!"

"Why would this Willie tell you that and put his ass out in the wind?"

"Because he's got it in for Green and Ali-Ben," Nalo answered.

One-Ear Willie, a black man, had been Al Green's trusted numbers runner. When playing the numbers, a bettor must guess any combination of the last three digits of a racetrack's *handle*, the total cash receipts of the daily nine horse races. Because of the long-standing relationship he had with Willie, Green dropped his guard and became lax in enforcing the post time for Willie to turn in the numbers sheets, the bettors' picks. Willie saw that as a hole in the fence; a safe opportunity to cheat Green by not delivering the sheets until the racetrack announced the final tally, the handle. Willie could then bet on behalf of a fictitious customer, and thus his wins were guaranteed. At some point, Green scented something was amiss, and sent Ali-Ben to shake down Willie. But the numbers runner did not fess up to his scam, and Ali-Ben sliced off his right ear, hence the nickname One-Ear Willie, and his grudge for Green and his henchman.

A thought budded in Comfort's mind. "Sammy, I'm gonna come down to the city and hook up with Frankos. He should be able to get our stuff back from those bastards."

"Yeah, and we gotta make Frankos happy before that crazy Greek whacks me," Nalo said, fear in his wobbly voice.

But Comfort was struck with the flu, and had to delay his rendezvous with Frankos.

Nalo was in turmoil over Comfort's illness, and his inability to come to Manhattan and sit down with Frankos. But Nalo, maintaining a low profile, curbed his wanderings into topless bars and Middle Eastern clubs, and stayed off the streets. On Sunday mornings, though, he was in the habit of eating breakfast at the Market Diner on Manhattan's West Side. Driving there in his Volvo on the Sunday before Christmas, a misty day, Nalo was in the company of informant Bill Comas, who as of late had become his shadow. Still without an inkling of Comas's undercover alter ego, Nalo snuggled the Volvo into a parking spot behind the restaurant. He switched off the engine, and he and Comas started walking toward the front steps of the diner. To his dread, Frankos was fast-stepping in his direction. The Greek, in sweat pants, a green parka, and a black wool cap, stuffed his hand inside the jacket inner pocket, and drew a .22 caliber snub-nose revolver. In what seemed a fraction of a moment, Nalo saw the point-blank blue flash of gunfire, though not registering the loud explosion, and felt a burning jolt in the left temple.

"And this is just a love tap, Sammy," Frankos said. "That's why this time I only used a .22."

Comas, terrified, expecting a second bullet intended for him, thought these were the last seconds of his life. Instead, as if he had died and resurrected in the span of an instant, he was watching the Greek, who could've been presumed to be a jogger, trotting away nonchalantly.

Nalo staggered backwards, arms flailing, and slumped over his car's fender. Confused, he pressed a palm against the bleeding wound on his left temple, ears ringing from the detonated gun blast. But he soon realized he had also a bullet hole in the right temple. How could this be? Frankos had fired one shot, not two.

Comas bewildered, his heart pounding as though it were about to break through his chest cavity, looked around him for anyone who might've seen the shooting. Thanks to the rain, no one in sight. He slid both arms under Nalo's armpits, and dragged the limp, traumatized man inside the automobile and onto the rear seat. He picked up the car keys off the ground, got in the driver's seat, and hit the accelerator, gravel and dust rising in the wake of the Volvo.

Comas sped south on Seventh Avenue en route to New York Presbyterian Hospital on William Street in lower Manhattan. Weaving through traffic—typically scarce on a Sunday morning, and glancing frequently back at the moaning Nalo, his face sopping with blood—Comas was getting nauseous. His stomach was sensitive to goriness, and he was fighting a surge of regurgitation in his throat, the speeding over bumps and potholes aggravating the nausea.

The hospital came into view, and Comas coasted to a halt in front of the entrance to the emergency room. He pulled Nalo off the car seat, and staggering and lurching, walked him into the receiving area of the ER. No one paid attention to Comas and the wounded Nalo, blood streaking on the sides of his face, and dripping onto the tan vinyl floor. The doctors, nurses, and the supporting staff were bustling hectically, gurneys everywhere, and patients in green gowns lingering to be examined. Pungent odors of antiseptic in the air, Comas propped Nalo in an armchair near a receptionist, who had two phones in her ears. Without speaking to anyone, the informant hastily hightailed it through the swinging doors of the emergency room, hid the keys to Nalo's Volvo above the sun visor, and flagged down a taxi.

Inside the ER, where Comas had sat him, now unconscious, mouth slackened, Nalo's head rested on the back of the chair, arms dangling over the sides.

CHAPTER 76

ncredibly, Nalo's point-blank gunshot injury to the head required two Band-aids. The bullet had entered the left temple, spun around his head under the skin, and faintly grazed the side of the cranium, exiting through the right temple. An unfathomable stroke of luck.

In a room at the hospital, three NYPD detectives at his sides, Sammy Nalo swore he had never before seen the shooter and did not know him. The cops doubted his story.

"You can think what you want, but I told you the truth," Nalo said to the investigators.

The doctors discharged him, and he tottered out to the parking lot on his own power. Groggy, Nalo found the ignition key above the visor, and drove home to the Bronx, his temples and cheeks smeared with the brownish tint of iodine, and covered with gauze pads.

On learning of his partner's miraculous survival, Comfort thought of an irony: Sammy "the Arab" Nalo cheated everyone he came in contact with—even death.

Cured from the flu, and time running out before he had to begin his prison bid, Comfort returned to New York City. He and Frankos had set up a tryst. "Greek, you're blaming Sammy for not giving you what you're due . . . and maybe you think I'm screwing you as well. But it's Al Green and Ali-Ben that you gotta go after. They took off with . . . oh, I'd say around eleven million in stones and gold. Those fuckers took everything Sammy and I had." Comfort, unaware Frankos knew that Sacco and Furnari had recovered the jewels Piccarreto had copped from him, added to his woes, "Another thing, Greek, this wiseguy from Rochester, Rene Piccarreto, fucked me out of another four-and-a-half mil in jewelry. Diamond bracelets, necklaces, you name it. He got it all."

The Greek was straining to keep a straight face.

Though Comfort had been forthright, Frankos wasn't buying that he and Nalo had lost all of the Pierre riches. "So, what're you sayin', Bobby? You can't pay me? I'm tellin' you right now, I'm gonna get my end in three possible ways. Either in cash, or in diamonds, or in blood. I know that *mouleenian* Green and that low-life Turk Ali-Ben may not be in the country, and nobody knows where they are."

"Wrong, Greek. They're back, and I know where you can find those two sons of a bitches," Comfort said, smirking.

Frankos slapped Comfort's shoulder. "You know where those two crooks are?"

Comfort nodded. "I'll make a deal with you. You get back what is mine and Sammy's, and we'll split fifty-fifty anything you come up with. How's that?"

"That's fine, but I ain't givin' Sammy a penny. He's lucky I didn't kill him."

"That's another thing, Greek. You gotta lay off Sammy. Just leave him alone. I'll give him something from my cut."

"Bobby, I don't know why you're covering up for that lowlife. I bet he'd rob his own mother."

"He did," Comfort said, chuckling. "Look, let's just say he can't help himself. All right. Now do we have a deal?"

Frankos held out his hand for a shake, as did Comfort. "Bobby, where do I find those rat bastards?"

Comfort told Frankos the whereabouts of Green and Ali-Ben. "Oh, Greek. You did not get this from me."

"You don't gotta worry about that. I work alone and nobody knows my business."

Frankos put on his contract killer hat and launched a pursuit for the black man and the Turk. Comfort's tip as to where they were roosting had served Frankos well, and in thirty-six hours, he zeroed in on his prey.

Although Green and Ali-Ben had, so far, skirted Frankos, and averting Comfort and Nalo, they thought it best to leave New York and fade away in a remote region of the country, or the world. Ali-Ben, who had been married to Green's sister, decided to repatriate to his native land, Turkey; Green was set on relocating to Atlanta and merge into one of the black quarters of that city. And even though in Europe the reckless tourists had frittered away a king's ransom, they managed to conserve a sizable portion of the satchel—sufficient assets to live happily ever after elsewhere, far from Donald Frankos.

But Ali-Ben had a new toy. He'd been courting one of the shameless cocktail waitresses at a Turkish restaurant–night club, the Sahara Sunset. His designs were to whisk her off to Turkey and desert his wife, Green's sister, a numbers runner. And so Ali-Ben and his scandalously dressed girlfriend were in his rooming house, a decrepit tenement in Astoria, Queens, where they had been packing suitcases, and of far greater value, strapping and sealing the priceless duffel bag with half of the jewels. Green was in possession of the second half. Ali-Ben and his paramour had reservations on a Turkish Airlines flight to Ataturk Airport in Istanbul. In haste, they abandoned the roach-infested room and scrammed to a pay phone in the unheated lobby of the tenement. Ali-Ben phoned for a car service to take him and his babe to Kennedy Airport, a twenty-five minute ride.

Inside of fifteen minutes, the taxicab was in front of the entrance of the rooming house, and the driver beeped the horn.

"That must be the taxi. Let's go," Ali-Ben said to his girlfriend. They stepped outdoors onto the sidewalk, a drizzle wetting the ground, and the driver opened the rear door. He assisted the girl into the automobile, and helped Ali-Ben load the luggage and his duffel bag into the trunk. When Ali-Ben bent his waist to get into the cab, he saw someone wearing a red beret in the front passenger seat. *Why do we have another passenger riding with us?*

CHAPTER 77

A li-Ben got into the car, and in a boorish manner asked the driver, "Who's this guy with you?"

The answer came as the taxi sped off. The man in the front passenger seat spun to face the rear of the taxi, pointing a silencer-equipped .44 Bulldog revolver. Ali-Ben's mouth fluttered, and he pleaded, "No, Greek don't . . . we can work it out."

Composed, Frankos said, "You're damn right, *we are* gonna work it out, right now."

The cocktail waitress belted a shrill, her hands out at chest level. "*NOOOOO!*" Ali-Ben yelled, waving his palms in hopelessness.

"Which one of you wants to go first?" the Greek asked sardoni-cally. No answer, but more hysterical pleading from the trapped elopers as Ali-Ben fought to unlock the door to his right, a futile try.

Frankos chided, "Since you two have no preference, I guess it's ladies first." And he shot the woman in her cleavage, the loud explo-sion quaking inside the car. A splatter of blood splotched her beige blouse and face, and the head blasted back onto the backrest, eyes rolling into the lids.

Frankos blew on the smoking end of his gun barrel, and bore a second bullet into Ali-Ben's forehead, skull fragments and red pulp spraying the rear window. A haze of gunpowder reeking of an asphyxiating gaseous stench clouded the air in the taxicab.

The second casualty slumped forward, slowly tumbling onto the floor of the car, greenish fluids seeping from his mouth.

On the Belt Parkway, below the speed limit, the taxi was on a due west course advancing toward Brooklyn. There the operator of an auto wrecking yard—the one who had destroyed the limo used in the Pierre—would crush-compact the cab. And the corpses of Ali-Ben and the waitress were to be laid in the trunk, their final resting place.

As for Al Green, his relocating to Atlanta was not in the cards. Ali-Ben's body wasn't cold yet when Green met a similar fate at Frankos's hands.

His goal fulfilled, the Greek telephoned Sacco. On seeing each other in person, he told the Cat, "Those two deadbeats are gone."

"Who?"

"Al Green and Ali-Ben," Frankos said matter-of-factly. "Nobody's lower than a thief who steals from another thief."

"Don't tell me anything else, Greek."

Frankos waved away Sacco's concerns. "I just wanna tell you I got the satchel back. That's all," he said as if exterminating three humans was no different than swatting three flies.

"You got Comfort and Nalo's jewels back?"

"Oh, yeah! My deal with Comfort is that we're splittin' what I got back from Green and Ali-Ben right down the middle. But I don't know where to go with this swag. So I thought if I give you some of the jewels you can help me unload mine."

Stealing from the rich was a harmless misdeed, but killing for profit . . . well, that was one of a different order. And Nick "the Cat" Sacco didn't subscribe to it. "Nah, nah." Sacco raised his hands and shook his head. "I got enough from the Pierre, Greek. You keep it. And if you want, I can give you the names of a couple o' fences that'll be fair with you. But I don't want none o' that."

Besides, Sacco was financially comfortable. Plus, he had benefited from the bundle of gems he and Furnari reclaimed from Rene Piccarreto.

"All right, Nick." Frankos nodded and winked smilingly. "You're all right in my book. Look, tomorrow I'm gonna hook up with Comfort and square away with him."

Frankos, a man of his word, did divide the repossessed goods with Comfort, though the Greek spared him of the gory details.

January 2, 1973, the anniversary of the Pierre Hotel robbery, was the first day of Bobby Comfort's imprisonment in a New York State penitentiary, Attica Correctional Facility.

Nalo even though the probabilities were ninety-nine percent that the seven-year sentence would be overturned on appeal, it didn't sit well with him, and rather than accept the inevitability of his incarceration, he delayed the commencement of his sentence. He remained free on bail, equivocating whether to withdraw his guilty plea and apply to the court to set a trial date. But despite this seesawing period, and the recent fatal near-miss with Frankos, Sammy Nalo's moral fiber couldn't be rid of his vices and tendencies to be deceitful. An ancient European proverb accurately touches on Nalo's incorrigible mindset: *The wolf's fur changes seasonally, but its color is always the same.*

And not far into the future, his debts to a bookmaker had surmounted $200,000, and Nalo found himself again staring at the deadly end of a weapon. The bookmaker's collector, Bill Arico, a callous bank robber, spied Nalo's routines and daily schedules. Nalo received his phone calls in a pay booth stationed on the sidewalk near the entrance of a bar, the University Pub, on Broadway three blocks north of Columbia University. Habitually, in the afternoons Nalo lunched at this watering hole, and there he also consorted with his associates. On March 11, 1973, a turbulent day of lightning and torrential downpours, Nalo was in that booth, rainwater dousing the glass panes of the stall.

Arico and a second man drove past the phone booth. "That's him!" Arico said to his driver. "That's him, all right. Turn the car around and make a slow pass as close as you can get to the phone booth." Arico rolled down the car window partway, the wind-swept rain whipping his face. He rested the muzzle of an AK-47 on the top edge of the window and peered through the barrel sights with one eye, his forefinger on the trigger.

CHAPTER 78

The car crept past the booth at two to three miles per hour. Nalo was absorbed by his phone call. Arico took aim, and in a deafening *rat-ta-ta-ta* emptied the AK-47 magazine, a shower of glass shards flying in every direction, spent shells ejecting from the assault weapon. In a spontaneous panic of jerky motions, Nalo kicked open the sliding double-doors of the booth and buckled onto the sidewalk, writhing spastically, his overcoat and pants dotted with red holes. According to a bystander, the fracas lasted less than six seconds, ending in a sudden silence. Nalo lay supine on the drenched ground, one foot shoeless, arms and legs outstretched, raindrops landing on his cheeks and brow.

The booth was reduced to smithereens, and the shooter and his driver raced off south on Broadway and swung east on 110th Street.

Onlookers who had watched or heard the ambush huddled over Nalo. At least seven or eight bullets had penetrated his torso, stomach, and legs. And it seemed likely that Sammy Nalo no longer had to sweat out whether his seven-year sentence would be commuted on appeal. Actually, today all his troubles might've been over as he lay on the sidewalk, straining for gulps of air.

APRIL 1973

The Pierre Revue had been bumped to the sidelines. Bobby Comfort had gone to prison, Sammy Nalo barely clung to life, his bullet-perforated body resembling a pasta strainer, and the whirlwind began fizzling.

Meantime, Nick "the Cat" Sacco was venturing into a succession of thefts. But his rising reputation as one of the top-ranked jewel thieves in the country was a fast-brightening blip on the FBI and NYPD's radar screen. More glaringly, in fashionable suits he was womanizing at elite night clubs and restaurants from one end of town to the other: the famed El Morocco, the Rainbow Room, the iconic Copacabana, the ultra-exclusive Regines, and the legendary Xenon Disco Club. And in Sacco's line of work, such limelight, and spending pockets full of cash in the swirl of the New York nightlife, was as hazardous as tap dancing in a minefield.

"Nick," Christie Furnari warned, "you gotta slow it down, kid. You're drawing attention to yourself."

Furnari's sermons were unheeded, and Sacco's philandering became his signature. One morning in May of 1973, the Cat found a crumpled piece of paper in his wallet. He unraveled it and read: Joanne Rinaldi 212-288-7124. (Throughout the late seventies, the 212 area code was designated to not only Manhattan but to the five boroughs as well.) Joanne was the gorgeous Pierre captive, the Brazilian's mistress who had given the classy Sacco her telephone number.

Should I phone her or not? What if she calls the cops and sets me up?

Against his better judgment, Sacco's libido prevailed. "Hello, you may not remember me, but I was one of the robbers at the Pierre that night. The one you gave your number to."

"Oh, yes, yes. You're the tall handsome guy with the brown bedroom eyes. Well, what a surprise," Joanne said in that melodic voice when someone is ecstatically surprised and rendered speechless by an unexpected caller.

"Did I get you at a bad time?"

"No, no. But you never told me your name."

That knocked Sacco off balance. *Should I give her my real name? What if she does set me up?* "Eh . . . Donnie. Yeah, Donnie."

"Okay, Donnie. Surely you have a last name. Only pets have just one name."

This broad is a wiseass. "Caputo . . . Donnie Caputo."

"I'm so glad you called, Donnie. You're Italian, like me."

"Yeah. I wanna apologize for that night. Hope we didn't scare you."

"Not at all. You did me a favor because I found out that . . . that two-timing, ex-boyfriend of mine, the Brazilian asshole, had just gotten married. And that night, remember when you and I were in the black chick's room waitin' for her to get herself together in the bathroom, even you said he was stringin' me along. I was just too blind to see through his bullcrap." Joanne softened her tone. "But I'm so glad you called."

"I'm glad too. Uh . . . can I take you out to dinner tonight?"

"Sure. Where are you takin' me?"

He wouldn't tell her the restaurant he'd chosen. If she were to turn him in, why chance walking into a SWAT team? "I'll surprise you."

"All right, surprise me, Donnie."

"I'm gonna send a limousine for you, and the chauffeur will know where to take you." This was a precaution in case Joanne might have the police at her home lying in wait for him.

"Wooh, this sounds exciting."

"Give me your address, Joanne."

If Furnari caught wind that Sacco was scheming to date one of the Pierre hostages, he'd castrate him with a rusty hacksaw blade, and feed the testicles to his German Shepherd.

Sacco the Cat knew a limo operator, Lenny, a skillful driver who, if tailed, could easily lose the chasers. He had another quality well suited for this assignment; he was *a street guy* and wasn't timid in dealing with nosy cops. And Sacco's instructions were for him to go to Joanne's apartment in Long Island City, Queens, and bring her to the Palm, an upscale steakhouse on 50th Street between Broadway and 8th Avenue. But Lenny was not to map out a straight route to that restaurant. Instead, he backtracked east to the Long Island Expressway and rode it west to Van Dam Street, the last exit before the Midtown Tunnel. The exit ramp is an eighth of a mile long, and if another vehicle was following the limo, Lenny would've known it. He looked through the rearview mirror and no other cars were behind him, but admiringly he saw his beautiful passenger's emerald-green eyes staring out the side window, her modestly made-up face exuding radiance. He loved her bobbed auburn hair and pearly cheeks. *If only she wasn't Sacco's property.* He drove on for a mile to the underpass crossover that leads to the tunnel's toll booths. The deft chauffeur paid the twenty-five-cent toll, and the tunnel devoured the black limo. Once again, Lenny looked behind him and saw nothing odd. His destination, where Sacco was waiting for his date, was fifteen minutes into Manhattan.

As the limo was nearing the exit of the tunnel, Lenny peeked into the side-view mirror, and to his startle a black Plymouth was tailgating him. Possibly an NYPD unmarked car.

CHAPTER 79

Sacco was at the bar in a three-piece, blue-violet suit, and the headwaiter of the Palm came to him. "Sir, anytime you're ready. Your table has been ready."

The Cat peered at his watch. "I'm still waiting for someone to show up. It must be traffic."

"Very well. At your convenience." And the waiter walked away.

The limo raced through the exiting mouth of the Midtown Tunnel, and Lenny switched on his right-turn signal. He checked the mirror, and the tailing Plymouth's left-turn signal was blinking. He exhaled and turned right onto Third Avenue, as the suspicious car steered left for 34th Street.

The chauffeur walked Joanne into the Palm, and this pampering electrified her. Watching her hips wag as she sashayed in his direction, Sacco put down his drink on the bar and stood. He thrust his hand for Joanne to take, and she rose on her toes to peck him on the cheek. He was instantly drunk with her perfume.

Lenny stepped away to lend Sacco and his lady friend privacy. But the Cat called him back and slipped him a fifty-dollar bill. "Thank you, Nick. I'll be outside in the limo."

"No problem, Lenny." Sacco then said to Joanne, "Do you wanna have a drink here at the bar?"

"Why not, *Donnie*," Joanne answered in an off-note as though she didn't believe Donnie was his real name. But she keenly understood that, in light of how they met, Sacco would have to be *totally* crazy to have told her his real name. As it was, asking her out, a person he had held at gunpoint, had been a chancy pursuit. A chancy pursuit! No, it was insanity on his part. When it comes to women, the most sensible, intelligent men, even those in high positions, lose common sense and dive headfirst into the stupidest situations.

They sat on barstools as the bartender mixed the cocktails, a whiskey sour for the lady, and scotch on the rocks for the Cat. She was side-glancing him, approving his taste in clothes, and admiring the neatly parted, ear-length, brown hair. Sacco, too, was surveying Joanne. He couldn't keep his eyes off her cleavage. And those pouty, painted lips.

They clinked glasses, and she said, "Cheers. To us."

"To us," he echoed, sipping his scotch. He rested the drink on the bar top, and took a gift-wrapped box the size of a book from the inner lining of his vest "I have a little somethin' for you. Nothing fancy. Just a thought." He handed it to her. "Go ahead, open it."

Taken aback, she smiled and patted her heart. "What is it?"

"Hope you like it," he said bashfully.

Joanne removed the wrapping paper and opened the lid of the box. Her pretty mouth fell open. "Ohhhhh!" As if suddenly overheated, she vented her face. "This . . . this is . . . I don't know how to say it." She was looking at a gold necklace with emeralds set in a platinum pendant. Unable to find befitting words, Joanne kissed Sacco on his mouth.

The Cat was slightly embarrassed. He hadn't foreseen her planting a kiss on his lips. "The emeralds match your beautiful eyes." *No investment yields a higher return than that of complementing a woman.*

Joanne spread the necklace on the upper part of her bosom, a pair of pear-shaped breasts. "It's . . . it's unimaginable that you would give me such an expensive gift on our first date."

"Oh, it's nothin'. I'm in the business, remember?"

"I don't know anybody who'd give me something like this . . . so expensive." She kissed him again. "I mean, I don't even know your real name." And she winked. "And that's another gift you could give me. Your real name."

They laughed into silliness, and he placed his hand on her thigh. She didn't object. "At some point, I'll tell you my name. But I gotta play it cool. Know what I mean?"

"Aha, aha."

They swilled the cocktails and then moved to the Palm's dining section, a stately oak-wainscoted room lighted by crystal chandeliers over each table set. Preceded by the flavor of broiled beef, a uniformed waiter in a dark tan server jacket doled out to Sacco and Joanne evenly cut chunks of a two-inch-thick Porterhouse steak. Side orders of roasted red potatoes and creamed spinach complemented the scrumptious meal. As a final touch, Sacco ordered a bottle of Joseph Drouhin Cabernet.

He was beginning to feel more tranquil; Joanne had flouted his fears and not notified the police. He was eying her, and she seemed genuinely smitten by him. They ate, drank, shared jokes, and enjoyed each other's company, an upwelling coziness loosening the jitters of a first date.

They moved on and boarded the limousine. Lenny asked from the front seat, "Sir, where to?"

"Regine's on Park and 59th."

"You got it," Lenny said.

Joanne snuggled into Sacco and wound her arm around his. "Wow! We're going to Regine's? I always wanted to go there, but it's so hard to get in. You think they'll let us in?"

The Cat took Joanne's hand and looked at her with a devious smile. "*Of course* they'll let us in."

Regine's Night Club and Discotheque was the elite of the elites, playground for the rich and famous, "the beautiful people." A cadre of celebrities, Roger Moore, Liza Minnelli, Andy Warhol, Truman Capote, Richard Harris, Mick Jagger, and Elizabeth Taylor were fixtures at Regine's.

The limousine parked a few yards from the club's entrance, above which extending over the sidewalk and to the street curb was a burgundy awning displaying the famed Art Deco–style lettering, Regine's. At the entryway, in a visor cap and brown uniform, the doorman admitted the few he'd choose from the long line of people hankering to be part of "the happening."

A misty drizzle twinkled in the night air. The Cat and Joanne—who was sheathed in a tempting black-and-white hip-hugging dress, baring tan-bronzed shoulders and three-quarters of her succulent thighs—waded through the crowd, making their way to the front of the line. The doorman spotted Sacco, who towered above everyone else, and waved him in. "Nick, is that you? Get yourself and that knockout redhead out of the rain. Come on in."

Oops! The doorman had *let the Cat out of the bag*, pardon the pun. He called him Nick. Joanne looked at Sacco and gave him the widest grin she could muster. "Well, pleased to meet you, Nick," she mocked in a mode that said *I caught you*. "Now all you have to do is tell me your last name."

If Christie Furnari only knew!

"Oh well. "I guess you had to find out sooner or later." He leaned down and kissed her on the forehead. "But we'll wait a while for my last name."

Sacco paid the entry fee, and the heavyset doorman said, "Good to see you, Nick. Who's the green-eyed hot mama on your arm?" And he winked at the Cat.

As they made their entrance into Regine's, Marvin Gaye's hit, "I Heard It Through the Grapevine," was reverberating off the walls, the floor and ceiling of the world-famous discotheque. Joanne, prideful to have Nick flanking her, was starstruck when she recognized Sammy Davis Jr., and boxing champion Joe Frazier, both lounging on one of the red velour settees. And there goes Cher, and Roman Polanski, and . . .

It had been a dazzling evening, and a costly one for the Cat, finalizing the night in Joanne's bed.

CHAPTER 80

H e had plastic tubes in his nostrils, penis, throat, and ears. An IV needle was inserted in the left arm, and his head and naked torso had been bandaged. Lying immobile in the hospital bed, swathed head to toe in sterilized gauze, the patient could've been misconstrued for an Egyptian mummy, his chest barely inflating and deflating as he breathed weakly. The attending physicians had listed Sammy Nalo in serious condition. The bullet count they had carved out of his legs and stomach was eleven. And the surgeons could not understand how Nalo was still alive. Everyone who knew him said he had nine lives; and if that were true, he had already extinguished three of the nine: the crippling beating outside Sirocco, the short-range shot from Frankos's pistol, and the telephone booth sniping barrage.

Nalo would linger precariously on the critical list for three months, wavering between life and the brink of death.

Comfort had adjusted to Hotel Attica's unstable environs, where a minor disagreement as trivial as cutting into the line waiting to use the pay phone could trigger a prison-wide riot. Wisely, Comfort didn't socialize with other inmates, and kept his distance from the danger zones: the television room, the card games, the monopolizing of the daily newspapers, and the library, where fighting over a book was an everyday happening. Those were the primary sources of outbreaks, quarrels that often sparked violence.

Coached by his attorney, Bobby Comfort drafted and filed the appeal to strike out the seven-year sentence. But this had a double purpose: it'd also quell the rumors that bribery was why Judge Tyler had manipulated District Attorney Frank Hogan into accepting Comfort and Nalo's plea deal. And Comfort and his lawyer, Greenspan, concurred on a positive outlook: the Appellate Court would rule in his favor. As for Nalo, if he might live to hear that verdict, he, too, would've had his wish.

Sacco and Joanne's dalliance carried on for two months, and as a toy that no longer fascinates a child, he had grown tired of her. The Cat was concentrating on following a lead that might've been lucrative. Through an inscrutable contact, Frankos had heard that Detective George Bermudez, still living in Miami, Florida, needed to liquidate the jewels he'd filched from Nalo's apartment. Bermudez had been in search of a fence who'd purchase the ill-gotten gems, but had failed to find one willing to pay his price. Typically, a fence pays ten to twelve percent of the retail value of stolen products, but Bermudez had been asking no less than forty-five percent.

NOVEMBER 1975

Contrary to his physicians' prognostications, Sammy Nalo had recuperated and the court remanded him to Attica to begin his four-year sentence. He and Bobby Comfort had won the appeal, and in January of 1976, Comfort, who had gone in fourteen months earlier, was paroled. For the first ninety days of Nalo's incarceration, the warden had placed him in the hospital ward, and for that reason he and Comfort hadn't bumped into each other at Attica.

The warden cleared Comfort for freedom, and Millie was at the gates of the penitentiary. The sheer anxiousness of whisking her husband away and taking him home to Rochester was irrepressible. She had been praying he'd never again leave her and the two girls—the two-year old she had been pregnant with, and little Nicole, who wasn't so little anymore. The missy was three months shy of seven, and in her mind going on sixteen. Daddy couldn't have been prouder, and the first time he kissed the little one his eyes pooled.

"Millie, this is the first day of our new life. I'm a changed man, and from now on my income is going to come strictly from legitimate businesses. And that's a promise."

They kissed, and she got into the driver's seat of her maroon Buick Riviera. Her Bobby was the passenger as she drove south on Route 684. But no sooner had Millie shifted the selector lever into drive, he lit a cigarette.

"But one thing will never change, Bobby. You'll never quit smoking. Will you?"

"Probably not. What're you want, everything? Who's perfect?"

In three hours, they'd be in bed, feasting on one another.

In February of 1976, George Bermudez borrowed $50,000 from his credit union to invest in a parcel of "highly desirable real estate" in Fort Meyers, Florida. But to his chagrin that "sought-after property" proved to be worthless land, an alligator swamp. Thus Bermudez's need for immediate cash. But so far, no fence had offered more than twelve percent of the retail value of his jewelry.

At last, a miracle, which he believed in, happened. A supposed South Miami hustler, Clint something or the other, whom Bermudez had met in a bar, said he knew a "big time buyer" of gold, who was predisposed to paying much more than *street money*. The fence's name was Waldo Jaegermeister. And for a five percent broker fee, Clint volunteered to coordinate for Bermudez and Jaegermeister to meet at St. Thomas in the Virgin Islands.

The Bermudez and Jaegermeister meeting was set, and the ex-detective boarded a Pan Am flight from Miami International to Cyril E. King Airport in St. Thomas. From wheels-up to wheels-down, the Boeing 707 had been in the air for two hours and twenty-five minutes. The landing of the four-engine aircraft on the relatively short 4900-foot runway was hair-raising. The full blast of the jets' reverse thrust, and the two pilots' weight on the brake pedals were necessary to bring the airplane to a halt before skidding into Moravian Highway. Bermudez's heart was in his mouth, and as the Boeing 707 slowed to a roll he made the sign of the cross. *"Gracias, Dios mio. Gracias Dios Mio."* Puerto Ricans are devoted Catholics and adore Jesus, even though none of them ever met him.

A flight attendant opened the cabin door, the warm tropical air wafting into the aircraft, and Bermudez climbed down the roll-up steps onto the tarmac. He was surprised to see that the extent of the terminal was a twenty-by-eight-yard open barrack, and a shack for a customs office. Bermudez only had a carry-on briefcase and trotted to the taxi stand, running ahead of the other disembarking passengers, anxiousness in his steps.

The seven-mile cab ride along Bovoni Road to the Bolongo Bay Beach Hotel was not scenic but quite bumpy; so rough that Bermudez felt as though he were on the strenuous Mexican Baja off-road racing circuit. Saturated in sweat from the jungle-like ninety-seven degrees, he thought for sure his dentures might rattle loose. He hung on to the safety strap handle, his knuckles white as sugar. The taxi had passed four to five miles of bramble and shrubbery on the sides of the road when it came to a clearing. "We comin' up da hotel, mohn," the black driver said in a cross of French and Haitian accents.

The Bolongo Bay Beach Hotel, where Jaegermeister awaited Bermudez in a suite, was a two-story string of rooms and bungalows overlooking the splendid Bolongo Bay, the sun in the azure sky sizzling as if it were a giant heat lamp. The term *suite* was an overstatement; these were small rooms with bathrooms and terraces. Within the multiplex of buildings were poolside bars and cabanas, chaise lounges scattered on the beach, palm trees swaying mildly in the damp southerly zephyr.

Clint had insisted for Bermudez to bring his entire assortment of the jewelry and not just a sample or two. If Jaegermeister's expert valued it minimally at $950,000, he, Jaegermeister, would button up the sale right there and then, and tender Bermudez forty-five percent of the appraised sum minus Clint's five percent commission. Hence, the sly cop would fly home resting his head on a hefty $380,000 in US dollars.

CHAPTER 81

The concierge directed Bermudez to Waldo Jaegermeister's suite, one that fronted an enthralling view of the bay. Bermudez knocked, and Jaegermeister opened the door in a brown velvet house robe and slippers. "I'm Waldo. Mr. Bermudez, I presume?"

"Oh yeah. That's me. Been that for forty-nine years, and hope I'll be George Bermudez for the next forty-nine years." His worn clichés amused him, and he thought they amused everyone else. He felt the welcoming coolness of the air conditioner, his skin quickly drying of perspiration. "It's a hell of a lot more humid here than Florida."

"Well naturally, here we're closer to the equator," Jaegermeister said.

Bermudez saw a second and a third man on a couch. Nodding toward the two, he asked Jaegermeister, "Who are they?"

"Good question. Adam on the left is my appraiser. And a damn good one. And the one on the right is my manservant, Lance."

The three greeted warmly, and the appraiser, a six-foot-two, wide-shouldered person who spoke in a rugged Brooklyn accent, said to Bermudez, "Make yourself comfortable and let's see what you got. This may take a while."

"Oh yeah. I brought everything." Bermudez, dressed for the tropics in khaki shorts, a flowery short-sleeve shirt, and sandals, dumped a briefcase full of gems onto the coffee table, confidence beaming in his eyes in knowing the high quality of his cargo.

"You brought it all! Good!" Jaegermeister said, a thrill in his voice as if nothing could've made him happier.

Adam the appraiser took a loupe out from a pouch and reached for a pad and pen on a side table. Someone knocked on the door, and Lance, who hadn't spoken a word, opened it for the caller. It was a waiter carrying a platter of hors d'oeuvres and a bottle of Moët & Chandon. He laid the food tray on a coffee stand and dunked the champagne bottle in a metal ice bucket, droplets of condensation forming on it.

The waiter walked out, and Waldo Jaegermeister, pointing at the delicacies, said, "Mr. Bermudez, please have some. You must be hungry. That's why I ordered somethin' to nosh on and champagne for your parched throat."

"Eh . . . thanks. Call me George."

Jaegermeister's manservant poured the Moët in two fluted glasses, handing one to him and the other to Bermudez, who raised it as a toast. "*Salut*, Mr. Jaegermeister."

"*Salut*, George. Welcome to St. Thomas." The host gestured with the glass at his guest. "I think we'll do business today, and we'll all be happy." And he smiled amiably as though Bermudez was the most important person to him.

Adam, humorless and immersed in inspecting the contents of the briefcase, passed on the champagne. He was itemizing each piece of jewelry, a painstaking chore.

Jaegermeister and Bermudez were engaged casually in elementary talk, consuming an hour, in which the former New York detective had downed three glasses of champagne. Before arriving at Jaegmeister's suite, Bermudez had had no idea what kind of individual this buyer might've been, and an uneasy feeling perturbed him. But the alcohol helped soothe the tension.

The room was the size of a lion's cage, and four people occupying it restricted everybody's movements. Thankfully, Adam finished his assessment of Bermudez's possessions. "Waldo," he said, "I wanna talk to you in private. Why don't we step outside?"

Jaegermeister said to Bermudez, "George, you mind if he I and have a private talk?"

Bermudez, feeling lightheaded, shook his head slowly. "Not at all. Take all the time you need. I'll have another glass of . . . what're you call it? Moe Shanghai?"

"It's Moët & Chandon. Drink as much as you want," Jaegermeister offered magnanimously.

Adam closed Bermudez's briefcase and went out into the common breezeway, Jaegermeister behind him. Bermudez found himself alone with Lance, who, stone-faced, hadn't yet said a damn word. *Why is this manservant so quiet? Maybe he's an introvert. But who cares?*

Ten awkward minutes clicked by, and at last Adam and Jaegermeister came back into the so-called suite. They stood practically over the dodgy detective for what felt to him too long a pause in silence. Sensing a forthcoming line of questions that he'd rather skirt, Bermudez shifted squeamishly in his seat. Jaegermeister snorted through his nose and asked, "George, I need to know where this treasure came from. I don't wanna peddle hot merchandise to the wrong person, or bring it to the wrong place. Know what I mean?"

"This is not hot material," Bermudez replied with an air of conviction as if he were offended. "It's inheritance from my wife's side. It's *not* hot."

"Well, that's good news, George." Jaegermeister joggled his chin in Adam's direction. "He says everything you got in that briefcase is worth all of 950 grand, just as you said. I must tell yah, you're a straight shooter."

Bermudez, parked sloppily in his chair beside the couch, smiled disingenuously. "I told you. So what're you gonna give me for all this?"

"We're going to make you the deal of a lifetime, and you're gonna be very, very appreciative," Adam said. "Yes, you're gonna be very appreciative. A sweet deal."

"Oh yeah?" Bermudez uttered somewhat cheerfully but in a doubtful tone.

"This is the deal: We'll take all the jewelry. We're not goin' to pick and choose the cream and leave you to worry about gettin' rid of the lesser pieces. No, we'll take all of it. Okay?"

"Uh, uh," Bermudez mumbled, rocking his head as if it had come unhinged from the neck. "And what're you guys gonna give me for everything?"

Jaegermeister cut in, "I'm a man of my word, too, George. Didn't I say we're gonna give you the deal of a lifetime? And we are. We're takin' all the jewelry, and we're givin' you your life."

"What're you mean?" Bermudez asked, a knot in his throat.

Jaegermeister looked at Adam, who side-glanced Lance. A still silence was hanging, and a bolt of apprehensiveness struck Bermudez, his heart pulsating faster. A sudden instinct alerted him something was wrong. And his perception was justified. Waldo Jaegermeister, a fictitious name, was really Donald Frankos. And Adam was Nick Sacco. In an instant, Lance yanked out a sawed-off shotgun from under the pillow of the couch. In sync, Sacco cocked his revolver, and Frankos dug his hand into the pocket of his house robe for his semiautomatic. And swiftly, the artillery was trained at Bermudez.

CHAPTER 82

T he three gunners stared menacingly at Bermudez, his intestines in a convulsion. Sacco leaned down to him eye to eye. "I always had respect for cops and always will. But you're a dirty cop, and somebody should've drilled a bullet in your temple a long time ago. And you're a liar, too. Inheritance from your wife's family, my ass. We know where you got that swag. Sammy Nalo's pad."

"No, no . . . I swear . . . nothing was found when we searched Nalo's place."

"That's because you had already cleaned out the joint before your pals got a warrant. So save the bullshit, George," Frankos said.

"I would never do that. Even . . . even Nalo told Lieutenant O'Neil that he had no jewels in his house," Bermudez said feebly.

"I gotta tell you, George, you'd make a great lawyer," Frankos teased.

Bermudez saw no humor in the Greek's joke, his face perspiring like a wet sponge.

Sacco scooped the jewelry off the coffee table and layered it neatly inside the briefcase. In the next second, Frankos leaped forward and tied Bermudez in a bear hug, and Lance, a collector for loansharks, patted him down. "He's clean."

Frankos said, "George, we're gonna go for a ride and take you to where you can enjoy the rest of the afternoon in the sun." The Greek dropped his hand hard on Bermudez's shoulder, and he flinched.

"When we leave here, don't try any cute tricks. Just walk along with us, and keep in mind that my friends and I have guns in our pockets, and we'll blast some lead into your skull if you do anything stupid," Frankos warned.

Frankos and Sacco were in stride alongside Bermudez as they walked through the ground floor terrace of the Bolongo Bay Beach Hotel, Lance following behind. They piled into a rented Chevy Nova, Lance at the wheel, and he drove onto a narrow, unpaved trail, a pathway pocked with ruts and potholes, Bermudez in the rear seat sandwiched between Sacco and the Greek. The bumpy three-mile road ended at a desolate fishing dock. A lone, old fishing trawler was lashed to two wharfs, rocking gently on the water. Lance parked in a dirt lot, and Frankos said to Bermudez, "All right, George. We're goin' fishing, but I gotta tie you up."

"What're you gonna do to me?" And Bermudez flew into a thrashing fit, struggling to free himself from his captors, kicking furiously the back of the car's front seat. "Where're you takin' me? You bastards, where're you takin' me? I'm gonna have you all arrested."

"Is that right, George? Are you gonna tell the police we stole your jewelry that you stole from Sammy Nalo?" Sacco asked cynically.

Bermudez didn't think that was funny; he elbowed Frankos and the Cat, frantically thrusting and twisting his upper body to the left and to the right. The scuffle wasn't under control until Lance climbed over the driver's seat and lent a hand. Sacco managed to bind Bermudez's wrists and feet, and Lance and the Greek carried him to the edge of the dock, hurling him onto a seventeen-foot Boston Whaler. It was tied to the stern of the trawler, a wooden fishing boat in disrepair, engine clunking, blowing blue smoke from the smokestack. Bermudez bellowed a scream, and Frankos screwed a silencer into the barrel of his pistol. "*You* do that again, and you're gone, George."

The captain of the trawler, Reginald Stoneham, a black, gristly-faced seadog, a crop of nappy, white hair grazing on his scalp, stuck his head out the window of the pilot house. "I'mma ready to shove off. Y'all be ready to go?"

On the island of St. Thomas, Captain Stoneham was not known to do much trawling for fish; his niche was hauling contraband, drugs, stolen items, illegal immigrants, assault rifles, etc. In this instance, Frankos and Sacco had commissioned him and his rotting boat to tow Bermudez in the Boston Whaler twelve miles out to sea. Stoneham climbed down from the pilot house and jumped onto the dock to unfasten the lines from the wharfs. "I theenk you better put a lifejacket on dat dude. Jus in case, you know?" He pointed to the stern deck of the trawler. "You'll find one over there."

Lance took one of the lifejackets from a stowage bin, and he and Sacco jumped into the Boston Whaler. They untied Bermudez's wrists, and Lance passed the yellow life vest to Sacco, who wrestled to strap it onto the wriggling detective. "If you don't hold still, my buddy's gonna whack you over the head with that huge gun of his," Sacco said.

Captain Stoneham eased the fishing vessel from the dock and spun his tiller wheel, setting his magnetic compass on a northerly eighty-four degrees for the twelve-mile sail into the Central Atlantic, the Boston Whaler bouncing on the surface of the waves as the trawler towed it at nine knots (about eleven miles per hour). Frankos was standing on the stern of the fishing boat, his gun at his side. "Don't make a sound, George. We don't need to attract anybody's attention. Do we?"

Captain Stoneham, a cigar in his toothless mouth, hollered from the pilothouse, "We're six miles out."

"Keep goin' 'til we're about twelve miles offshore," Sacco said. "Keep goin'."

But why do they wanna go so far out? wondered Stoneham.

CHAPTER 83

Twelve miles into the deep ocean, the air was cooler, and the waves had grown to eight-foot swells, the trawler and the Boston Whaler in tow climbing and descending as if they were on a mini roller coaster. Standing on the aft deck, feet apart, Frankos holstered his revolver and stared down at Bermudez, who was lying on the fiberglass floor of the seventeen-foot runabout, grimacing and wiggling, trying to loosen the twine restraining his ankles and wrists. The Greek held a palm horizontally as a visor above his forehead and did a 360-degree scan of the horizon. No land in sight. "All right, George, now you can scream all you want. Only the sharks will hear you."

"What're you gonna do with me?" Bermudez asked in tears.

Stoneham eased on the throttle, and the trawler backed down to a near standstill, the Boston Whaler crashing into its stern. Floating motionless on the crests of the eight-foot swells, the fishing boat and the relatively small runabout were pitching and yawing fiercely as if they were toys in a bathtub. "Shit, it's rough out here," Sacco complained. "It feels like this thing's gonna capsize."

"No, mohn, it won't capsize. Me boat built by me grandpappy," the captain yelled back from the pilot house.

The scrawny Stoneham stepped down the ladder to the stern deck, a twelve-inch serrated knife in his mouth. He had his T-shirt off, and you could count his ribs, the man's skin darker than dirty motor oil. The captain bent over the transom of the trawler and severed the line to the Boston Whaler.

"Don't leave me here. Please don't leave me," Bermudez begged, angst on his face. "You can keep my jewelry . . . I won't report you. Pleeeeease don't leave me."

Although it was late in the afternoon, the sun was intense. "This'll give you a chance to get a good suntan," the Greek derided. "And if you get thirsty, you got plenty of water around you. Adios."

Stoneham went up to the pilot house, shifted the transmission forward, and shoved the throttle lever ahead. He rotated the tiller to a 272-degree heading for the return trip to shore, the diesel engine growling loudly, emitting dense smoke from the smokestack.

"*Noooooo! Noooooooooo!*" Bermudez howled, the trawler shrinking in the distance as the Boston Whaler soared and plummeted into the mountains of swells.

CHAPTER 84

On touching land, Sacco, Lance, and the Greek made haste to the airport. At the terminal, Sacco phoned the St. Thomas marine constable and reported that approximately twelve miles off the northeast coast of the island he had spotted a small boat adrift, a man possibly in it.

"What were you doing out there?" the constable asked.

"I was on a speed boat."

"What is your name, sir?"

"Look, I don't wanna get involved. I'm just tellin' you what I saw." And Sacco terminated the call.

JUNE 1976

Nick Sacco retrenched from the nightlife in Manhattan and focused on his family. His bride, Nora, a pretty woman fashioning shoulder-length, wavy brown hair and big hazel eyes bore him two children, a pair of girls. He was loyal and loving to her, and cared immensely for the lovable tots.

The Pierre was a long-forgotten event. Bobby Comfort had become a homebody in Rochester, and Sammy Nalo was serving his prison sentence. Bermudez, who had been rescued safe and sound, never recounted his calamity offshore in the Atlantic Ocean, praying the authorities wouldn't reopen the investigation into Nalo's lost jewels. And the timing was right for Sacco to resume his burglaries.

The Cat had befriended an insurance broker, Jay Burger. For a fifteen percent "referral fee," Burger, who was in the know of his clients' valuables he insured, was supplying Sacco the names and addresses of those customers. One such target was a house in Hewlett, a ritzy town on the south shore of Long Island, where a widow had a safe full of Tiffany & Co. designer jewelry. "Nick," the insurance broker said, "this job is a cinch. The broad lives alone in a big house, and she's never home during the day." He waved Sacco into the coffee room of his office. "I don't wanna talk out there. Anyway, her name is Lauren Baker, and she used to tell me that in the morning she goes to the gym, then to get her hair and nails done. Then she goes shopping in the Five Towns, spending her dead husband's money. She's running around the whole day." Burger gave Sacco a piece of paper. "Here's her address. Good luck." And he slapped the Cat on the back.

Sacco and a novice burglar, John Marino, who was under the Cat's tutelage, were set to undertake the robbery at the widow's residence. The intended victim was an attractive woman in her early thirties. Recently, her rich husband had died at the age of fifty-nine. Sacco and Marino pinpointed Ms. Baker's property. In the unlikely event she might've been at home, they had dressed as mailmen pretending to deliver a package. Marino knocked on the front door. No one answered, and on jiggling the door knob it was unlocked. He and Sacco looked at each other and shrugged. They poked at the door, and it opened. The two burglars entered and tiptoed about the ground floor to pinpoint the master bedroom. They did, and with the minimal illumination of a night lamp it was rather obscure in there. They could hear a faint hissing of running water. "Sounds like the sprinkler in the backyard," Marino said.

But to the burglars' shock, the homeowner stepped through the bathroom door naked and walked face-to-face into Sacco, her breasts bumping into his chest. Sacco wound his arm loosely around Ms Baker's slim waist, pulled a sheet off the unmade bed, and draped it over her. But an oddity astounded him and Marino. The walls in this bedroom were painted black; the windows covered with black curtains, and if all lights were turned off the room would've been darker than an abyss. Then something unimaginable overcame the two burglars; they saw an open but empty coffin lying abreast the foot of the king-size bed.

"What the fuck!" Marino blurted, visibly shaken from the ghoulish sight.

CHAPTER 85

Nick Sacco and John Marino, affected by the macabre spectacle of the coffin, were winded as if they'd seen the devil before them. The Cat reshuffled the sheet he had thrown over Ms. Baker so her head was uncovered. "I don't know what you got goin' in here, but all I want you to do is to open the goddamn safe you've got somewhere in this bedroom." The voluptuous widow didn't seem fazed by the trespassers, probably because of how gingerly Sacco had handled her.

She nodded at the nightstand beside the bed. "It's in there."

"Well, open it."

"What if I don't?"

That baffled Sacco. "If you know what's good for you, open it."

"What if I don't know what's good for me?"

Marino closed in on Ms. Baker, and raised his gun high over his shoulder as though he were about to wallop her on the head. Sacco quickly moved in front of her as a shield. "Hold it, hold it." He then said to Ms. Baker, "Look I don't wanna see you hurt, but this kid is like a bull in a china store. See how big he is? Sometimes I can't control him. So do me a favor and please open the safe."

Ms. Baker stared audaciously at Sacco, and he perceived a faint smirk on her lips. "All right, I'll open the safe." She looked at Sacco as if she were undecided about something. "On one condition. If *you* guarantee me that you'll take what you came here for, and go without touching me."

I sure would love to touch you. "I *personally* guarantee we won't lay a hand on you."

Give or take $840,000 in gems and platinum wares were in the safe, and Sacco emptied it. He then carefully handcuffed Ms. Baker to the bedpost, Marino cut the phone lines, and they fled, the ghastly impression of the casket causing goose bumps on their skin.

"What the fuck is this weird bitch doin' with a coffin in her bedroom? And those black walls and curtains," Marino said warily.

Sacco shook his head. "I don't know, but I'm gonna talk to the insurance broker. He might know what that's all about."

Sacco, who seldom sold his spoils to fences, consigned Ms. Baker's Tiffany collection to a jeweler on Canal Street, who later paid him sixty percent of the gem's $840,000 trading value. It was a hell of a score, and he should've been reveling in it. But incompatibilities with his wife, who was afflicted by an acute bipolar condition, had corroded the marriage. She was combative and irrational, and arguments exploded every night, emotionally scarring the children. One night, Sacco came home late, and realized he had forgotten his house key on the kitchen counter earlier that afternoon. "Great! Now I gotta wake her up." He rang the bell. No answer. He rang it again, this time repeatedly. A minute passed, and he could see a light through the top window of the door. "Phew. She's up."

The safety chain clanged, and Nora opened the door. "Why the fuck did you wake me up? And where have you been 'til two o'clock in the morning?" The bipolar disorder had worsened since she gave birth to the first baby, a typical side effect, and her once serene countenance had soured to that of a witch. As it is not unusual for a bipolar sufferer to be in denial of his or her mental flaw, Nora was adamant about medical intervention and treatment, which was viable and available. "You have no consideration for anyone. You think everybody has to be at your beck and call," she ranted on. Without fail, she'd cast blame on anyone she interacted with, one of the symptoms of that illness.

"I forgot my keys. Sorry."

"What whore have you been with? Aha?"

"I wasn't with a whore, but maybe I should've been."

Nora saw red, and at a meager five-foot-five had the gall to slap her husband across the cheek, blood bubbling in his nostrils. But it wasn't courage; in that moment, she was in the upswing stage of the bipolar cycle, a phase in which an overdose of adrenaline had altered her chemical balance, distorting her perception of invincibility. Sacco tried to squeeze into the doorway, and she clocked him a second, a third, and a fourth time. He shoved Nora aside, but she tugged at the tails of his jacket, tearing one. "You son of a bitch, you're out with whores all hours of the night, and then you got the balls to wake me up," she bawled at the loudest capacity of her lungs.

It took discipline for Sacco to ignore her provocations and not smack her. Furnari's slogan came to mind: *A real man doesn't beat his wife; he just kills her.* But the Cat didn't have it in him to do either. Not to disturb the neighbors in the attached brownstones, he closed the door and locked it. As usual, Nora's cantankerous banter wakened the little girls. "See? You ain't happy 'til one of the kids hears you. If you wanna take out on me whatever goes on in that sick mind of yours, that's fine. But why do you have to put the children through it?" he went to his daughter's nursery, looked into her crib, and embraced the toddler, kissing her. "It's all right. Don't cry. Mommy doesn't feel good. It's okay."

And that was exemplary of how Sacco's household would erupt on any given day. But what could he do? He wouldn't consider leaving the girls, not in the hands of a woman whose volatility was as ignitable as dynamite. He had one alternative: to play it day by day. *Maybe she'll get medical help.*

But for now, Nora's emotional instability and the unpredictability of her pendulum mood swings, were a distraction to Sacco, and a detriment to his distraught children.

NICK SACCO

I tried everything to make my wife happy and keep her from going off the handle. It got to the point where I couldn't think straight, and that meant I couldn't plan a job. When I did a robbery, I had every little detail worked out. That's why I never got pinched. But if my head wasn't clear and straight, I was handicapped. So I decided not to do anything until I figured out how I could get Nora to understand she had to go for help. It was a blessing that I could afford to stay on the sidelines.

But unlike me, John Marino needed a score, and now this bungling rookie was on his own. And God forbid John should get caught, he had no stomach; he was all bark and no bite, and who knew how he'd take it if he were looking at thirty years in a federal joint. One thing Christie Furnari always said, "If you're gonna pull off a crime, either do it alone, or do it with someone you trust enough to be your codefendant. Because if the shit hits the fan, you don't wanna get locked up with someone who'll rat you out to save himself."

CHAPTER 86

John Marino, a five-foot-eight, two-hundred-pounder in his twenties, who had more muscles than brains, broke into a mansion in Sands Point, Long Island. The private police of that upscale village arrested him for burglary and possession of an illegal weapon. Marino, who had the shape of a refrigerator, was booked at Nassau County Police Headquarters in Mineola, and because he was armed during the commission of the burglary, the district attorney upgraded the charges to a Class A felony.

"Judging by what we got on you, you're in deep shit, John," Detective Peter Van Holt said to Marino, who, ruffled and scared, didn't hold out too long before folding his stoic pretense. Van Holt, blond-headed and beer-bellied, dangled a document in front of the prisoner's face. "This here, Johnnie Boy, is a criminal complaint and sworn affidavit from the arresting officer who got you red-handed." He spat his chewing gum into a waste basket underneath his desk. "Yeah, you're going way for a long time."

Submissively, the neophyte burglar had been staring at his shoes, knowing the charges he was burdened with were indefensible. Scared of the rigors inside a penitentiary, eyes glossy with fear, he looked upward at the tallish, blue-eyed Van Holt. "Can we work somethin' out?"

"Like what?"

"I can tell you some things about this guy, Nick Sacco. He's a burglar. They call him 'the Cat.'" Marino was about to inform on someone who had been mentoring him, and a spell of repentance wedged a lump in his throat.

Van Holt popped another stick of gum in his mouth. "I don't know of him, but if this Sacco is a two-bit burglar, I don't want to waste my time."

John Marino, handcuffed to a radiator, shook his head as if the detective couldn't have been more mistaken. "Oh no, he's not a small-time thief. The Cat is plugged into the Lucchese people," he said, his voice a bit higher. "And sometimes he works with 'Fat Tony' Salerno."

This is organized crime, and Sacco might be a big fish. "Let me look into this, Johnnie Boy." Outward, Van Holt didn't seem too interested; inward, his adrenaline had spiked as if he had just hit a jackpot. He then said to his partner. "I'll go to my office to make some calls and see who this Nick Sacco is. Watch our friend here."

It was warm in the airless, non-air-conditioned station house, and Van Holt's partner loosened his tie and vented his face with a folded newspaper. "What're you know about Sacco?"

"A lot," Marino answered in clipped words as though he wasn't willing to delve into it deeper unless it'd be to his favor.

Van Holt's inquiries with the NYPD resulted in a mouth-watering discovery. Nick "the Cat" Sacco was a person of interest whom the NYPD presumed to have ties to Lucchese Consigliere Christie "the Tick" Furnari. The detective, jubilant, rushed back to his office, an ear-to-ear smile on his flabby face. "Johnnie Boy, we may have something here. Mr. Sacco is known to the NYPD. They say he's an armed robber." He sat on his desk and faced Marino, who for the past two hours, still cuffed to the radiator, hadn't been able to stand. Van Holt nodded the way one does when light begins to shine on an elusive solution. "So Johnnie Boy, what can you tell me about your buddy Sacco?"

"What's in it for me?"

"Aha!" Van Holt yapped as if he had the right answer for Marino. "If you can give me enough information to arrest Sacco for a crime he committed here in Nassau County, I'll recommend to the DA to put a plea deal on the table for you."

"What kind of a deal?"

"Well, as things stand you'll get convicted of armed robbery, and you already have a nice rap sheet. So it'll be bye-bye Johnnie Boy for a *loooong* time. But if what you got on Sacco is juicy, I think I can get you a plea to a misdemeanor, and ninety days in the county jail. Now you can handle that. Right?"

Marino, whose brow was pleated like the head of a bulldog, didn't seem quite ready to take the plunge.

"I'm giving you back your life, and I can't believe you have to think about that," Van Holt said.

"Yeah, I'll take that," Marino answered.

Of course, the fledgling burglar gladly jumped at three months in the county jail versus twenty-five years in a Supermax prison. And Van Holt began debriefing Marino. The detective, eagerness in his movements, set up a tape recorder on his desk, and switched it on. "So where do we start, Johnnie Boy?"

Marino asked for a glass of water and a cigarette. Halfway through a Lucky Strike, the jitters subsided, as did his remorse. "Three months ago, Sacco and me robbed a woman's house out here on Long Island. She was home when we walked into the house and had to take her at gunpoint."

This is an excellent start. "Do you know the victim's name?" Van Holt asked.

"Lauren Baker," Marino answered in a low voice.

"What's her address?"

"I don't know the address, but I can show you where it is."

NICK SACCO

I read about Marino in the papers. I talked it over with Furnari, and the first thing he said was to whack him. Furnari wasn't just worried about me; if Marino flipped, the ripples could wash over the Lucchese consigliere as well. I could've asked Frankos to kill Marino, and the Greek would've done it in a minute. But I didn't want to take that route. I never hurt or murdered anybody, and I wasn't about to start now. I had to sit tight and hope Marino would be a man and take his lumps without taking anybody down with him.

CHAPTER 87

The Nassau County Robbery Squad inducted John Marino in the "stoolies den of rats," and he detailed to Detective Van Holt his and Sacco's violation at Lauren Baker's home.

"And where can we find Mr. Sacco, Johnnie Boy?" asked Van Holt.

"He lives in Brooklyn on 18th Avenue. I don't know the number of the house, but I'd recognize it if I saw it."

Van Holt swore out a warrant. But in compliance to protocol, in order to arrest Sacco he had to obtain permission from the captain of New York's 70th Precinct, which had jurisdiction in the section of Brooklyn where the Cat resided. It was 1:00 A.M. and raining. Sacco lived on the second floor of a brownstone, and one of Van Holt's cops rang his bell. The Cat was not asleep and tramped down the stairs to see who could've been calling so late at night.

He opened the door, and based on Marino's descriptions Van Holt knew who was standing before him. He showed Sacco his gold badge. "Nick Sacco, I'm Detective Van Holt from Nassau County. These other officers are from NYC's 70th Precinct. I guess you know why we're here."

"Am I supposed to know why you're here? What is this, a riddle?"

"Does a Lauren Baker from Hewlett ring a bell?"

"I haven't got the foggiest idea what you're talkin' about. But what're you want from me?"

"I'm arresting you for armed robbery, possession of an illegal weapon, and unlawful captivity."

Sacco didn't speak another word; a hardened felon knows not to make any statements to the authorities if he is the target of an investigation. And smartly, he didn't resist and complied with Van Holt's body search. At the 70th Precinct, detectives fingerprinted Sacco and detained him overnight. Within twenty-four hours, the Nassau County district attorney forwarded the necessary paperwork to extradite him to that county.

Sacco was arraigned in district court in Hempstead, Long Island, and remanded to the Nassau County Jail without bail. His lawyer drafted a motion for reconsideration of bail, and the arraigning judge granted it, setting the hearing two weeks thenceforth. In the interim, Van Holt scheduled a lineup in which Sacco would be placed on display for Ms. Baker.

Three days into the county jail, and at 6:00 A.M., four deputy sheriffs removed Sacco from his cell, and wrists and ankles shackled, transported him to police central booking where the lineups were conducted. Van Holt sent one of his underlings to call on Ms. Baker and chauffeur her to the station house. The woman's sweet perfume heralded her as she made her entrance into central booking, tempting the gawks of the wishful cops who would've given the world to this stunning hunk of a female, if only they could have her for one night.

"I'm Detective Peter Van Holt, Ms. Baker."

"Under these circumstances, I'm not so pleased to meet you," Lauren Baker said, extending a hand bent at the wrist for the detective to take, her bracelets jingling.

Van Holt seemed a bit flustered by the elegantly dressed brunette, whose complacent demeanor suggested financial comfort and culture. "This won't take long, Madame."

The lineup was soon underway, and Ms. Baker's alluring hazel eyes skipped from one suspect to the other, five in all. She scanned the quintet of figures behind the one-way glass window, noting the height markings in inches on the backdrop wall. The tallest of the subjects, who had the number two tag pinned onto his chest, was the second from the left. He was six-foot-two and solid. And handsome. As Ms. Baker's gaze swept from left to right scanning the suspects, Van Holt saw her pausing on number two. "Ms. Baker, do you see anyone in the lineup who might've been the robber?"

"I . . . I can't be sure."

Van Holt said, "Take all the time you need. Can I get you some coffee?"

"Tea, please."

Tea was not on hand at central booking, and Van Holt sent for it. Lauren Baker considered the five men, who were now fiddling restlessly, twitching and scratching. She stole another glance at number two. Van Holt said, "I'll have these characters turn sideways. That may help you." Through the intercom system, he directed, "All right you guys, turn to the right." And to impress Ms. Baker, he joked, "C'mon fellas, show your Alfred Hitchcock profiles."

As the five men turned, number two had a unique feature that Ms. Baker immediately distinguished, his aquiline nose. A delivery boy carried into the room her fuming-hot tea on a tray, and she took it with her lotion-softened hand, her pinkie jutting into the air. She slurped it with short sips so as not to burn her naturally cherry-red lips. Unable to remove her eyes off that same person behind the one-way window, Van Holt asked, "You seem to go back to the tall one toward the left. You think he's the one?"

She sipped her tea again but didn't answer. Lauren Baker was now positive that number two, the one who had the longish but cute nose, had been one of her burglars. Number two was Nick Sacco.

CHAPTER 88

L auren Baker had scrutinized Sacco at length in the lineup, and she knew beyond doubt he had been one of the encroachers in her home, though they hadn't touched a hair on her lithe body, a well-maintained specimen. But appreciating Sacco's gentility during the holdup, and besotted by his striking and imposing stature, she declined to identify him.

"Ms. Baker, are you sure none of these thieves is the one we're looking for?" Van Holt asked skeptically. "These people there behind that glass are all known burglars, and three are violent."

Was it possible John Marino hoodwinked Detective Van Holt? No, that line of thinking contravened common sense. When Ms. Baker had reported the robbery, she described one of the gunmen as tall, polite, and civil. And on meeting Sacco, Van Holt did find him well-mannered and gentlemanly, whereas Marino was not tall and had a gruff demeanor, typifying a street hooligan. Then who was lying, Lauren Baker or John Marino?

Van Holt had grown frustrated and started acting it. He forfeited his pretentious sophistication, and his tonality heightened to one of rudeness and harassment, his body language suddenly jumpy and hostile. "Lemme ask you this, Ms. Baker." He indicated the glass window. "Did anybody threaten or approach you?"

She gave the detective a stare as though that was an absurdity. "Absolutely not!"

"I have a feeling you're not being truthful. And if it turns out you're not telling me the truth, you can be charged . . ."

"You're irking me, detective. I said I don't see anyone in this lineup that faintly resembles the men who robbed me. Period."

Van Holt was wordless. *Someone is lying. Either Marino or this rich bitch. Which one is it?*

"If we're done here, detective, please have your lackey drive me home. I've had enough of the body odors in this place." And she fast-stepped out into the hallway, her high heels clacking on the pavement.

Van Holt scented a foulness of collusion; had he, Sacco, bought her silence? Perhaps. But despite the detective's reservations, he had to release him, even though Marino had proffered a sworn affidavit affirming Sacco's role in the robbery. Pursuant to New York State laws, the testimony of someone who partook in the same crime as the defendant is not admissible unless it is corroborated by independent evidence; that is either a witness who had no involvement in the felony, or additional supporting facts. And Van Holt, bound by the law, had to disregard the allegations against Nick Sacco.

It had been a close call for the Cat, who had picked up on Ms. Baker's attraction to him. Her resoluteness pretending not to have recognized him was a magnanimous act, and he was fascinated. He thought about Lauren every minute, and visions of her were imbedded in his brain; the svelte figure; the defined outline of her jaws that was unpadded by excess flesh; and those large eyes, black as polished marble. Sacco felt a flutter in his heart for her, but was she a dead end for him? It was a godsend that she hadn't pressed matters, and it'd be wise for him to let sleeping dogs lie.

At times, however, the heart does not obey the mind. *This is the day I go for broke.* The Cat showered, splashed on cologne, and donned a double-breasted Pierre Cardin. Preened and shaved, he cut the figure of a Hollywood actor, and drove to Lauren's home—a risky impulse.

CHAPTER 89

The white sign on the curb of Peninsula Boulevard read: ENTERING HEWLETT, ONE OF THE FIVE TOWNS. Sacco's pulse raced as he turned right onto Kew Avenue, the street where Lauren lived. He parked his powder-blue Lincoln Mark III across the street from her house. It was a dreary, drizzly day, and chances were she was at home. He strutted to her front door, a bouquet of red roses in his hand. The Cat rang the bell, and thirty seconds passed. No answer. Disappointed, and about to leave, he heard the door knob clang. Lauren Baker, in an orange satin blouse and a black skirt, looked at Sacco unsurprised. "I've been expecting you." Unconsciously, she patted the side of her hair, a subliminal sign when a woman is awestruck by a man. "Please come in. This time you don't need a gun." She gave Sacco an unrestricted smile and waved him into the black-marbled vestibule, vivaciousness illuminating her face.

To say Sacco felt awkward would be an understatement. "I . . . didn't mean to barge in on you. If . . . if I knew your phone number, I would've called first."

"You should've asked for it the last time you were here. But you left in a hurry."

Almost negligent, Sacco gave her the flowers. "Oh, these are for you."

She sniffed the bouquet and closed her eyes. "Red roses! My favorites. Thank you! So thoughtful of you . . . and romantic. Come into my den."

"You're not gonna call the cops, are you?" he asked half jokingly.

Lauren threw her head back, feigning drama. "I wouldn't think of it. Or maybe I should. No, don't be afraid. Come, come."

As Sacco followed Lauren, he was admiring her womanish hips and roundish buttocks, and those silky, beautiful legs whose calves funneled nicely into her mocassined feet. The den was wood-paneled and painted white, the seating all red leather. Lighted candles emitted a sweet scent, and Lauren motioned him to sit on the couch, her hands long, slinky, the fingernails red and lacquered.

"Uh, I wanna apologize for, you know, everythin' that happened. And, well . . . I wanna thank you for what you did last week at the lineup. Eh, thanks, I really appreciate it. And I won't forget it."

Lauren's sleek, pointy tongue touched the tip of her nose. "Does that mean you're going to give me back what you stole from me?" she asked in a harmonious voice as she unwrapped the bouquet, the cellophane crackling.

"I can't give you back your jewelry 'cause I sold it, but I do wanna pay you for it."

"That's fine." She sat on an armchair and crossed her legs, the skirt creeping up her thighs. She cast her eyes at the sofa. "Please, sit."

Sacco did, and seemed tongue-tied. Lauren saw this and asked lightheartedly, "Now that we've taken care of business, are you going to take me out to dinner?"

Her cleverness was becoming apparent to the Cat. She was infatuated by him, not only because of his physical prowess, but also due to her underlying attraction to him as a criminal. But the young widow's ulterior motivation not to have thrown Sacco to the dogs at the lineup was her bet that he'd be appreciative and would come calling. He'd surely reimburse her for the jewelry; and if he wouldn't do so she could always tell Detective Van Holt that she had been fuzzy, but now was certain Nick Sacco was one of the armed robbers. Above all, Lauren knew that if he were sent to prison, she'd recoup the limits of her insurance policy, $250,000—a far cry from her $850,000 stolen jewelry.

Sacco looked at his watch, a gold Rolex he had traded a jeweler for swag gems. "Sure, soon it'll be dinner time, and we can have a bite somewhere."

He and Lauren were warming to each other, dining at a French restaurant. But apparitions of the coffin in her bedroom, well, that was dampening the evening. He'd been delaying asking her but he could no longer resist: "Hope you won't mind, but I gotta ask you . . ."

Lauren adapted a naughty look and interrupted him, "Why do I have a coffin in my bedroom, right?"

Sacco blushed at her candidness. "Well . . . yeah. I mean it's kind of . . ."

"Weird?"

"Well, yeah."

She waved her hand in understanding and chuckled, silliness in her giggle. "It was a fetish of my late husband. Eh . . . he . . . he liked for us to make love in the coffin." And Lauren laughed in a ticklish cackle.

Sacco laid down his knife and fork, a startled look on his face. "I'll be damned . . . I'll be . . ."

"Don't worry. Tomorrow, someone is coming to take it away."

"Thank God, 'cause I ain't into nothin' like that. Know what I mean?"

She was fiddling with the top button of her blouse, her cleavage bubbling beneath it. "But I have some sex fetishes of my own."

Christie Furnari's position as consigliere of the Lucchese Family was a powerful rank but one that mandated fairness and unwavering determination, traits requisite for one to be respected in the underworld societies. "Nick," Furnari had instilled upon Sacco, "Your word is your bond. When you say you're gonna do somethin', you gotta live up to it. You know me well enough that if I tell you I'm gonna put you on the moon, you should buy yourself a space suit. And if I tell you I'm gonna kill you, you better get in your coffin and try it on for size. Understand?"

And Nick Sacco was a man of his word who could be relied on. Two weeks into his relationship with Lauren Baker, he invited her to a Sunday brunch at Tavern on the Green, a famous Manhattan restaurant. It's on 67th Street and Central Park West, and boasts an enchanting panoramic view of Central Park. Before ordering, sipping champagne mimosas, Sacco gave Lauren a greeting card in an envelope. She sliced open the flap with her fingernail and the brass key to a safe deposit box spilled out. She read the card:

> To my one and only sweetheart, Lauren,
> The stars will fall from the sky before I stop loving you.
> This is the first of many promises to you that I will keep.
> The key that came with this card is to a safe deposit box that
> has $850,000 of your money.
> And you know what it's for.
> With love, Nick.

Overcome by Sacco's noble promise, Lauren, wide-eyed in wonderment, placed a hand on her bosom. "I don't know what to say. You are a marvelous man. But you know, I already got some of the money from my insurance company."

"Yeah, but the insurance company didn't give you the replaceable cost of the jewels. Right?"

"I got $250,000."

"Well now I made you whole and plus."

Lauren looked up at the ceiling in thought. "Then why don't we take the difference from this and buy ourselves a beach house where it's warm in the winter?"

"Deal!" Sacco said.

Nick and Lauren became inseparable. His marriage to Nora couldn't be restitched together, and not for his lack of trying. What had been adding salt to the wounds in the long-existing conflicts in Sacco and Nora's matrimony were the early nuances of infidelities on his part. Those insinuations materialized into a reality as Nora was now aware of Nick's *commara*, his mistress.

CHAPTER 90

Livid and highly combustible, Nora Sacco was bent on unleashing her scorned woman's wrath. But how could she inflict the worst damage to her disloyal husband? She could inform the police of Sacco's criminalities, but she didn't know any specifics and had no proof of any wrongdoing. Nora then thought of alerting the IRS about his underreported income, but that posed a problem for her. They had been filing joint returns, and that would make her an accessory. What else could she do to avenge his indiscretions? Nora, in a perpetual state of disorientation, and feeling denigrated, her bipolar disorder muddling her thinking, devoted every waking minute to that thought.

Lauren still didn't know that Sacco was married and had two toddlers; and should those eye-openers have come to her attention, she'd blast off into an explosive temper. But today, September 18, 1976, it was her thirty-fifth birthday, and she had woken to the placid whirring of crickets, sunlight filtering through the black blinds of the master bedroom. On the prior evening, Lauren and Sacco had celebrated at a restaurant and then at the movies, viewing the film *Rocky*. But she spent the rest of the night alone. For reasons she couldn't justify, he always had somewhere to go or something to do in the middle of the night that couldn't wait until tomorrow. Lauren longed to have Nick in her bed and wake beside him in the morning, and here on her birthday she was alone, again. She felt malaise and grogginess, the aftermath of the cognac she had drank after Nick left at 2:00 A.M. Still in bed in her white satin nightgown, she was nursing a cup of tea, gazing vacantly through the window into her colorful backyard, an array of lovely flowers coloring the green grass.

Suddenly, remembrances of Lauren's marriage to her late husband, Roy Baker, intruded upon her sullenness. She and Mr. Baker had been a world apart in age, and he was more a father figure than a spouse to her, though she genuinely adored the man and did not marry him for his wealth. Her dad, a financially well-heeled textile industry executive, had been an absentee parent. In redemption, though, prior to his death he erected a substantial trust fund for his only daughter; thus she never had to rely on anyone's support, husband or otherwise. But Lauren's father had failed to provide her with the four human essentials a child instinctively craves, paternal attention, guidance, love, and affection. And Roy Baker unwittingly became the subliminal fatherly companion to her.

Lauren looked at the clock on her nightstand: 8:30. Then she heard a heavy thumping at the front door. Surprised, she laid the teacup on the stand and scuttled to answer the harsh knock. She opened the door, and a haggard woman dangling a gallon-size plastic jug at her side was standing there, feet apart, no makeup, and disheveled brown hair. The caller's eyes had the look of an untamed animal, and to Lauren's dread it was instantly palpable that this stranger was emotionally unbalanced.

"Who . . . who are you, and why are you here?"

"I'm your boyfriend's wife, you filthy bitch," Mrs. Sacco announced.

"You mean Nick?"

"Yeah, Nick, as if you didn't know, you whore."

Confusion and the raw news of betrayal ripped into Lauren, siphoning the air from her lungs. Heart pounding, she wasn't hearing all the vilifying words spewing through the intruder's mouth, though she understood the core of her harangue.

"Don't you know he has children who need a father at home and not running around with a two-bit slut?" Mrs. Sacco berated, wielding the plastic jug.

A wife, children, why didn't Nick tell me about all this? He misled me. But now, in the heat of this confrontation, Mrs. Sacco's tirade began to register in Lauren's head, and her boyfriend's strange behavior came into focus. He had been leading a double life, and she could never have seen herself as the mistress of a married man, a father no less. But she was Nick's *commara*, as the Italians label a mistress, and it repulsed her. Sounding like reproaching voices echoing inside her head, Lauren couldn't squelch Mrs. Sacco's profanities, loud vulgarities that were within earshot of her neighbors. And in those rampant seconds, the dignified Ms. Lauren Baker felt as low as a streetwalker.

"You think you're gonna take my husband from me and his kids? You may have his cock, but I have him by the balls," Mrs. Sacco hollered in a snarl for all to hear as she splashed the liquid in the plastic jug in Lauren's face.

It was muriatic acid, and unable to protect herself, Lauren's eyes and skin burned as if they were on fire. She screamed, rubbing her eyelids. The attacker, wild with vengeance, lunged at her rival, brandishing a barber's razor, slashing the blinded Lauren's forehead, hands, and arms. It was 8:35 in the morning, and this spectacle unfolded outdoors on Lauren's front steps. She pushed herself away from Mrs. Sacco, backpedaling into her doorway, intending to lock out the crazed woman. But the incensed wife, overtaken by fury, was out-powering the wounded Lauren, blood splattering the white nightgown, daylight blackening in her vision.

CHAPTER 91

L auren tripped to the ground, and Mrs. Sacco straddled the fallen lady's waist, doggedly hacking at her. Lauren was tightly covering her face, begging Nick's wife to stop. Instead, she kept punching and slitting, and the shrilling grew louder. A postal worker who was on his daily route saw the clash and knew someone was seriously hurt. He threw the mail sack in his truck and ran to Lauren's aid, unscrambling the two females.

"She's nothing but a whore," Mrs. Sacco yelled to the mailman.

He had known Lauren, and here she was severely lacerated, deep cuts on her cheeks, forehead, and hands, the nightgown shredded and bloody. More serious, the acid might've injured her pupils. Four or five neighbors rushed in, and two men restrained Mrs. Sacco, who hadn't refrained from growling venomous ramblings, thrashing her arms and legs, wriggling to free herself. An off-duty nurse saw to Lauren's first aid to the best of her ability. Someone who had witnessed the sadistic attack phoned 911, and in minutes two Nassau County police cruisers and an ambulance raced in.

The police officers handcuffed Nora Sacco, and the paramedics wheeled Lauren into the ambulance. At South Nassau Communities

Hospital in Oceanside, Long Island, a team of doctors and nurses in the trauma center hovered around Lauren's gurney, and in a choreographed effort stabilized her. Having analyzed the seriousness of her injuries, the chief physician saw fit to send for an ophthalmologist and a cosmetic surgeon.

At police central booking in Mineola, too, the morning awakened to a hectic pace. Coincidentally, on that day Detective Van Holt had been on rotation, and it was he who booked Mrs. Sacco for aggravated assault. "Well, well, well. What're you know? This yarn is really spinning," Van Holt said to his partner, Detective Hans Warner. "Something is goin' on here." He slurped on a can of Coca-Cola and put a hand on top of his head. "First Marino rats on Nick Sacco. Then Ms. Baker can't *or won't* pick him in a lineup. And now, Sacco's wife splashes Baker's face with acid and cuts her into a hamburger. What're you make of all this, Hans?"

Detective Warner was stumped, but Van Holt was positive that Nick Sacco, Lauren Baker, and who knew who else were in the epicenter of a conspiracy.

In her cell, Nora Sacco wasn't talking to anyone, and descended into a catatonic state.

That afternoon, the Cat had gone to his home to find a babysitter with the children. "Where's Nora?"

"I don't know, Nick. She called me this morning at seven o'clock and asked me to come here. She said she had an appointment somewhere."

"An appointment!" Sacco questioned. He smelled feces and said to the teenage girl, "I think you should change the kids' diapers. And please don't ever let my children lie in shit. You hear me?"

The phone rang, and in a tone of self-importance a man's voice asked, "Is this Nick Sacco?"

"Yeah. Who's this?"

"This is Detective Van Holt. I have a lot of questions for you."

Sacco was shocked to hear from this cop again. "You can ask all the questions you want, but you're not gonna get any answers. Now what is this about?"

Van Holt told him what had happened at Lauren's house. Sacco couldn't believe his ears and slammed the phone onto its cradle. And the detective was so baffled by the increasing complexity of the Lauren Baker robbery case his head was spinning.

Sacco hastened to the hospital to console his lover, though she was sedated and semiconscious. The day after, following a three-hour cosmetic surgery to obliterate Lauren's facial wounds, eyes bandaged, she wakened to hear Sacco's voice at her bedside.

"How're you feelin'?"

"Nick?" she said in a hush without moving her dried, chapped lips.

He petted Lauren's hand, a medley of medicinal odors in the room. "Yeah, it's me. Right now you probably hate me more than anyone else in the world."

"Why didn't you tell me . . . ?"

"I was going to, but I wanted to wait for the right time. I'm really sorry. I've been livin' with that nut only because I didn't wanna walk away from my kids." His chin was on his chest as he fought back tears. "I . . . I want you to do me a special favor."

"Why would I want to do you a favor after what you've done to me?"

"Because I'm ready to get rid of her and marry you. And what I'm asking of you is not to press charges."

That prompted Lauren to react by lifting her head off the pillow, though she couldn't. "I can't believe what you're saying to me. Just look at what she's done to me!"

"I know how you feel, and I can't blame you. But I want you to do it for my kids. I don't want them to be without their mother."

"I wish I never met you, Nick," Lauren whispered, despondency in her strained voice.

CHAPTER 92

S eventy-two hours after the ferocious butchering, Sacco posted $5,000 cash bond for Nora. One of the bail stipulations ordered her to be committed to a clinic and examined by psychiatrists. This lightened the weight off Sacco's shoulders, his fear that in one of her stormy fits Nora might've harmed the babies. Against her will, he and two friends, who lived on the ground floor apartment of his brownstone, were driving her to a medical clinic. "You want everybody to think I'm crazy, Nick. Don't you? But I'm not the one who's crazy. Take me back home, you bastard, and you can keep your whore," Nora shrieked in a prolonged scream, pounding madly on the ceiling of the car. "Take me home, you *baaasssstard!*"

"It's not my decision to commit you to a clinic. You heard what the judge said," Sacco answered, the two neighbors cringing at the emotionally disturbed Nora as they sat on either side of her in the rear seat. "Besides, don't you want help so you can feel better?"

"I don't need help. Now get me home, you fuck."

Nora was admitted in a psychiatric ward for a two-week period, and Sacco's mother cared for the children. Lauren was discharged from the hospital, her eyes still bandaged, though the ophthalmologist's prognosis of her vision had been encouraging. Sacco took her home in Hewlett, and throughout the ride she didn't talk. She was sore from the cosmetic surgeries, but her most painful soreness was from the deception she had suffered. "Honey, I know it's hard to get over it, and I understand you're still mad at me." Sacco kept his eyes on the road as he spoke. "But as I already told you, I was gonna come clean. I was just waitin' for the right time."

His girlfriend didn't acknowledge him and turned her head into the window. He decided not to belabor the point, and remained quiet. At Lauren's house, he parked in the driveway. "I'll get the wheelchair out of the trunk. The nurse should be comin' soon. She'll be with you through the night, and then another one will come at eight o'clock in the mornin'."

She finally spoke and said dryly, "The nurse has to stay with me because you can't."

Sacco sat the debilitated Lauren in the wheelchair and rolled her to the side door, the woman's eyes moist and languid, her face expressionless. He had festooned the living room with cheerful banners of well wishes and set a vase of red roses on the coffee table, even though she couldn't see any of it. He pushed Lauren to where the fresh flowers were and let her inhale the fragrance. But she began crying. "You can be so sweet, and I just don't understand how you could have lied to me." And she reached for his neck to hug. Her boyfriend knelt, and they embraced, Lauren weeping, tears leaking under the bandages.

"It's all gonna be okay, baby. And as soon as my divorce goes through, we'll get married."

She nodded gratefully.

The cosmetic surgeon was buoyant about Lauren's recovery; on removing the stitches in her face, the scars would fade to unnoticeable, pencil-thin lines. And she and Sacco were hopeful her eyesight would return to near normal, though prescription glasses might've been needed.

"Do you mean what you said? Are you really going to leave her?" And she searched into Sacco's eyes for reassurance.

"There's nothin' between Nora and me anymore. I only stayed with her because I'm afraid that one day she'll go off and hurt the kids. Look what she did to you."

"But don't you see, Nick. You scorned her. And . . . I . . . I can almost forgive her."

"Forgive her! Honey, you know how many scorned women are out there," he said, his arm stretched, pointing to somewhere beyond the walls of their concubine. "Does that mean every wife whose husband cheated on her should go out and cut up the *other* woman?"

"Everyone handles things differently. I don't know what I'd do in the face of infidelity."

"Well, you don't gotta worry about that with me."

"I hope not . . . I hope not, Nick."

As time passed, and Lauren's wounds healed, her vision eventually clearing to normality. At Sacco's insistence, she consented to withdraw the charges against his estranged wife. His divorce was consummated, and he took a hiatus from his burglaries. But he had something in store for Lauren, a gift: a Tiffany diamond necklace, and for good measure a Burma ruby platinum bracelet. She was in seventh heaven, but more so at his proposal to marry her. And Lauren was up on her toes with happiness as if she were a little girl whose daddy had given her a new doll. "Will I marry you? Of course, I will." And they kissed, Sacco leading her to the bedroom.

The wedding was a private ceremony at a chapel in downtown Las Vegas on North Bruce Road off Route 515. The newlyweds took pleasure in their honeymoon holed up at the Flamingo Hotel & Casino. But the faces of Sacco's children kept crossing his mind, and he couldn't leave those images behind. He went out onto the terrace of the suite to be alone with his thoughts, the Nevada scorching sun sinking into its cradle of mountains that encircles the City of Sin.

Lauren, a sensitive soul, knew her Nick was in anguish. And beneath the hardness of his manliness, she understood the cause of his torment. Lying in bed, she called out to him, "Nick, are you all right?" No answer. "Come in from that hot sun before it burns you to ashes. It must be 110 degrees out there on that furnace of a terrace, honey. Come back to bed. We're not finished and still have a long way to go."

Sacco, guilt-ridden and remorseful, rested his two hundred and twenty pounds on a chaise lounge, watching distractedly the flaming orange sun sliding into the earth behind the mountain range. "My kids are scarred emotionally for life. Goddamn it!" he murmured to himself. "I knew somethin' wasn't right with that Nora, and I shouldn't have married her. Never mind having babies with her."

CHAPTER 93

The December winter had crept in, and the new Mr. and Mrs. Sacco purchased a beach house for the winter in the sunny Florida Keys, a soothing place for Lauren's convalescence. But a heartache was vexing him, those feelings of self-blame and repentance that stubbornly refused to wane. The home his kids lived in stood in a bustling neighborhood of Brooklyn, populated by drug-abusing teenagers, young prostitutes, and criminally prone adolescents. He thought about it, and after many sleepless nights he decided to relocate his children to where it'd be better fit for their upbringing.

Sacco was now in the market for a house in a respectable, bucolic town in Long Island devoid of petty criminals—environs bordered by serenity. He was in high spirits, eager to talk about it with his ex-wife. This resolve, though, brought on a queasiness, the disquieting polarity of anxiousness and relief; anxiousness from fear that Nora might not have been in accord; and relief in knowing that his children and their mother would fare better in a safer environment and a privileged lifestyle.

Sacco called his ex-wife, and what followed the third ring shot a shuddering pain into his stomach. Nora's latest act of spitefulness rocked him and he screamed into the phone, "That senseless bitch. Why did she do this?" He glowered at the receiver as if it were at fault.

CHAPTER 94

T o Sacco's devastation, the recorded message on Nora's telephone line said, *"Sorry, this account is no longer active. Please check the number and dial again."* She had run off with the toddlers. She was gone. He was crushed and felt life was no longer worth living. But the Cat, a man of resilience who did not cower to tragedy, was not to surrender to this fate. He'd search and scour every corner of the country until he'd find his two little darlings.

Lauren was on a Delta flight to Fort Lauderdale, and her ultimate stop would be the beach house in the Keys, a splendid home. The cresting ocean was its backyard. She was flying alone; her groom, grief-stricken over the disappearance, or as he declared it, the *kidnapping* of his children, embarked on a quest to locate Nora. But Sacco's efforts were a futility. Nora, perhaps, had moved to another state, if not to a foreign country. Resigned he'd never rekindle with his girls, the Cat rejoined Lauren in Florida but couldn't wipe away his sorrow.

Maybe . . . just maybe one day Nora will be in need of money and resurface.

As for the fates of the Pierre protagonists, no one can run from his or her destiny, and as mortals they all yielded to theirs.

Al Visconti, the eighth member of the Pierre marauders, was incarcerated for an unrelated offense in Sing Sing, a New York State maximum-security prison. Studying the statutes in the prison law library, Visconti devised a foolproof means to escape. How? He composed a typewritten, officially formatted Habeas Corpus writ—an order issued by a court to release a prisoner. Visconti then mailed it to a friend on the outside, who was in possession of a judge's seal—one that he stole. This comrade of Visconti affixed the judge's seal and forged his signature on the phony Habeas Corpus brief, and pretending to be a process server duly served it on the warden. The warden examined the document, and having reviewed numerous court orders throughout his tenure, had no doubts about its authenticity. Within forty-eight hours, pursuant to the provisions set forth in the writ, he released Visconti.

And here's why this diabolical feat should've been in the Hall of Fame of Escapees, if such an award existed: Al Visconti hadn't escaped through a tunnel or by scaling a wall and wasn't listed as a fugitive. Thus he wasn't being sought by the authorities. And so, Visconti vanished into the blue yonder.

In 1984, he once again tested his luck. Visconti was operating an illegal poker game, a nightly affair, and his dealer was a *card mechanic*, a cheater. One evening, because of a sore loser the poker game got out of hand. A shootout ensued, and Al Visconti lost his life in the process.

Donald "the Greek" Frankos was thriving as a contract killer, whose primary employer was a Mafia capo, "Fat Tony" Salerno. In 1982, the Greek was indicted for a string of murders, and in prison he coauthored a book titled *Contract Killer*, though it did not sell in volume. The end for the Greek came in 2011; he died in a New York State maximum-security penitentiary, the Clinton Correctional Facility.

Bobby Germaine, a consummate stickup artist, was on the run, the result of a botched holdup at a jewelry store on East 57th Street in Manhattan. But his magnum opus, in concert with the infamous Henry Hill, was the burglarizing of Estée Lauder's New York penthouse, stealing $8,000,000 in furs, silverware, and artwork. In 1979, still in partnership with Hill, he was distributing narcotics, and on the premise of his son's testimony Nassau County detectives arrested him. Posing as a writer, Germaine claimed to the police that he wasn't Bobby Germaine, though his fingerprints confirmed otherwise. On his release from prison, he moved to Florida and in 1989 died of heart complications.

In 1987, Christie "the Tick" Furnari was sentenced to one hundred years. He met the common fate of many Mafia bosses; they're either murdered or imprisoned for life. Those who preserve freedom and die peacefully are as rare as a white fly. But Furnari may die in his bed at home after all; due to a grave medical illness the Federal Bureau of Prisons freed the aging consigliere in 2014. As of this writing he's still among the living.

Detective George Bermudez did not enjoy his early retirement. FBI Agent Matt Hammer never dropped Ol' George from his crosshairs, reminding him that the NYPD might've closed its files, but not the Bureau. And it was for this unofficial ongoing reminder that the former detective could not sell Sammy Nalo's jewelry. But mercifully, after Sacco and Frankos had ditched him floating out at sea, thanks to the kindhearted Sacco for alerting the St. Thomas authorities, a local Coast Guard vessel spotted the shady detective adrift, and rescued him.

George Bermudez, who had since been existing on his pension, passed in 2009.

Judge Andrew Tyler, in the course of his judgeship managed to slip out of a few nooses. In 1971, prior to his post on the bench of the State Supreme Court he had assumed an unpaid position as the chairman of the Harlem Anti-Poverty Program. Not long into this occupation, he was criticized and forced to step down for misappropriating welfare funds. And that began the marring of Tyler's reputation.

On with Judge Tyler's soap opera: in 1976, he was arrested for perjury, though through clandestine manipulations of the justice system, the charges were overturned on appeal. At another point in his career, Tyler was under scrutiny for accepting bribes. But following much-publicized accusations, he was cleared to resume his judgeship and reinstated to reign as the Honorable Judge Tyler. He died in 1989.

Assistant District Attorney Doug Pope, shortly after the Pierre case, resigned from the Manhattan DA's Office and joined a circus . . . no, just kidding. His last known move was that he had blended into the legal circles, and evidently never attained his wishes to achieve fame and wealth.

Nora Sacco and her two girls, to date, have not had any contact with Nick Sacco, and he hasn't seen his children in forty years.

Lauren Baker, the second Mrs. Sacco, loved her husband dearly. The marriage flourished, though she often regretted the Cat's felonious livelihood. Sadly, she was killed in an accident. Lauren was bicycling on a summer evening along the shoulder of Atlantic Boulevard in Key West, and a drunken motorist fatally struck her. She was 37.

FBI Agent Matt Hammer, an earnest lawman, solved a multitude of high-profile crimes. Preceding his participation in the Pierre case, he had spearheaded the investigation into the armed break-in at Sophia Loren's suite at the Hampshire House hotel in Manhattan. But Mr. Hammer, who's currently still alive, contributed wholeheartedly to fighting crime throughout his tenure with the Bureau.

Bobby Comfort retreated to his home in Rochester and tended to his wife and daughters, who were now attractive, well-bred teenagers. He had renounced his vocation as a master thief and ventured into a legitimate jewelry store in the Rochester area. But the relentless harassment from police snoopers was an obstacle. They believed the stock in Comfort's store was mainly of stolen items. Not the case, but Comfort chose to dismantle and shut down the operation. After all, despite the losses he had incurred, he had squirreled away a substantial nest egg.

In 1987, Bobby Comfort succumbed to lung cancer and passed on in peace in his home.

Millie Comfort lived on to rear her daughters, but missed her Bobby. They had been undivided soul mates. She prayed and fought for him to quit smoking, the likely catalyst that fed the cancer. And all she has for consolation are those placating memories of Bobby. Health-wise, Millie aged gracefully, though the passage of time had bloated her.

The tears Sammy Nalo shed over the loss of his onetime ally, confidant, and savior, Bobby Comfort, could've been counted on a fingerless hand. It was 1988, fourteen months since the painful death of his former partner, and Nalo burglarized a furrier's warehouse in the Manhattan Fur District. In Naloesque tradition, he double-dipped into his cut of the robbery, and his co-robber retaliated by murdering him. Coincidentally, minutes apart from when Nalo had been fatally shot, one of his creditor bookmakers had set out to stalk and kill him. But the bookie was let down; Nalo's murderer had wakened earlier.

Nick "the Cat" Sacco amassed considerable wealth, though his life had been peaks and valleys of exhilaration and heartache. Already dejected over the separation from his children, Lauren's tragic death demolished him psychologically. He mourned his love, and she is permanently lodged in his heart. The grief for her and his little girls lingered like a stalled, dark cloud. But as the years wore down the calendars, Sacco lightened his heavy heart.

In 1974, to his dismay, NYPD detectives ensnared him, and through a plea deal he testified against a pair of the cruelest, vicious killers in the crime history of New York City. And the Cat is currently tucked away in the Federal Witness Protection Program. Prior to vanishing into the Witness Program, he did a magnanimous deed in redemption of his past.

Sacco's lucrative days as a jewel thief had ended, as did his multimillion-dollar earnings, and cognizant of his faults, rather than squandering his savings on gambling binges, he donated a large percentage of his assets to a foundation dedicated to building orphanages for homeless children.

But how long could Nick "the Cat" Sacco, a man accustomed to the type of life that the vast majority of the population know only through movies and television, tolerate the constraints and restraints of the Federal Witness Protection Program?